Happy Fathers Day
June 1989
Ian

LIFE WITH LYLE

His Caddie's Diary

LIFE WITH LYLE

His Caddie's Diary

DAVID MUSGROVE

with

JOHN HOPKINS

HEINEMANN KINGSWOOD

Heinemann Kingswood
Michelin House, 81 Fulham Road, LONDON SW3 6RB

LONDON MELBOURNE AUCKLAND

Printed and bound in Great Britain by
Richard Clay Ltd, Bungay, Suffolk

The photograph numbered 2 in this book is reproduced by kind permission of Charles Briscoe-Knight and those numbered 4, 6, 7 and 8 by kind permission of Phil Sheldon.

To the Hollinwell caddies
with whom I grew up

CONTENTS

INTRODUCTION

At any major contemporary golf tournament in Europe (and a good few in America as well), the interested spectator can see the tall, sturdy figure of Sandy Lyle. The big Anglo-Scot, who was born in Shrewsbury of Scottish parentage, is easy to pick out. He's probably among the leaders, which is no more than you would expect from one of the world's best players. He'll be supported by a large gallery from which, from time to time, will come shouts of, 'Come on, Sandy' or 'Well done, Sandy' or 'Good old Sandy' because he is among the most popular of golfers in Europe. And by and large he'll remain impassive to all but the most outrageous of his own strokes.

Alongside Lyle will be a shorter man, burly with iron grey hair, a studious expression on his face, carrying Lyle's bag. His name is David Musgrove and since 1981 he and Lyle have formed the most successful partnership of player and caddie in the world of golf. During that time Lyle has won two major championships (the 1985 Open and the 1988 US Masters), eight tournaments in Europe including the Dunhill Masters in June 1988 and the Suntory World Match-play in October 1988, not to mention a further four in the US, one of which was the 1987 Tournament Players' Championship, an event that could be called the fifth major championship. Other players have won more titles in this time but no other partnership has been as successful and is as enviable as Lyle and Musgrove's.

They are two men who, though separated by fourteen years, share a mutual respect, a love of golf and a wry, uncomplicated approach to the game and to life. 'Who's got the best job in the world, then?' Musgrove is fond of asking before he answers his own question: 'Sandy Lyle, of course. Who's got the second best job in the world?' he continues. 'Dave Musgrove.' And he grins, his normally rather stern face dominated by its beetling eyebrows breaking into a wide smile that is as warm as it is unexpected. Musgrove is a yeoman of England, straightforward, honest to a fault and able to see through the pretences and fabrications of others quicker than the time it takes him to say hello. Spend an hour with him in a pub or waiting at a railway station and you'll find him asking many questions, listening intently to the answers, anxious to learn. Never mind that he left school with few qualifications, he's an intelligent man with a deep well of honest-to-goodness common sense.

His life revolves around Kirkby-in-Ashfield, near Mansfield, where he lives blissfully happily in the terraced house in which he was born. From the front room he can see the school he attended as an infant, the doctor's surgery he was taken to when he was ill and the dentist he has gone to for years.

Thanks to golf he has experienced a lifestyle dramatically different from the one he would have known had he remained a draughtsman. He's visited four of the five continents and stayed in luxury hotels he could otherwise only have dreamed about and, at present at least, earns far more than he had any right to expect. But there couldn't have been a better demonstration of how down-to-earth he is and how solid his values are than occurred at Christmas 1987.

Musgrove and his girlfriend Hilary were in Tenerife on holiday and much against his will had been prevailed upon to attend a sales breakfast given by timeshare salesmen, 'timeshare touts' he calls them. The virtues of one exotic venue after another were extolled and the more exotic the venue the less impressed Musgrove became. Finally and with a growing sense of frustration a salesman turned to him and said: 'Well, where would you like to live?' Musgrove didn't need to think for a moment: 'Kirkby-in-Ashfield,' he replied.

'This is what life is all about, isn't it?' he says, looking around his front room at home. 'The heavy gang at Coxmoor [his regular golfing friends at his golf club] are more in touch with reality than the sort of posers one comes across so often in golf. What does it matter what sort of a room you've got in your hotel? You know, they're offering rooms in The Lodge at

Pebble Beach, California, with fireplaces, and everyone's falling over themselves to get one. They're not lit, of course. It's just so they can say to one another: "Have you got a fireplace in your room? You haven't? I'm surprised. I've got one in mine and I'm only paying $280 a night."'

'Where's the chuffing sense of reality in that?'

His eye is caught by a book he was given recently – *What They Don't Teach You At Harvard Business School* by Mark McCormack. 'Three of the main headings he comes out with early in this book are: "Listen aggressively", "Observe aggressively" and "Talk less". But I can clearly remember the first two things my grandmother ever taught me. The first was how to tie up my shoelaces. The second was what the three brass monkeys who sat on our mantlepiece represented – Hear All, See All and Say Nowt. Here's McCormack who's spent thousands and thousands of dollars on his education and written all these clever words just to say the same thing.'

Musgrove met Lyle during the Benson & Hedges tournament at York in 1981. He had been caddying for the Spaniard Manuel Calero but was out of work, Calero having missed the halfway cut. (At pro tournaments only the leading seventy scorers compete in the third and fourth rounds.)

Musgrove was cooling his heels on the putting green when Lyle approached him. 'Would you like to work for me for a while?' he asked as he stroked putt after putt towards a distant target. Musgrove was dumbfounded but recovered quickly enough to mumble agreement.

The agreement was in principle; details still had to be worked out. 'The thing I don't want from a caddie is a yes-man,' Lyle said.

'That's all right,' Musgrove replied. 'You've not got one. The last thing I am is a yes-man. There are two things I want from the golfer I work for: I can't caddie for a golfer who quits, and I want to be paid regularly.'

A few minutes later, as he stood on the putting green contemplating his luck at getting a job with the most consistent money-winner in Europe, Musgrove was approached again. 'Would you work for me in the US next year?' Nick Faldo asked.

If Musgrove was dumbfounded at Lyle's approach, he was speechless at Faldo's. From beginning the day with no work he had now found employment for the rest of the European season and the early part of the following year. 'I always go to the Benson & Hedges with some friends from home,' he says. 'They drive me up, I supply them with tickets, car park stickers and so on. I said to them as we were going home that night: "I've had the most fantastic day of my golfing life."'

The meeting of Lyle and Musgrove was a meeting of two men outstandingly talented in their own fields. Lyle's ability had long been apparent. After a glittering amateur career he turned pro in 1977 and won that year's qualifying school. Finishing 49th in the 1978 order of merit was good enough to earn him the rookie of the year award. He leaped to the top of the order of merit in 1979 – when he also appeared in Europe's Ryder Cup team – and again in 1980.

Musgrove was a good golfer who had caddied off and on for nearly twenty years since starting as a 12-year-old at Hollinwell, the Nottinghamshire course near his parents' house.

'It was my mother who suggested it,' he recalls. 'When I got to between the ages of playing with Dinky toys and not knowing what girls were for, she said to me one day: "Why don't you go caddying and make yourself useful?" Me and my friend Hugh Monro set out on our bikes to Hollinwell and halfway there we got caught in a cloudburst. My first memory of the famous Hollinwell golf club is going down the drive in the slashing rain, parking our bikes in a shed and drying ourselves as best we could.

'A lot of my friends did paper rounds or butchers' rounds. That always seemed too much like hard work to me, getting up early in the morning and distributing papers. Anyway, I used to earn as much in one morning's caddying as they earned in a week. I would get six shillings for a round and that was a lot of money for a 12½-year-old, which is how old I was when I first went there in August 1955.'

Musgrove learned the rudiments of golf by watching the men for whom he caddied, as so many caddies have done before and since. He has hardly had a golf lesson in his life. 'On a Sunday if there were no members about we could play the first four holes, walk across to the 17th fairway and play that as a par three, and then go down the 18th. We used clubs from the pro's shop.'

He is still a good golfer and has retained a single-figure handicap since 1967. Yet suggest to him that a handicap of eight is something to be proud of and he will snort with that streak of realism and self-deprecation that is typical of him: 'I can't play golf. I can hit it forwards and upwards and generally finish a round with the ball I started off with, which is the main thing. I can scrape it round. But that's about all.'

In the mid-1950s Musgrove was one of a group of boys who would gather on weekend mornings and while waiting to start work amuse themselves by putting pennies on the railway line near the golf course as the Master Cutler steam engine passed on its southward journey from Sheffield to London. Then they would report for caddies' duties at Hollinwell by 9.00 a.m.

'Most of the old caddies at Hollinwell have gone now. Every time I go home I hear of another one that has died. Dal Warren, who used to caddie for John Jacobs, died this year. Dal's brother Joe taught me the most, I suppose, of the humorous side of golf.

'He would say: "You take the short cut when you can."

'I asked him once, "But what happens when they hit the ball and you never see where it goes? Then what do you do?" His simple answer was, "You have to stand there and confess you haven't a clue where the hell it is."

'Another caddie, Charlie Cherry, was a good player. The man he was caddying for once at Hollinwell asked: "What club is it?"

'"It's a six iron," said Charlie.

'"I can't get there with a six iron."

'"I could get there with a six iron," said Charlie.

'"No you couldn't."

'"Yes, I could. I'll show you." And he did.

'Another one was old Foster Chapman. He was caddying for Smiler Greaves, so-called because he never smiled. Smiler was also known as the Spangle Man because after twelve holes he always used to give out Spangle sweets.

'Foster Chapman was broke and hadn't been able to buy any

cigarettes for a week. Smiler made the mistake of throwing his cigarette down on the ground while he played his shot. As Joe Warren said: "Foster Chapman's hand came out like a cobra and grabbed this cigarette and hid it for later." Smiler, meanwhile, hit his shot on to the green and couldn't understand where his cigarette had gone.

'Then there was old Dr Sparrow. After six holes he'd tell his caddie to go and find him some balls in the woods. When the caddie brought some back old Dr Sparrow would be able to start again.'

Musgrove worked as a draughtsman for the National Coal Board, and for several years he took part of his annual holiday to go to the Open and caddie. He worked for Jean Garaialde, the French pro, at St Andrews in 1964 and for the last two rounds they were paired with Tony Lema, the winner.

In 1971 he caddied for Roberto de Vicenzo, the great Argentinian, in the Open at Royal Birkdale. 'In the third round we were paired with Mr Lu,' recalls Musgrove. 'On the 13th, a par five, Roberto hit a drive and a six iron and reached the green, and Mr Lu hit a drive and a screaming three wood and his ball just reached the green. Roberto three-putted and Mr Lu holed his for an eagle.

'Going up the next hole, Roberto turned to me and said: "They put me out with a Chinaman to improve my English." At which point Mr Lu suddenly disappeared over a boundary fence to try and find a toilet. "Hey," Roberto shouted at me. "Lu go and make shit."'

While still caddying part time, Musgrove left the Coal Board in 1966 to join the aerospace engine division of Rolls-Royce at Hucknall, near Derby, also as a draughtsman. Six years later, in January 1972, he took a decision that changed his life. He was offered voluntary redundancy. To a man who had lived his life in a rented house, the security of continuing with a firm as large as Rolls-Royce was appealing. On the other hand, Musgrove, by now in his late twenties, was a good golfer and he knew that if he didn't take this chance to try his luck as a caddie, then he would never do it. It wasn't a hard decision to make and he hasn't regretted it for a moment since.

For four years from 1976 Ballesteros and Musgrove were a

regular partnership during which time Ballesteros won the Open at Royal Lytham in 1979. But not the least of Musgrove's qualities is a pride in what he does, and after several tumultuous years with Ballesteros he could no longer tolerate the abuse that was heaped upon him at, it seemed, almost every turn. Caddying for Seve at the Open at Lytham was hell, he was to say later. 'Three weeks later he was still chewing me out. But there were also wonderful moments with Seve. He is so gifted it's not true.'

But a change there had to be, and in Lyle, Musgrove found the perfect employer. 'Sandy is the best bloke in the world to caddy for,' Musgrove said in the *Sunday Times* after his victory in the Open at Sandwich in 1985. 'I'll tell you what my life's like with Sandy – my wages must be the best on tour, must be, and when I stay at his house at Wentworth he brings me tea in the morning. That can't be bad, can it?'

The two of them go through a well-rehearsed routine before every shot. Lyle stands alongside Musgrove and the golf bag. They talk quietly for a moment. For a golfer and his caddie this is a moment as intimate as confession for a Catholic. This is when a caddie must enjoy his boss's confidence or he is on his way to being fired. At this moment the caddie must know the answer to anything he is likely to be asked. He must know what to say and, just as important, how to say it. He mustn't talk too much. The caddie must know whether his employer needs a little boost in confidence. Some caddies have been fired for talking too much at this moment, just as others have been fired for saying too little.

At first all Lyle asks for is the yardage. Sometimes, as on the ninth hole of the last round of the 1988 US Masters for example, the yardage suggests the club he should use. 'How far is it?' Lyle asked Musgrove who was standing by the bag waiting.

Musgrove had already taken his yardage book out of the back pocket of his overall. '173 yards,' he replied.

'In that case it's a seven iron,' said Lyle.

The decision was simple. There was no wind worth taking into consideration, no other factors to influence the shot. It was the distance for a seven iron, and so a seven iron it was. As Lyle moved to address the ball, Musgrove lifted the big white bag out of Lyle's sight. Moments later the shot came to rest two feet from the hole. A birdie three was inevitable.

That particular shot, however, was a formality. Lyle's mind was made up as to the club he wanted and the distance he wanted to hit it the moment he was told the yardage to the hole. The skill of one caddie over another comes in helping his player choose the right club for the distance. He might say, 'It's a soft five,' or 'If you take eight, then it's got to be a good one.'

There are those who say that in this respect Musgrove is the great controller. He chooses the club, tells Sandy how to hit it and then stands back and awaits results. 'Some people think I do everything bar hit the ball,' says Musgrove. 'They make him sound like a robot controlled by me. That's not true. I say things to him and he says things to me. I give him my opinion when he asks. I don't tell him what to do. It's not like that at all.'

It is undeniable, however, that part of the skill of a caddie as good as Musgrove is knowing when to interfere with his player's club selection and when to keep quiet, and when and how to give those brief few words of encouragement.

Take the 12th hole of the last round in that 1988 US Masters at Augusta. Lyle, having bogied the 11th, had just hit his tee shot into the water on this beguiling short hole. After leading the tournament for nearly forty holes, he was now certain to forfeit his position. He was furious with himself as he strode off the tee, showing all the signs of getting himself into a state. At this moment Musgrove needed two heads. One to count the distance from the tee to the dropping zone, thus working out how long a shot Sandy's third shot would be, the other to reassure his boss.

Born like most of us with only one head, Musgrove nevertheless had to handle both issues. 'I'm trying to do two jobs at once,' he says at the appropriate passage in the following pages. 'I've got to keep a cool head, otherwise we'll make another mistake. I was trying to measure from the tee to wherever he was going to drop, but at the same time I'm trying to calm him down. I told him: "Don't worry about what's happened. That's done, ancient history. Just make sure you get a five."'

Lyle took his medicine on the par three 12th, failed to birdie the 13th, narrowly missed a birdie on the 14th and by the 15th was getting anxious again. It was time for Musgrove to step in once more.

There was a lull in play and Musgrove, part-time psychiatrist and counsellor, first drew Lyle's attention to the view. 'I wanted to get his mind off the golf for a moment.' Then, as the players began to leave the green, Musgrove performed a second piece of man management with such skill it suggests he has a future in dealing with lots of people and not just one when he decides to give up humping golf bags around the world.

'Look, Sandy,' he said, putting his face close to Lyle's to emphasize the importance of what he was saying, 'you've lost your lead and you're chasing now. A weight's been taken off your shoulders. Put that to your advantage. Let somebody else do the work for a change and we'll chase them.'

History records that Lyle stood on the 16th tee needing to complete the last three holes in two under par. He did so; and the US Masters, one of golf's four major titles, fell to a Briton for the first time. It's as impossible to say that he wouldn't have done it without Musgrove's solid sustaining presence by his side as it is impossible to say he would have.

The Oxford Dictionary definition of the word caddie is, '*a.* a lad or man who waits on the look-out for odd jobs (def. 1730), *b.* Golf. A boy (or man) who carries the clubs etc. (def. 1857)'.

One version of the word's origin is that it comes from *cadet* in French, the word used in France at that time to mean an officer apprentice, i.e. someone not commissioned. The Scots adopted the word cadet and with their burr it became known as caddie or cadie, meaning messenger or errand boy. The earliest drawings of caddies depict men standing with a bunch of clubs under their arm.

Whatever the origin, the implication of the word caddie is someone to serve, to fetch and carry, to help and advise, a person best described as a cross between a valet, confidant, messenger, bag carrier, companion. In the autumn of 1988 Lyle and Musgrove celebrated their seventh year as a partnership. In that time Lyle has been at his lowest ebb, when his wife Christine announced she was leaving him, and at the peak of his powers, winning the Open in 1985 and the US Masters in April 1988. In their years together Musgrove has been a constant in Lyle's life; certainly Lyle spends more time each day with him than with anyone else apart from his companion Jolande Huurman.

If Lyle has been good for Musgrove, then Musgrove has been good for Lyle. He is the first to say that it's the player who hits the ball, who holes the putts, who does the difficult part; but he is always there, ready. He knows the starting times, has packed the golf bag with items ranging from dozens of tees, several pencils, both waterproofs and a spare sweater, a dozen balls and a yardage chart of the course. Musgrove has yardage charts of thirty-eight American courses, twelve maps of courses in Europe done by a firm called Strokesaver and a further sixty-six yardage books he has compiled himself using his own measuring wheel.

Only once has Musgrove made a serious mistake while working for Lyle. It came during the 1987 Phoenix tournament in the town of that name in Arizona, USA. The two of them had played golf with friends the day before the tournament and Musgrove borrowed an eight iron from Sandy and forgot to replace it. 'We got out the next day in the tournament, weighed the shot up for an eight iron and couldn't find the club. I finally twigged where it was.

'That's probably the worst mistake I've made with Sandy. I've never overslept. That's the game, isn't it, to be there on time and ready to go. You can only be late once. My whole day is geared to getting up in the morning to be ready for playing whatever the time. The player has probably come 3,000 miles as well. You can't make a muck up then.'

The traditional concept of a golf caddie is of a man burly enough to be able to carry a 50 lb golf bag. He'll probably have tattoos on his forearms, will drink a lot, perhaps spend nights on end sleeping rough. Income tax is what everyone else pays; the only VAT he'll know is VAT 69 whisky. The old caddies were wonderful characters, likeable rogues many of them, who lived on their wits and drank their savings. These were the men who invented the rhyming slang that remains a part of a caddie's vocabulary. 'Fruit and veg' is a wedge. 'You'll need the furniture' means you'll need a wood. 'Lady Godiva' is a driver, 'Tom Mix' a six, 'Garden Gate' an eight, 'Doctor's Orders' a nine.

'The image of a caddie is of a man with no collar and tie who can't speak properly,' says Musgrove. 'That may have been the case once but it is less so now. The increase in prize money has made caddying for a top-class pro a lucrative proposition, so there is more competition than there once was. The pressure is greater and so are the rewards. A missed putt can lose a player £5000. One shot saved can earn a caddie enough to live on for a month. It's become serious business.

'Some of us just want to do our job properly. It doesn't start on the first tee and end on the 18th green, you know. That's why we want to be able to get into the clubhouse locker-room to collect the clubs in the morning and return them in the evening – to do our job better. I don't want Sandy to have to do anything more than change his shoes.'

This diary begins in the late summer of 1987, the start of a rich time for Lyle – and an equally rewarding period for Musgrove. Their lives are hectic but enjoyable. Lyle is at the peak of his powers, Musgrove a picture of contentment most of the time. A lot has happened to the third longest partnership on the European tour (only Manuel Pinero and his caddie Jimmy Cousins and Sam Torrance and Brian Dunlop exceed the Lyle–Musgrove partnership). Turn over and start to read about some of it.

London, November 1988   John Hopkins

Tournaments in which David Musgrove caddied for Sandy
Lyle between 1 September 1987 and 13 November 1988

1987

3–6 September   Ebel European Masters, Crans, Switzerland.
Winner: A. Forsbrand. Lyle sixth.

10–13 September   Panasonic European Open, Walton Heath, Surrey.
Winner: P. Way. Lyle joint forty-ninth.

17–20 September   Lancôme Trophy, St Nom-la-Bretèche, Paris.
Winner: I. Woosnam. Lyle joint third.

25–27 September   Ryder Cup, USA v Europe, Muirfield Village, Columbus, Ohio.
Winner: Europe beat USA 15–13.

1–4 October   Dunhill Cup, Old Course, St Andrews, Scotland.
Winner: England beat Scotland 2–1.
Faldo, England's captain, defeated Lyle, Scotland's captain, 66–69.

8–11 October   German Masters, Stuttgart, West Germany.
Winner: Lyle after a 2-hole play-off with Langer.

15–18 October   Suntory World Match-play Championship, Wentworth, Surrey.
Winner: Woosnam defeated Lyle by 1 hole.

5–8 November   Kirin Cup, Yomiuri CC, Tokyo.
Winner: USA beat Europe 10–2.

11–14 November   Isuzu Kapalua International, Kapalua, Maui, Hawaii.
Winner: A. Bean. Lyle third.

18–21 November	World Cup, Kapalua, Maui, Hawaii.
	Winner: Wales (Woosnam and D. Llewellyn) beat Scotland (Lyle and S. Torrance) at second play-off hole.
	Individual event winner: Woosnam. Lyle second.

1988

14–17 January	MONY Tournament of Champions, La Costa CC, Carlsbad, California.
	Winner: S. Pate. Lyle joint eighteenth.
20–24 January	Bob Hope Chrysler Classic, Palm Springs, California.
	Winner: J. Haas. Lyle joint twenty-fifth.
28–31 January	Phoenix Open, Scottsdale, Arizona.
	Winner: Lyle defeated F. Couples after three-hole play-off.
4–7 February	AT&T Pebble Beach National Pro-Am, Pebble Beach, California.
	Winner: S. Jones. Lyle joint thirteenth.
3–6 March	Doral Ryder Open, Doral CC, Miami, Florida.
	Winner: B. Crenshaw. Lyle joint fifteenth.
10–13 March	Honda Classic, Eagle Trace, Florida.
	Winner: J. Sindelar. Lyle joint second.
17–20 March	Hertz Bay Hill Classic, Bay Hill Club and Lodge, Orlando, Florida.
	Winner: P. Azinger. Lyle joint fifteenth.
24–27 March	The Players' Championship, Jacksonville, Florida.
	Winner: M. McCumber. Lyle missed the cut.
31 March–3 April	K-Mart Greater Greensboro Open, Forest Oaks CC, Greensboro, North Carolina.
	Winner: Lyle.
7–10 April	US Masters, Augusta National GC, Augusta, Georgia.
	Winner: Lyle.

14–17 April	MCI Heritage Classic, Harbour Town GL, Hilton Head Island, South Carolina. Winner: G. Norman. Lyle joint thirteenth.
5–8 May	Panasonic Las Vegas Invitational, Las Vegas, Nevada. Winner: G. Koch. Lyle missed the cut.
12–15 May	GTE Byron Nelson Golf Classic, Las Colinas, Irving, Texas. Winner: B. Lietzke. Lyle joint thirtieth.
27–30 May	Volvo PGA Championship, Wentworth, Surrey. Winner: Woosnam. Lyle joint seventh.
2–5 June	Dunhill British Masters, Woburn G & CC, Bedfordshire. Winner: Lyle.
9–12 June	Manufacturers Hanover Westchester Classic, Westchester CC, Rye, Connecticut. Winner: Seve Ballesteros at first play-off hole from Greg Norman, David Frost and Ken Green. Lyle missed the cut.
16–19 June	US Open, The Country Club, Brookline, Massachusetts. Winner: Curtis Strange after eighteen-hole play-off with Nick Faldo. Lyle joint twenty-fifth.
23–26 June	Peugot French Open, Chantilly, Paris. Winner: Faldo. Lyle missed the cut.
7–10 July	Bell's Scottish Open, Gleneagles Hotel, Auchterarder. Winner: B. Lane. Lyle joint second.
10 July	St Mellion Trophy, St Mellion, Cornwall.
14–17 July	Open Championship, Royal Lytham & St Anne's, Lancashire. Winner: Ballesteros. Lyle joint seventh.
4–7 August	Benson & Hedges International, Fulford, York. Winner: P. Baker after a two-hole play-off with Faldo. Lyle sixth.

18–21 August	Carroll's Irish Open, Portmarnock, Dublin. Winner: Woosnam. Lyle tied for seventeenth place.
25–28 August	NEC World Series of Golf, Firestone CC, Akron, Ohio. Winner: M. Reid. Lyle fifth.
1–4 September	Ebel European Masters, Crans, Switzerland. Winner: C. Moody. Lyle joint twentieth.
8–11 September	Panasonic European Open, Sunningdale, Berkshire. Winner: Woosnam. Lyle joint third.
15–18 September	Lancôme Trophy, St Nom-la-Bretèche, Paris. Winner: Ballesteros. Lyle joint third.
22–25 September	German Masters, Stuttgart, West Germany. Winner: J-M Olazabal. Lyle joint fourteenth.
6–9 October	Suntory World Match-play Championship, Wentworth, Surrey. Winner: Lyle beat Faldo by 2 & 1 in the final.
13–16 October	Dunhill Cup, Old Course, St Andrews, Scotland. Winner: Ireland beat Australia 2–1. Scotland, captained by Lyle, were defeated by England, captained by Faldo, in the quarter-finals. Lyle lost to Faldo 68–67.
27–30 October	Volvo Masters, Valderrama, Sotogrande, Spain. Winner: Faldo. Lyle third.
10–13 November	Nabisco Championships of Golf, Pebble Beach, California. Winner: Curtis Strange. Lyle joint seventeenth.

WHO'S WHO

A reader's guide

Richie Alimo	American friend of Lyle
Paul Azinger	American pro
Peter Baker	British pro on the European tour
Jimmy Ballard	American teaching pro
Seve Ballesteros	Spanish pro on the European tour
Chip Beck	American pro
Brian Bellenger ('Big Brian')	British caddie
Michael Bonallack	Secretary, Royal and Ancient Golf Club of St Andrews
Gordon Brand Jnr	British pro on the European tour
Ken Brown ('The Vicar')	British pro on the European tour
Mark Calcavecchia	American pro
José-Maria Canizares	Spanish pro on the European tour
Creamy Carolan	American caddie
Mike Carrick	American caddie
Howard Clark	British pro on the European tour
Peter Coleman ('Pete')	Bernhard Langer's caddie
Fred Couples	American pro
Jimmy Cousins	British caddie
Neville Cramer	Friend of Musgrove and Lyle
Ben Crenshaw	American pro
John Davidson ('The Prof')	British caddie
Rodger Davis	Australian pro on the European tour

Nick DePaul	American caddie
Jimmy Dickinson	British caddie
Brian Dunlop	Sam Torrance's caddie
Nick Faldo	British pro on the European tour
'Fish Finger'	British caddie
Ray Floyd	American pro
Billy Foster	British caddie
David Frost	South African pro on the American tour
Angel Gallardo	Vice-chairman, PGA European Tour tournament committee
Peter German	Tournament organizer, International Management Group
'Golf' Ball	American caddie
Tony Gray	Director of tour policy, PGA European Tour
Ken Green	American pro
'Gypsy Joe' Grillo	American caddie
Jay Haas	American pro
Willi Hofmann	German teaching pro; Langer's coach
Terry Holt	British caddie
Jolande Huurman	Sandy Lyle's girlfriend
Tony Jacklin	Captain, the European Ryder Cup team
Mark James	British pro on the European tour
Tom Kite	American pro
Gary Koch	American pro
Brad Krosnoff ('White Russian')	American caddie
Barry Lane	British pro on the European tour
Berhard Langer	German pro on the European tour
'Laughing Boy'	British caddie

David Llewellyn	British pro on the European tour
Davis Love	American pro
Alec and Agnes Lyle	Sandy Lyle's father and mother
Gary McCord	American tv golf commentator
Mark McCumber	American pro
Andy McFee	Tournament director, PGA European Tour
Dave McNeilly ('Irish Dave')	British caddie
Mark McNulty	Pro from Zimbabwe on the European tour
Neil and Bridget Macpherson	British friends, resident in the USA, of Musgrove and Lyle
Mick Maull	British caddie
Steve Melnyk	American tv golf commentator
Chris Moody	British pro on the European tour
Hugo Monro	School friend of Musgrove
Philip Morbey ('Wobbly')	British caddie
Larry Nelson	American pro
Jack Nicklaus	Captain, the 1983–87 US Ryder Cup teams
Greg Norman	Australian pro on the American tour, who also makes regular visits to Europe
Andy North ('The Duke')	American pro
George O'Grady	Managing director, PGA European Tour Enterprises
Mac O'Grady	American pro
John O'Leary	Chairman, European Tour tournament committee
José-Maria Olazabal	Spanish pro on the European tour

John Paramor	Director of tour operations, PGA European Tour
Harry Parker–Brown	American caddie
Calvin Peete	American pro
Manuel Pinero	Spanish pro on the European tour
Don Pooley	American pro
Martin Poxon	British pro on the European tour
Nick Price	Pro from Zimbabwe on the American tour
Andy Prodger ('Prodge')	Nick Faldo's caddie
Glenn Ralph	British pro on the European tour
José Rivero	Spanish pro on the European tour
Ivor Robson	Starter at several European tournaments
Chi–Chi–Rodriguez	American pro
D. J. Russell	British pro
Ken Schofield	Executive director, PGA European tour
Tony Sher	Friend of Musgrove and Lyle
'Silly Billy'	British caddie
Scott Simpson	American pro
Joey Sindelar	American pro
Jeff Sluman	American pro
Des Smyth	Irish pro on the European tour
Paul Stephens	British caddie
Payne Stewart	American pro
Curtis Strange	American pro
Jim Thorpe	American pro
Sam Torrance	British pro on the European tour
Lee Trevino	American pro
Hilary Turner	David Musgrove's girlfriend
Bob Tway	American pro
Chuck Van Linge	American friend of Lyle

Lanny Wadkins	American pro
Tom Watson	American pro
Barry Willett	Club maker
Ian Woosnam	British pro on the European tour
Ian Wright	British caddie

1

31 August 1987–9 January 1988

Seven in a row – Ryder Cup triumph – Christmas holidays

Ebel European Masters, Crans, Switzerland

Monday 31 August to Sunday 6 September

Flew to Geneva for the European Masters, or the Swiss Open as we call it, at Crans-sur-Sierre. It's one of everybody's favourite places, a small, exclusive ski resort 4,000 feet up in the Swiss Alps with majestic views of the Rhone valley below and the mountains above. They had the world ski championships there earlier this year.

We all like it so much because of the continuity of the place. You go back to the same hotel each year, eat at the same table, have the same waiter. I've been there twelve times and this year M. Shallert, the patron of the Hotel Robinson, said to me: 'When you've been coming here for fifteen years we'll make a presentation to you.'

There are three big families in the town. Gaston Barras is the largest property owner and the driving force behind the tournament. His mother still works in a shop halfway down the main street. The others are the Reys and the Bonvins. Nothing much happens in the town without them being involved.

The hotel was fantastic. We had the flight from England, bus from the airport, four-star hotel with big swimming-pool and huge rooms with television and a fridge, bed, breakfast and dinner for seven nights. Good service. Cost us £350 each. It was done through Traveleads, who arrange most of my travel in Europe. They do a lot of travel arrangements for the tour and some of the deals they come up with are brilliant.

What I did this week is much the same as I do at each tournament. Went to the clubhouse and got a locker for Sandy before he arrived. Made sure there were enough new balls in the bag, and enough different-numbered balls to avoid a clash with Sandy's playing partners if they're using the same make of ball. The Dunlop balls are only numbered from one to four. Titleists go up to eight. Some people prefer to play with high numbers, some with low numbers, some won't play with threes, some won't play with fives. Sandy doesn't mind which number ball he plays with.

Before playing every day I clean the grips, the most important part of a golf club, and empty the dust out of the bag. Check the start times both for the pro-am and the tournament. Check who's playing in front of us so I can watch them getting ready to go to the first tee and so give ourselves enough time. If they're on the putting green I know we've got a few minutes. If they're on the tee we're the next up.

You need to be clear which tee you're starting from if it's a two-tee start – number one or number ten. Sandy went on the wrong tee at Monte Carlo once and wondered where Paul Way and Gordon Brand Junior, his partners, had got to. When he eventually found them they laughed so loudly that an official shouted at them for making too much noise.

Pros have been known to drive off with their putter, which is not always the right club to use on a par five. The caddie's been on one tee, the pro on another with a putter in his hand. Since it's the only club he has, he must hit the ball with it when his name is shouted.

I try and guess what the weather is going to be like. Can I leave the waterproofs out of the bag? I always carry a dry towel, a supply of new gloves in a plastic bag to keep them dry, tees, markers, pitchmark repairers. When I get on the course the main job apart from carrying the clubs, which you take for granted, is to give distances. The first distance is from the ball to the front of the green; the second is how far the flag is from the front of the green. Then you give the total. The player might ask: 'How many yards are there behind the flag to the back of the green?' And sometimes he might say: 'Is it tight left or tight right?' With tee shots he may want to know how far it is to carry a bunker or to remain short of a hazard, and where the features are on the course. The predominant concern is to try and figure out where the wind is coming from.

Sandy finished sixth. He has always had a good record in Switzerland. However badly he's playing, the thing about Switzerland is that, being 4,000 feet up, the air is so thin the ball flies a lot easier. It flatters your golf. It's like giving monkeys nuts up there, now there's no rough worth speaking of. The four par fives are all in Sandy's range in two shots and he can drive a couple of the par fours as well. It's good therapy, if you like.

Panasonic European Open, Walton Heath, Surrey

Monday 7 to Sunday 13 September
Flew back from Switzerland and drove home, getting in around tea time. Next morning we drove down to London again, to Sandy's house where we were staying for the European Open.

While Hilary and Sandy's mother sorted out the garden, planting a load of shrubs, bulbs and all sorts, we went with Sandy's father every day to Walton Heath. I've not been there since the Ryder Cup in 1981 but I keep cards of all the courses we play in a drawer at home. Normally I'd get to a course on a Tuesday and walk all eighteen holes. I've got my own measuring wheel. The coloured spots on the fairway are there to help us with our measurements.

I had no time to measure the course before the pro-am but there's a lad named Ian Wright that sells yardage books in Europe. So I bought a book off him for three quid. That meant I had measurements good enough to get round in the pro-am. I wasn't exactly getting there blind.

Sandy was paired in the tournament with José-Maria Olazabal and Bernhard Langer. Langer started off like a train. In fact I couldn't see him getting beat the way he played the first two days. Olazabal missed the cut but he didn't give up. He lost his temper and all sorts, but he still didn't give up. That impressed me.

Sandy struggled and struggled and finished on the Friday

night on the border for missing the cut. It was so dark the last group had the choice of playing on or coming back at half-past seven the next morning. Ross Drummond and Magnus Persson both had to birdie the last to knock the plus fours out, which included Sandy. They chose to play the next morning and as it happened they both bogied the last and knocked themselves out.

Ross Drummond said they'd been playing in the dark. This comes back to the fields being too big. There was supposed to be a proposal that the top 100 players be exempt from pre-qualifying rather than the top 125. They've just blindly copied this 125 from the US. What I think they should have done is work out what a golfer needs to break even in Europe – it's got to be £15,000 or £20,000 – and then see where that sum is represented on the money list. It'll be about seventieth or eightieth. Best to make them exempt and make the rest pre-qualify.

We're playing Saturday and Sunday. Sandy did some practising. The practice ground at Walton Heath is miles away, down the bottom end. And it isn't very good. All you can do is hit a few balls up the old first. His dad was there watching. He's always tried to follow his dad's advice.

He yanked it round on the Saturday but on the Sunday he hit it really well. Two four-iron shots were the best he'd hit all year. Of course he took seven going up the last which was dead depressing, but he wasn't going to make any money anyway whatever he did at the last. So it was a real good step in the right direction.

Sandy had a good crowd watching him because he was out early. One regular supporter is the old radio announcer from the Goon Show, Ronald Fletcher, who always follows him. He describes himself as Sandy's greatest fan. He's a very distinguished-looking fellow, plays at Royal Mid-Surrey. Every tournament in the London area he's there, watching Sandy.

Lancôme Trophy, St Nom-la-Bretèche, Paris

Tuesday 15 to Sunday 20 September
Flew from East Midlands. It's only about twenty minutes in

the car from home. Brilliant airport. No queues there, as usual.

Sometimes Mark James or Ian Woosnam or D. J. Russell are on flights from East Midlands but this time there's only me. Got my bags and walked round to the board to see what flights were due in from London. There were two and Sam Torrance and Brian Marchbank got off one and so I cadged a lift from them in one of the courtesy cars, big Peugeots.

Brian Dunlop, who carries for Sam, and I were in one and the rest squashed into the other. Took us to the players' hotel, dropped me off at where we stay in Versailles. I shared with Pete Coleman who caddies for Bernhard Langer. Hotel full of caddies. I generally share with Coleman, Andy Prodger, Nick Faldo's caddie, or Brian Dunlop, someone like that. Every time they had a shower in the room above, the flaming water came in our room. We complained to the manager and he said it's been like that for ages. The wallpaper was coming away from the wall. It didn't do any damage to us. We remonstrated, hoping for a discount, but it didn't do any good.

The players stayed at the Trianon Palace. We could leg it to their hotel via the scenic route through the chateau, take in the ambience, down across the gardens, look at the statues, come out of the gate and the hotel is right there. Only takes twenty minutes. You've got to have a bit of a constitutional before you start work. There was a bus to the course from there every morning. Made sure we got on it first, got a seat before the players.

So there we were at Trophée Lancôme. Of course, these worldly-wise experienced tour caddies have taken all their warm clothes and waterproofs with them, completely forgetting that this year the event was a month earlier than usual. In the past it has been wet, cold and windy but this was the hottest bloody week of the year. I've never drunk so much on a course as I did that Sunday, all that bottled water. Complete mistake, of course. I spent the next week going to the lavatory. No brain, you see.

Sandy shot twenty under par and finished joint third. As I say, he had started playing better on the Sunday of the previous tournament after a session with his father. Also this was his third week in a row and he thrives on playing. Actually he got within a shot or so level with Woosnam for about twelve holes and then Woosnam pulled away again.

Had to get home from Paris on the Sunday night in time to catch the plane to New York the next day for the Ryder Cup. Everybody was going to the airport on the Sunday night from the Lancôme so you've got to be unlucky not to get a lift of some description. I had plenty of time, actually, and I went on the Traveleads bus. I flew British Midland airways and got into East Midlands airport at 9.45 p.m. No sweat.

Ryder Cup, Muirfield Village, Columbus, Ohio

Monday 21 to Monday 28 September
Caught the 9.40 from East Midlands to London to get the 12 o'clock plane to New York. This is the hard part because after the Ryder Cup it's the Dunhill Cup. It was going to be difficult getting up to St Andrews in time to measure the course for Wednesday of next week, since we were not due to land at Heathrow until the Tuesday morning. But then Malcolm Hulley and Sandy Jones (officials of the PGA) changed our tickets so that we could leave immediately after the Ryder Cup and get back to England on Monday morning. They looked after us great.

We flew to New York on TWA and changed terminals to find the plane to Columbus, Ohio. Got to the desk, gave our tickets in. All ten caddies sat there (the other two were travelling separately) and when they said: 'Ladies and gentlemen, this plane is oversubscribed. Anybody that wants to wait for the next plane will receive $150 dollars', ten caddies dived at the desk. By this time it had gone up to $250 but it was in vouchers to be used on TWA so it wasn't any good to us. If it had been Nelson Eddies (readies, dollars) we'd have had them, snatched their hands off.

When we got to Columbus the transport was ready for us and we arrived at the Red Roof Inn at 7 p.m. Had a double room all to myself. The players only got there at 5 p.m. and they'd been on Concorde. We watched tv that night and it showed Woosnam and Sam and Sandy and some of the others on the putting green.

Early starts and long days, the Ryder Cup was. For some reason the practice rounds seemed to take forever. Mind, you had the halfway hut between the 9th green and the 10th tee. We could get drinks, sandwiches, even cigarettes in there at the right price – nothing. Once we'd eaten our sandwiches the idea was to give the crusts to the fish and watch them eat. Golden carp they were. Looked like piranha.

The caddies were flown to the Ryder Cup in 1983 but we weren't given any gear then. This time we had two pairs of trousers, real good ones, 50 or 60 quid a throw, two pairs of socks, three shirts (they told you which ones to wear every day), a black V-neck Glenmuir sweater, pair of Pro-Quip water proofs, pair of Foot-Joy shoes. You get those half a dozen times a year in the States anyway. Foot-Joy just turn up and give you a pair of training shoes. Normally they're $40 or $50 retail. If they've got any left when everybody's had one free pair, you can have another for $20. They're incredibly comfortable. They don't keep their shine very long if you're walking through wet grass all day but if you're getting that many pairs you can look respectable.

The caddies didn't see why Europe shouldn't win. We thought we'd got as good a chance as they had. Over the years the Memorial tournament at Muirfield Village has been won with very high scores. They've had cold, windy conditions and the greens are fast and you couldn't play to the pins. But in the Memorial earlier in the year Sandy finished sixth. He loved it then.

He said after one practice round: 'The thing about this course is you can remember every hole. Some courses you can't. There's no gimmicks. You can see what you've got to do. The fairways are fairly generous. When you miss them you're in trouble but they're not narrow targets to aim at. It's very fair.'

After the first afternoon when we dry-rubbed them, four-none, the danger was thinking: 'We're in front and they can't pass us.' Jacklin had to raise the spirits every morning. Not that they were downhearted, but he had to get them into a fighting mood each morning, even more so when they were in front than when they were behind. When you're behind you *know* you've got to do it.

My best memory of 1983 is of Jack Nicklaus looking grey when he thought his team had lost on that last afternoon, but this time he looked resigned to it all week. My best memory of him this time is on the 14th hole on the Saturday afternoon. In front the Faldo/Woosnam match against Strange/Kite had finished with incredible golf by both sides and Nicklaus came and stood on that tee right beside me and said: 'I can't believe the scores you guys are doing on here. I thought this was supposed to be a hard course.' I said: 'It is a hard course.'

I think that Nicklaus was trying to fulfil too many roles. That course was designed by him and it's a masterpiece. Now, when you design a course the ultimate test is to have the best players in the world on it. He has that at the Memorial every year so he has actually got over that. But he acts as host then, doesn't he? He was also doing that the Ryder Cup week. Maybe he still felt he was host rather than captain. Where else have we been before where the captain lives there? It's not neutral ground.

A lot of the success of the event had to do with the fact that they were not playing for money. Everybody was there to play golf. In our two matches on the Saturday there were four millionaires playing as hard as they could, for nothing. What more do you want?

Saturday was the best day's golf I've ever seen. Sandy and Langer played Nelson and Wadkins, morning and afternoon. In the morning we won that first hole with a five. They're on the green in two. They put their second putt, not their first putt, off the green. It was the most diabolical pin position anyone had ever seen.

We'd had half an hour's delay for frost and then we played a long match in the morning, which we won 2 & 1. Then we were last out again in the afternoon. After nine holes Langer said: 'This vill be a long game. Ve have to have something to eat and then ve vill carry on.' You can just imagine him with a knife in his teeth crawling under the barbed wire.

If you look at him shot by shot he looks very ordinary but he was never out of the hole. The begger wouldn't give up. I had a wind map of Muirfield Village. I worked out which way the wind was blowing on the first hole and related it to the first nine and then checked it after nine holes to see if it had moved or not. I drew an arrow on it and me and Bernhard studied it every hole.

Langer drove in the trees on the 15th on Saturday afternoon where Sandy made that eagle. A right crap-'ole shot it was. Langer said to Sandy: 'You play your shot first and if you make a good job of it I'll have a go. Otherwise I'll chip out and try and make a five.' Sandy played a good shot and Langer had a go but it hit a few trees and came down on the side of the hazard. All he could do was hack it forward. Then his fourth shot went over the green and he went wild because he was out of the hole. He went hairless, couldn't handle it. Been at it all day and he hadn't been out of one hole.

The best example of what Langer's like was on the 11th hole in the foursomes. He came across and said: 'You have either got 227 or 228 to the front.' I said: 'Yes, it's 230.' He said: 'OK, it's 228 to the front.' He wouldn't give up two bloody yards. He's got a helluva sense of humour. I mean, him and Sandy were blowing kisses to one another at one point. He never asks you what you said because he listens. He might say: 'What did you mean?' but he's always heard what was said.

Wadkins birdied the last five holes in the afternoon. It hasn't been said much before, mainly because he didn't always hole out, but he was only a few feet away on the last and it was the same on the par five where Sandy made the eagle. As Lanny Wadkins said, Sandy killed them on the par fives, hitting a two iron on that 11th hole in the morning foursomes to a few feet. That was the turning point of that match.

Sandy played an eight iron to the last in the afternoon, helluva shot. Finished six feet from the hole and he said to Langer: 'Get inside that.' When Langer's ball ended only eighteen inches from the hole, Jacklin and Gallardo started jumping up and down like dervishes by the side of the green. We wondered what the hell had gone off because we couldn't see. It virtually finished in the dark. We won by one hole. Perfect end to a fantastic day.

Langer and Sandy were an ideal combination. Sandy wants to get on with it but Langer wants to think about it. Langer's speeded up a bit and Sandy's slowed down a bit. They got on well together because one wasn't trying to play the shots for the other. They discussed each shot and then left the other one to get on with it.

In the singles Kite wasn't playing very well but he's the sort of player that once he gets confident, once the breaks go with him, then he's away. That's what happened. Sandy was one up but lost the par five, the fifth. He hit this three iron and it buried in the bank of the water hazard. Another yard and it would have been a chip and a putt for a four. Of course, he lost that hole. The next hole Kite got up and down and Sandy didn't. Kite missed the green on the short eighth and got up and down. Now it's starting to go with him. Our last chance was at the 12th where Kite buried it in the bunker near the pin and still got up and down. Then he birdied 13 and 14 and he was away. The turning point was that par five. If Sandy's ball had carried a bit more he had a chance of going two up and then Kite's still struggling with his game. Sandy said: 'Once you let this bloke get on top of you that's it, you're wasting your time. Just like Lanny Wadkins. Once he starts you can just pack your boots.'

Saw the presentation and left for the airport. I had taken my camera but ran out of film after the presentation ceremony and had to borrow a new film off Phil Sheldon (a British golf photographer). We got two bottles of Johnnie Walker whisky each and all the champagne we could carry when we left. One bottle actually got to St Andrews.

We were guzzling this whisky and champagne on the way to the airport and we walked in there like a bloody football team. Everybody knows what's going off, you see, and they're saying well done, well done. At Chicago it's the same. Had great big pizzas and all this beer and it all vanished.

Two golf writers went out of their way to slag IMG (International Management Group, the management firm run by Mark McCormack) after the Ryder Cup. When the Cup was held at The Belfry in 1985 the team's waterproofs were supplied by Vent-O-Lite and pictures were taken of the team wearing the Vent-O-Lite clothing.

Later, Vent-O-Lite used the pictures of the team as advertisements many a time. Sandy, Seve Ballesteros, Sam Torrance and Nick Faldo were contracted to Sunderland, another manufacturer of rain gear, and with all this publicity that Vent-O-Lite were making Sunderland broke their contracts wtih Sandy, Sam and Faldo and refused to pay them. IMG, as managers of Sam, Sandy and Faldo, were caught up in the middle of this and blamed by Sunderland.

To prevent a similar row happening again this year, IMG said that their players who had clothing contracts with other manufacturers would not wear clothes supplied by rival manufacturers. Langer, Lyle, Faldo did wear the team clothes, actually, but they blacked out the logo of the manufacturer, Glenmuir, on the shirts and sweaters.

This was picked up by Peter Haslam of *Golf World* and John Ingham in *Golf Monthly*. Peter Haslam never mentioned the fact that the three lads had lost all their money from the Sunderland deal. And that's the point.

Flew to Chicago, on to London and landed at ten past ten. The flight to East Midlands went at 11 a.m. I had to get my luggage, change terminals and get a ticket to East Midlands, which I did. I'd got two bottles of whisky and a big bottle of champagne. I put 'em on a trolley and ran through customs. I couldn't have stopped if I'd wanted to.

I got home for one o'clock on the Monday and watched the Ryder Cup videos all afternoon. Hilary had taped about five hours' worth. This was the first time, strange as it may seem, that I'd seen the Cup matches as a whole and I hadn't fully realized what a great occasion it was and how tight it all got, specially in the singles on the last day. Months later, Lanny Wadkins said about the Saturday that even though he'd been on the losing side he was still proud to have taken part in such good matches.

Dunhill Cup, Old Course, St Andrews, Scotland

Tuesday 29 September
Me and Hilary drove up to St Andrews for the Dunhill Cup. Shared a flat in a house with Prodge, who was caddying for Faldo, and Brian Dunlop. We had picked the house out of a tourist board brochure.

— 31 —

Wednesday 30 September

When we came off the course there was a load of attractive girls standing around with their mother. One of them, little Evie, asked me to get Sandy's autograph. I said to her: 'You go and get it. He won't bite you.' The mother's name was Elsie Stewart and with her husband Wince they ran the Craw's (Crow's) Nest in Anstruther with their seven daughters. I asked if they did dinner for non-residents and when they said they did I asked if we could book a table for tomorrow night? So we went round there. Brilliant, it was, brilliant. Couldn't eat it all.

Thursday 1 October

Got on the tee at the Dunhill. There was Sandy, Sam and Brand Jnr and I said to them: 'You've played for glory, let's see you play for money.'

First round was against Zimbabwe. The full Zimbabwe team is Mark McNulty, Nick Price and Denis Watson, but none of them played. Instead Sandy played Tim Price, Nick's brother, who is a club pro at Royal Harare. Price was three under after four and Sandy was one under. Tim is a good golfer but a very slow player and that rattled Sandy slightly. He doesn't like slow players. In the end Tim three-putted a few times mainly because he was leaving himself so far from the pin, and Sandy played steady. Beat them, the Irish and the Americans to reach the final for the first time.

Sunday 4 October

Scotland against England. Sandy played Nick Faldo and Faldo holed a real good load of putts from 10 to 15 ft for birdies. He played slightly better than Sandy and he holed the putts as well. I think he shot 66; Sandy was 69. Behind were Sam and Gordon Brand and the turning point of the match came on the 13th where Gordon drove into the big bunkers. Sam hit his second shot stone dead while Gordon came out of the bunker sideways. Then Gordon holed his third shot with a five iron. He finished up shooting a 64. So that was the end of that.

Monday 5 October

I got back and everybody said: 'You've had a good trip. Where are you going now?'

And I said: 'I'm going to Stuttgart in the morning.'

German Masters, Stuttgart, West Germany

Tuesday 6 to Sunday 11 October
Had to get the 7 a.m. plane from East Midlands down to London Heathrow. D. J. Russell was also on the plane. My mate Willi Hofmann, Langer's coach, had said he'd arrange a place to stay for two or three of us. It turned out to be over a bakery. This old woman served us fresh bread every morning, cackling away to herself. Couldn't understand a word, mind. Every night we ate in a pizza place run by an Italian. So there we are in the middle of Germany saying *buongiorno* and *grazie* and all this.

We were standing outside the caravan provided by Mizuno [the Japanese sports equipment manufacturers] one day and there were some real tatty golf clubs on a trolley. Barry Willett, who is in charge of the caravan, looked at these clubs, which had no covers on them, and said: 'Whoever owns these is a rich man. The fellow that made these clubs is personal clubmaker to the King of Morocco. Barry recognized the clubs because they were made by Lambert Topping, who used to be clubmaker at St George's Hill, and Barry succeeded him. It turned out that the clubs belonged to former Chancellor Schmidt.

Then Seve came beaming up to Barry with this MacGregor driver he had bought at the Ryder Cup. Barry looked at it and said: 'Hmmm, it's not bad really – for a forgery.' It had a MacGregor soleplate on it but the insert wasn't MacGregor. And Seve had paid $500 for it. You should have seen his face.

Sandy hacked it round in the first three rounds and then played really well on the last day when he had a 66. Of course, Langer played the best he's played for ages but couldn't hole a putt, otherwise we wouldn't have been in a play-off. But anyway we are. Sandy hit a driver and a four iron on the first play-off hole, the 17th, which was playing very long. Langer chipped and putted and the crowd all roared. They would, wouldn't they? On the 18th, a par five, Sandy hit a good drive and Langer for some reason took a three wood. He'd got a very strong three wood but it still left him another screaming three wood to the green.

He had a downhill lie and he was trying to hammer it and he cut it, a low cutter.

Just to the right of the 18th is the practice ground, which is out of bounds. Langer's ball was heading that way and three rows of Germans were standing to attention, sticking their chests out for this ball to hit them. It landed and took a helluva kick up in the air and went over their heads. Their arms shot up to try and catch it but it looked as if it had gone out of bounds. He then hit another similar sort of shot. Sandy waited patiently to find out whether Langer's first ball was still in play or not. Andy McFee, the tournament director, said it was out of bounds. So Sandy was not going to risk anything. He hit a shot into a bunker near the green in two and Langer was fifty or sixty yards away in four.

We stood there waiting for everything to sort itself out. I said to Sandy: 'How many has he had?' Sandy replied: 'Four, so the best he can do is a six.' I said: 'No, no. You've got to look for him to hole it and get down in five.' That's what you have to do at the death in matchplay. You've got to assume the bloke's going to hole from the rough or something, and then you're not going to be deflated if he does. Langer had a good go at it but missed. So Sandy came out of the bunker and had two putts for it from four feet. Thank you very much. Next?

It was Sandy's first win in Europe since the Benson & Hedges at York in 1985. He's not one to show much emotion. His dad always taught him that win or lose he should stay the same. He's very even-tempered. His dad used to say to him, 'Tempo, not temper.' Sandy is 'thank you very much, take the money, get in the car and let's go'. You don't have to worry about Sandy. He'll win every now and then anyway.

Got back to Sandy's place about 9.45 p.m. and went to an Indian restaurant. I was staying with him for the World Matchplay next week.

Suntory World Match-play Championship, Wentworth, Surrey

Monday 12 October
Spent the day on the settee asleep. Had a pain down my chest and I was coughing. I reckon I picked up a bug in Germany last week and it was made worse by having to wear overalls while we caddied. Caddies hate overalls. They may look smart but we get so hot in them. Felt awful. Got worse all week. Sandy's father and mother were there and his father had a hip flask and so he kept me going. We used to have prearranged spots on the course where he'd give me a drop of whisky. In the evenings we had to toast the Ryder Cup team as well. We got through four bottles of Ballantine's between us.

All the competitors in the match-play are given a house for the week on the Wentworth estate and a cook provided by Suntory. But Sandy, Nick Faldo and Mark McNulty all live on the estate so they didn't need houses. Sandy said he'd rather stay in his own house and so Judie Simpson, the cook, came and lived there for the week. Normally she lived in Chiswick and ran a wine bar so we were in good hands.

Tuesday 13 October
Practice day. I remember nothing, I felt so ill.

Wednesday 14 October
Pro-am day. Sandy played with Sir Neil MacFarlane, the former Conservative Minister of Sport. We always have a bit of a joke with him. He fades the ball quite a bit you see, and so I said: 'I see you're still inclined to the right,' and he replied: 'Yes, ever since 11 June' (election day).

Something very unpleasant happened at the end of the round. As we were coming up the 18th we saw Prodge coming down behind the ropes with a cup of coffee in his hands. 'I've got some bad news,' he says. 'Terry's girlfriend [Holley Church] got killed in America.'

Terry Holt, another caddie, was carrying for David Ishii. He'd known her for a long while. We're all a bit odd at this game but Terry's a bit odder sometimes. He'd met this girl and she was the only real person he'd been accused of getting on with. They'd got a place right on the beach in Jacksonville, Florida. She used to work in an estate agent's office and would organize us a nice place to stay for the TPC. She'd been across to the Open at Muirfield.

I said to Prodge: 'How did you get to know?'

'There's been two phone calls.'

'Are you sure?'

'Yes. They've both come from different sources.' One of the caddies in America had read it in a Jacksonville paper and had phoned, and then somebody else had phoned as well.

'Well, he's got to be told. We can't not tell him. Where is he?'

We told Ishii and then we went into the players' changing room and took a glass of brandy with us. We sat there waiting for Terry. As it happened there was nobody else there. Terry came in all full of life. I said: 'Sit down, Terry', and then Prodge told him. He was distraught. Provision was made for him to ring Florida from the tournament office.

Something similar had happened to me. When the Martini tournament was at Lindrick in 1982 my mother died the night before it started. The last thing she said to me was: 'Go to the golf tomorrow', and so I did. Terry remembered that. I said the best thing is to do the work. It's good to have something to do.

Thursday 15 to Sunday 18 October
We're playing David Ishii and everybody kept asking me what he was like. I'd say: 'He's the second leading money-winner in Japan, he's a good golfer and he's a gentleman.' We were four down at lunch. After thirty holes Sandy had got back to all square. Ishii was getting tired but Sandy was getting stronger and stronger. The longer a tournament the better he plays because he gets down to it. Sandy drove into a bunker on the 13th. Then it started to rain heavily and we had to mark the ball in the bunker and go back there the next morning. It was the night of the hurricane. I didn't hear a thing. I had the flu, you see.

All the roads were blocked the next morning. There was a tree down over Sandy's shed at Lyle Towers. Couldn't drive anywhere. Seve got there for seven o'clock the next morning. He walked in to the clubhouse from the house he was staying in.

After clearing-up operations, play resumed in the afternoon and we beat Ishii at the third extra hole. Got up and down from the right of the 17th, which is impossible. The next day we beat Larry Mize who had been waiting, like Scott Simpson, for what must have seemed like days. These two plus Greg Norman and Nick Faldo had been seeded and didn't start until the second round.

I sat at the same lunch table as Simpson and Mize. Simpson was really taken aback by how aggressive Seve was when they played. He said that every time he got a birdie Seve got three. It was the same sort of startled reaction that Jack Nicklaus had in the Ryder Cup.

Played McNulty in the semi-final. We'd had it, hadn't we? Three down and four to play but ... finished up winning. Sandy said: 'You'll have to start calling me ice-man now.'

Monday 19 October
The final against Woosie. Lost on the last green. When Sandy is playing a friend, like Woosie, he doesn't play any less hard, don't try any less to win. Basically there's no difference except you know Woosie's not going to be a funny bugger. He's not going to pull any tricks. Not going to be a cry baby. He's just going to get on with it, fast. They're two fast players.

Same with us caddies. We played Faldo in the final of the Dunhill and Prodge was caddying for him. It don't make any difference. You don't try and beat individuals. You just try and win and you either do or you don't. You know one has to win and one has to lose. But there's no needle between us. We joke with one another about the players. It's the same every week. You've got to live and travel together so there's no point in any of that. In fact you do it the other way round because you're helping one another more than anything, even in match-play. At Wentworth in the match-play one year I dropped my yardage book and the other caddie, John Moorhouse, gave it back to me. I'd have been in trouble without it.

Sandy likes the match-play because it improves his putting. 'You don't have to worry about missing the putt back,' he says. 'You get more aggressive. It's either going in or it isn't. In stroke play you have to bear in mind that you're going to miss a putt every now and then, but in match-play it doesn't matter about missing. That putt for a birdie, bang. That's why the scores are so good every year.'

Back home that night, knackered. This was the end of a seven-week stretch of major competitions and a helluva lot of travelling. To Switzerland then back for the European Open at Walton Heath, Trophée Lancôme in Paris, back home, down to London, Ryder Cup, back to London, back home, up to the Dunhill, back home, Stuttgart and then back to London for the Match-play. We couldn't miss any of them and the Ryder Cup was the odd one out and that turned out to be the highlight.

At Home

Tuesday 20 October
I've got two weeks at home with the unsurpassable luxury of not having to go out for meals, being able to wash my own pots when I've had dinner, and not to have to feed a hungry suitcase. I'm away so much I think washing my own pots is a pleasure.

Friday 23 October
Down to my golf club, Coxmoor, near Mansfield. Must be the best value for money in the world except for the ratepayers of St Andrews who don't have to pay anything. Paid £163.86 plus VAT for 1988. It's a super course, heathland. It must be the best winter course there is, drains terrifically. I got 36 points in a stableford, playing off eight; well, 7.5 to be precise.

Sunday 25 October
Me and Hilary went to Mablethorpe. It was cold and windy, typical autumn weather. There was a man with all his family around him and he said to them: 'We're having a day out and you will enjoy it.' We had a good day. There's no poseurs there. Where we go, for the golf, there are always poseurs. Take the Masters at Augusta. It's mainly people who go somewhere to be seen and admired. At Mablethorpe it's just

ordinary people. The sands are wide, clean and stretch for miles. It's just the weather that's the trouble.

Kirin Cup, Yomiuri CC, Tokyo

Saturday 31 October
Left home at 8.40 a.m. and flew from East Midlands to London Heathrow. At East Midlands I checked my bags right through to Tokyo for the Kirin Cup. This is the successor to the Nissan Cup, an end-of-season event between teams of six from Europe, Japan, the US and Australia and New Zealand. It is played on a round-robin basis for the first three days. In each individual match you get two points for a win and one for a half. These are all totalled up and at the end of three days the top two teams play each other in the final and the others play for third and fourth place. The Japs won it last year, beating Europe in the final.

Plane took off for Tokyo thirty minutes late. When I've been before we've had to fly to Anchorage, stop there for an hour and a half and then fly on to Tokyo. The flight took something like eighteen hours. But we got on this one and I couldn't figure the times we were to arrive in Tokyo until I realized it was a direct flight across Russia, been open since June. Flight took eleven hours directly over Copenhagen, Helsinki and then across Siberia. That's the best thing to do with Siberia, fly over it.

Landed at Tokyo and me and Wobbly (Philip Morbey, Ian Woosnam's caddie) got a bus to Tokyo's central bus terminal. It cost us ten quid. Taxi to the Akasaka Prince hotel, the tournament hotel. We got caddies' rate of $100 a night, which works out cheaper than if we had stayed in a smaller hotel. Arrived there at 12.10 p.m. on Sunday, Japanese time, which is 3.10 a.m. on Sunday morning back home. Immediately went to McDonalds for Big Mac and big flies.

First day was measuring day. Took Prodge's wheel. On every hole they have two different greens, one bent grass and one Koria grass. We played on the bent grass greens.

The Lions baseball team had their quarters at our hotel and they had these great big buses. On board was a girl in uniform and when we go to the course in the morning she brings you coffee and in the evening all the beer you can drink. It's Kirin beer, the tournament promoters. Not bad, actually. It's like a decent bottled beer in England.

Tokyo is a big sprawling city that looks featureless. All you can see is rooftops and buildings. The only landmarks are golf driving ranges. They look like big overgrown tennis courts. As you approach the Yomiuri course, which must be the hilliest course there is, there are three big billboards of Seve drinking Sapporo beer. One of them is opposite the entrance to the club, so on one corner you see this big advertisement of Seve drinking Sapporo beer and on the other there's Tommy Nakajima with some Kirin beer.

A new clubhouse, started the day after last year's tournament, was completed two weeks before this year's. They spent 180 million yen on it, which turned out to be £7 million. It was what I call a high-tech clubhouse. You know you have brushes to clean your shoes at courses in Europe? In Japan there's a line of little compressed air hoses and you squirt compressed air on your trousers and shoes. And when you go to the urinals there's a little electronic eye watching and when you've finished it automatically flushes.

Last year I noticed the toilet seats were electrically heated. This year I noticed there's a control panel at the side with buttons and lights. I thought I'll have a go at this, and I was playing about with these buttons when all of a sudden there's a little pipe comes from underneath and squirts a load of water all over just like an automatic bidet. So I got Faldo and Langer and said: 'Come and look at this', and squirted them with water.

The remote-control caddie cars run on a path which has a metal strip in it to act as a guide. The lady caddies wear brightly-coloured uniforms and white silk gloves and have buttons to start and stop the cars. Each machine can carry up to four big bags, costs $40,000 and there are ninety of them at this club. There are two places where it's a steep climb from green to the next tee and so they've built automatic walkways, like you see at airports, for the players. They must want something to spend their money on, I reckon.

There's a big craze for pachinco in Japan, a sort of equivalent to bingo. You see these halls packed with these machines, vertical bagatelle. The Japs sit there in rows. You put your money in and you get a load of ball bearings that are fed in automatically. All you do is control the rate they come out at. You have to aim for a certain nail at the top. Once you get one in, little doors and windows start opening up and make it easier for you to get your ball bearings in. If you win they start lighting up and bells ring. You press a button and a fellow comes with a dish. When you've got a load of ball bearings you take 'em down the end of the hall and pour them into an automatic machine that counts them. That gives you a ticket which you take to the counter and behind this counter are a load of prizes, as if at a funfair. You pick out what prize you want.

Tuesday 3 November
Practice day. Sandy played with José-Maria Olazabal and gave him a lesson. Sandy had been saying all year that Olazabal had been hitting the ball too low, swinging too short. So he used Jimmy Ballard's method on him. Got him playing a lot better by making him use more width on his backswing. Sandy helps people quite a lot. He's got the method and the strap, or connector, that he got from Ballard and he gets everybody tied up in the strap and defies them to hit the ball. Bloody funny. 'Teach' Lyle, I call him.

He had also given Seve a lesson in the Ryder Cup. We'd stood watching Seve on the practice ground at the Lancôme and he'd been swaying too much on his backswing. Sandy put him right the day before the Ryder Cup started.

Wednesday 4 November
Pro-am day. Rain reduced it to nine holes. It still took three hours. Sandy has a colour code for each amateur to help him remember them – red hat, glasses, yellow sweater, that sort of thing. You blast off with your four and they spread out to the four different corners of the earth. You never see them until you hear them shouting, 'caddie-san, caddie-san'. There's only one caddie and she's running about with clubs telling them how far it is, the lines on the green, raking bunkers. The Japanese

ladies run rings around us. They caddie for four, we caddie for one and they come and fill in our divots and take the pin and are laughing like hell all the time. A scream, they are.

The caddies got treated very well this week. We signed for breakfast – bacon and eggs, cornflakes, toast. In the afternoon we picked what grub we wanted – beef curry, beer, ice-cream. You needed a cast-iron constitution to cope with it all.

The bus journey to and from the hotel took approximately one and a half hours going out in the morning because we were going away from the city, and two and a half hours coming back. Some of the caddies found a way of getting to the course by train. It was about an hour quicker and a lot of them went that way. But it suited me to be on the bus. There was tv and sometimes the sumo wrestling was on and I could have a beer and relax.

Thursday 5 to Saturday 7 November
Played the Americans – again. They had their caddies with them, many of whom had come from the Nabisco Champion-ships in San Antonio, Texas. The American caddies checked the pin positions without realizing they were the pin positions used in the pro-am and would later be changed for the first day's play of the competition proper. They went whizzing about the course acquiring duff info and it led to one or two mistakes. In fact it happened at least once with Lanny Wadkins who Sandy played on the first day. Sandy shot a 68 and Lanny a 72. There was one hole where Sandy got a birdie and Lanny put his ball where he thought the pin was and it wasn't there; it was higher up the green.

So we beat America again, this time 3½ to 2½. Second day Sandy was 67 and Nakamura 72 and Europe beat Japan 10–2. Third day against Australia Sandy had a 67 and Graham Marsh a 71 and the team won 7–5.

The Australians were crying all night about the scoring system. It has been the same for three years. They won 1½ matches and America won one match, but America had more points than Australia. It has always been the teams with the most points that get first and second places.

I said to Graham Marsh: 'It's going to be a good tussle

between Australia and the US to get into the final.' He said: 'We're in the final because we've won more matches overall then they have. We've won two and lost one. The United States have only won one match overall.' But that didn't count because it has always been decided on individual points in a match rather than on team points.

George O'Grady and Tony Gray from the European tour were there and they were jumping up and down because we were in the final for the third year running. Langer was a very good captain. He discussed different holes with the players and how they should be played. He asked everybody's opinion about where they wanted to play. And he put Sandy and Woosie out first because they are fast players. He's a good bloke, Langer is.

The last day we got beat by America 5–1 or 10–2 in the end but at one stage when Sandy's match had finished we were up in three and down in three. If that had been the final score we'd have drawn 3–3 with America and lost because the first countback goes on scores for the day. Then we'd have had far more cause for complaint than the Australians because we'd have won three matches and halved one and still got beat. So that shut the Australians up.

So we were beaten in a third successive final. The Dunhill Cup, the World Match-play and now the Kirin Cup.

In three years Sandy has played twelve matches in this competition. Of those he has won ten and halved two. Mind you, it's stroke-play.

Who should turn up in Tokyo but Dave Thomas, the former Ryder Cup player, and his son Paul? We reminisced with Dave about the Ryder Cup, about how over the years it was the British that had made a balls-up of the last hole in every match and this year it was the Americans. We never lost the last hole at Muirfield Village. Dave had played in Ryder Cups over the years and had many disappointments and so he felt that he'd been on the winning team as much as anybody.

Checking out of the hotel is all organized there. You leave your case in your room, put your label on it with which terminal and what flight you're on, and they tell you what bus to catch. When you get to the airport, there's your case.

I paid my hotel bill with a Visa card. You get a better rate by paying with Visa and settling up at the end of the month than changing sterling into yen at the hotel. I reckon this is true in many countries and so I always try and use a credit card.

Bus to the airport took two hours and forty minutes so I wrote my diary, watched the Sumo wrestling. Because of crossing the dateline we left Tokyo at 8.45 p.m. on Sunday and arrived in Honolulu at 8.30 a.m. on the same Sunday.

Isuzu Kapalua International, Kapalua, Maui, Hawaii

Sunday 8 to Sunday 15 November
When we arrived I discovered I had lost the winder on my watch. I just had my alarm clock, which was all I needed to get me to the course in time.

I didn't need a car and for me it's a blessing not to need a car. No telephone, no watch, no television. There was television but it was full of US football and films. You can't really count that as television. No newspapers so we didn't hear all the bad news. Perfect two weeks. What more do you want?

Monday morning, a beautiful sunny day. We were all in shorts. Sandy played a four-ball with John Mehigan, a representative in California for North-Western, the equipment manufacturers, versus Howard Clark and Bruce Keplinger. This fellow Keplinger was interesting, a left-hander. He is a rep for Lake Tahoe Casino and he travels around the west and the mid-west of the US playing with high rollers, those they want to get into the casino. This fellow shot 72 and Lyle shot 73 off the same tees. What could be better than a four-ball in Hawaii on a Monday morning in November?

The first two days of the tournament were a pro-am. If you wanted to play it cost you $5000 which got you two rounds of golf and a week at the hotel, not including the grub or air fare from mainland US. One of our pro-am team on the first day was called Mr Williams. He was a big bloke, reminded me of Gerald Ford, the former US President. He said he had his practice there. 'What sort of practice?' we asked. 'I'm a brain surgeon,' he replied. This struck us as being very funny and we spent the rest of the day being as articulate as possible in case he was short of patients.

You played the two best balls of the five and after two days Sandy's team were 57 under par, which won it. So Sandy had played with the winning team for three successive years and not earned a penny because there was no prize money in the pro-am.

At this tournament they had pineapples for tee markers and little hedges around the junction boxes to camouflage the water pumps. They were selling pairs of flip-flops, like you'd wear on the beach only with spikes, for $35 a throw. That struck us as being different.

Sandy and I both like Hawaii for different reasons. I like it because it's the only tournament we play where the caddies are allowed to wear shorts, the reason being that when the tour stopped there years ago they could only get local caddies who wore shorts and no shoes. Shorts are more comfortable and practical than trousers in the heat.

Sandy likes Kapalua because he is a good reader of the grainy greens there. The grain grows towards the right-hand tip of Lanai island so he knew what every putt was going to do. They grow towards the setting sun. That's true of anywhere where there's grainy greens. That's why I always carry a compass in the bag, to be able to find west. In my yardage book I draw a line on every green to where the setting sun is.

Greens are cut in strips up and down so that one strip is dark and one is light. The light is because the grass is growing away from you and the dark because it is growing towards you. If you're putting along a light strip it's faster than if you're putting along a dark strip. Also if you're putting across the cut it's slower. Sandy weighs all that up. If you know what to look for it's easy to tell which way the grass is growing. At Kapalua, in Florida or any courses that have Bermuda grass greens, you get a ragged edge on one side of the hole and a very sharp edge on the other. So you make sure you look at the hole before you putt. Bobby Locke used to go up to the hole, peer carefully at it and plod back. He was looking to see which way the grain was growing.

— 45 —

Sandy started off well, shooting a 65, seven under in the first round but then was overtaken by Andy Bean. The last two rounds he played with Bean and Lanny Wadkins. He shot a 71 on the last day, which wasn't a good enough score to win. He was 16 under par with two bogeys and one double bogey for the week. So he had twenty birdies. And he finished third, winning $50,000.

World Cup, Kapalua, Maui, Hawaii

Monday 16 November
A day on the beach. Not very difficult.

Tuesday 17 to Saturday 21 November
The golfers started to arrive for the World Cup (a tournament for two-man teams from thirty-two countries). Some – Philippe Toussaint, Ernesto Acosta, Priscillio Dinez – I hadn't seen for years. We missed a chance to make some money selling yardage books. José-Maria Canizares and José Rivero for example kept asking us for the yardages. If we'd spent a few days working them out and copying them down we could have made a bob or two. But we never thought of it.

In the pro-am Sandy shot 66 and Sam Torrance 71 and they won it, splitting the first prize of $5000.

The Kapalua tournament and the World Cup both got national television across America and because of this the leaders were paired together even though they didn't go off last. In the first round of the Kapalua Sandy had a 68 with two bogeys, both three putts, and in the second round he was 69 with no bogeys. By now it had got wet and very windy and after two rounds Woosie and Sandy were tied in the lead in the individual competition, both seven under par. Everybody was saying that if Shropshire had sent a team they'd have won easily.

God, it was slow! The first day we got round in four hours and ten minutes. The second round was five hours and forty minutes and on the last round it took four hours just to get to the 12th tee.

In the third round Sandy was 71 with two bogeys and the

last round when there was the worst rain for twenty-five years he had two bogeys for his 71. We played with the Americans Ben Crenshaw and Payne Stewart. Crenshaw played fantastic but then he left two putts short and it destroyed him. Left them right in the jaws. They're both good fellows to play with, very considerate of the other players.

I said to them as we stood on the 1st hole that last day: 'I don't know how you can keep on pitching up and playing. Fly across the world and go out and play . . . I don't know how you do it. I'd have walked in.' It was windy and raining heavily and early in the morning, half-past seven sort of time.

After thirteen holes Scotland were three shots in front of Wales. Then Sandy three-putted the 14th and David Llewellyn holed a real good putt for a par, so we lost a shot there. Woosnam birdied the 15th and Sam dropped one on the 16th. On the 17th, Woosnam went within inches of hitting the cart path. If he had it would have gone into the water and been a double bogey. As it happens, the ball stuck in the grass and he made four. Sam also made four. Sandy and David made par.

Playing the last, a par five, Sandy was in the right hand bunker off the tee but chipped and putted for a four. Sam pulled his second right out of bounds and took six. So it was into a play-off and we lost that on the second extra hole. Sam probably thought he'd let Sandy down. Suzanne Danielle, his fiancée, was there. She's very nice but she was very upset, particularly about Sam missing that putt in the play-off.

We were on the course seven hours in that foul weather. Even though it was 75 or 80 degrees it was very uncomfortable. If it had been in Europe we wouldn't have been able to play. It was like the third day of the Open.

Sandy was very disappointed because he had been playing very well. He'd had twenty birdies in the first tournament at Kapalua, and six in the pro-am; six on the first day here, three on the second day, three on the third, and another three on the last. That's forty-one birdies in two weeks.

It was the fourth final he'd lost in nine weeks – Dunhill (lost to England), Suntory (lost to Woosnam), Kirin Cup (lost to the US), and this one. This was the worst, mainly because it was just one loss after another. Not much you can say at a time like that. You've just got to keep going: he was going to Australia the next day and I was going home.

When something has gone wrong you have to carry on doing the job. The job's there whether you're winning or losing. The caddie does exactly the same thing – carries the clubs, cleans the balls – whatever the score. You must look on the bright side, stop them getting depressed. You can quote Kipling, I suppose. 'If you can meet with Triumph and Disaster and treat those two imposters just the same . . .' As I get older and more experienced at the game I don't get so depressed. You view things more in perspective. I do, anyhow. I look at some of the young caddies in the States and if they have a bad round they're almost suicidal. And if they have a good round they're world-beaters.

I couldn't have been very good company when I took it bad. In those days, in the mid-1970s, we used to do four or five tournaments together. You couldn't get home and you couldn't get away from golf. But now we're home almost every Sunday night except when we're in the USA.

Elation? I can't wave my arms up in the air. It seems a waste of time. Some of them do at the slightest excuse. Some of them have a big face up front. The thing is, who hits the ball? Who is the golfer and who is the caddie? A lot of them think it's them who's playing. They'll say: 'I finished second with him.' Or: 'In my career with him . . .' And I'll say: 'How many times did you hit the ball?'

There was a lad who caddied for Scott Hoch (a leading American golfer) in Kapalua. Hoch holed in one at Las Vegas and won a white Roller. Bloody great long par three and Hoch holed in one. The caddie said: 'That was the highlight of my career with him.' I ask you, what a load of bollocks.

Rats' (caddies') quarters were good in Hawaii. I shared a room with Mick Maull from Newark who caddies for Mats Lanner. We stayed in the cheapest place there and it was still $60 a night but we had kitchens so we could do our own cooking. You can get three in a room if you like. There's the beach 200 yards away and a supermarket nearby. It couldn't be much more convenient.

At Home

Friday 4 to Thursday 10 December

Did my accounts. I get paid a weekly wage, and 5 per cent of Sandy's prize money. He gives me a cheque whenever we can sit down to work it out. I get all my money paid right there, in the hand. It's not top of the packet, as we say. Take someone that's got a job worth £20,000. They don't see anything like that because of tax. I pay most of my own expenses. Usually at the end of the year Sandy has a long trip to Japan and Hawaii and he pays my expenses for that trip. If he's on his own I stay with him in the hotel. He paid my air fare for a trip to the US in May and June as well. But otherwise I look after myself.

I've always been legal. I don't want the tax man haunting me. I've tried to do my accounts properly and keep everything in order. I've played golf with my accountant for years. In the old days he'd fill the bloody forms in and I used to give him a few balls and some waterproofs in return. But now he says it's got to be done every quarter as I'm VAT-registered.

I said: 'But what happens if I'm away for four months at a stretch?' They said in the local VAT office: 'Why can't you ring the information in?' I said: 'What, from Japan?' I don't know what sort of world they live in, but it ain't the real one.

At one time it was a bit of a skive, this caddying game. A bit of fun. But it isn't any longer. It's run like a business now.

I used to sit and watch golf from America on television. All winter I'd be playing at Coxmoor in mud and sludge and rain. You can't feel your hands and you've got three or four sweaters and waterproofs on. Easter was the worst because there had been no growth and the winter seemed to be going on for ever and generally there would be a flurry of snow. Used to try and play in the Easter Cup, stuff like that. And on the Monday and Tuesday night it would be the highlights from Augusta National or sometimes they were even live on the Sunday night.

You think to yourself, if only I could go there once. Well, I've been there no end of times. I've been to all these places. If I never go again at least they can't take it away from me.

The best thing that ever happened to me was when I got laid

— 49 —

off by Rolls-Royce. We said it at the time, those of us who were trying to make up our minds whether to leave or not. We said this is the big kick up the arse. You either do it now or you stop here for ever. I'm going out with some of my former workmates next week. I've missed the last two reunions but it's been arranged this year specially for me. I had to give them a date when I knew I was going to be at home.

I'm not complaining. What I'm saying is: 'You either win money or you're home early.' I can't lose. Let's face it, we're all in it for the money really. As Hubert Green said: 'I'm a whore and I don't mind admitting it. I'll go and play anywhere for money.' I agree with him. You might as well be honest about it. Somebody said to me: 'What about the glory?' I replied: 'Where do you keep that? In a bag or in your pocket, or where?'

Friday 11 December
Left to go down to Lyle Towers for a couple of days. Sandy had had a practice net delivered, a load of heavy tubular bars and netting and a drawing showing how to erect it. So I carted all this tubular stuff and the net and everything across the lawn to where he wanted it and got all the bits out.

It was a load of joints that you threaded in and tied with Allen keys, and the very first two joints were the wrong size. They'd sent the wrong parts. So we packed all that lot up and put it in the shed. Right, we'll go home, Hilary and I thought, so we get in the car and it won't start. We're in a right state. How are we doing now? Getting nowhere. Eventually, of course, we get it going and the right parts for the net did arrive and now its in pretty constant use.

For Christmas, I gave Sandy a book about the Red Arrows, behind the scenes, the men who fly and so on. I had found it in Nottingham. He'd been up flying with them. Sandy gave us a microwave oven so we had to take a course in how to use it.

Tuesday 15 to Tuesday 29 December
Away to Tenerife for the Christmas hols, three couples. The others were old golfing friends. We'd been there on holiday with one couple the previous year, to the same place, Los

Gigantes. We like it there. It's good weather, a nice quiet place, never wear a sweater.

When we got to East Midlands airport we found the plane had been diverted to Manchester because the clouds were too low. So we had to go to Manchester in buses and it meant that we arrived four hours late in Tenerife, in the middle of the night. Somebody on the coach said they'd paid £80 more to fly from East Midlands rather than Manchester.

Celebrated Christmas Day by going down onto the beach and having a swim. Opened our presents. Had our Christmas lunch – fillet steak and Christmas pudding brought out from England. The girls did the cooking between them – only simple things usually, for instance baked potatoes, corned beef, tin of veg. Took a lot of food with us because you can't get everything there. The supermarkets were good, though. I got a litre of whisky for a fiver in one. The so-called duty free at the airport was nearly as much as you would pay in England. It's a rip-off, duty free.

Didn't play golf. I deliberately didn't go near it. The others are all keen golfers but they just went for R and R and the old currant bun. Champagne, orange juice and brandy at tea time. A bottle of wine was only just over a quid over there. Brandy was about £2.50 a bottle and champagne was virtually bugger-all. We swam and read. I read a lot of Len Deighton. It's the detail he uses to describe people that I like. I read about five or six of his books. Hilary was reading about one book a day. Our friends bought us a book of *Telegraph* crosswords for Christmas.

It was like Hawaii. No car, no watch, no tv, no radio. Fantastic when you take them out of your life. Saw people with cars and all they were doing was driving about trying to find somewhere to park.

The only drawback was that we had to fight our way past timeshare touts every morning either on the way to the beach or on the way to the shops. One day we went to listen to them because they'd offered us 200 cigarettes, a bottle of whisky and breakfast to do it. At one stage they were showing us a film of different places around the world and I nodded off. The fellow didn't like that. What he really didn't like was when he asked me: 'You've been all over the world, where would you really like to live?' I replied: 'Kirkby-in-Ashfield.' That really pissed him off.

I thought about what it's like being a caddie. Some people might ask what are the prerequisites of being a good caddie. There is only one – having a good golfer to carry for. A good golfer is somebody who can keep the ball in play off the tee and hole from four feet on the green.

I travel a lot so I know about suitcases. My advice is don't spend much on them. They're going to get the hell knocked out of them however much they're worth. Avoid the ones with zips because the zips burst. Also you want a clip not only at the front but on either side to maintain the solidity. Should have wheels that are built in. Detachable ones break too easily.

While we were in Tenerife I read in the *Daily Telegraph* that Henry Cotton had died. I've got his autograph from 1957. I first went to St Andrews in 1964 and I carried for Jean Garaialde who played with Tony Lema in the last two rounds of the Open that Lema won. The Open ended on a Friday in those days so the club pros could get back to supervise their shops at the weekends. After the Open finished we went down to the station and earned a few bob helping people with their suitcases on to the train. Got Cotton's cases, took them in the carriage and put them in the rack for him and he gave me half a crown. A few years ago we were in Paris and Sandy was practising his putting. Cotton was there and he said to me: 'Are you related to Sandy?' I said: 'Only financially.'

Saturday 9 January 1988
Down to London ready to fly tomorrow to San Diego for the first tournament of the season in the US, the Tournament of Champions.

I'm looking forward to it. It is always nice to be getting back to work. It's the old itchy feet, you see. It's great to get home and when you've been home for two weeks you want to go again. You work in weekly cycles. You wake up every Sunday morning and want to pack your suitcase.

At the end of the year you say: 'I've got away with it for another year. I beat the system for another twelve months.' It's the variety that I like. I haven't got to go to work in an office on a Monday morning and see the same old faces in the same old places and work out what my pension is going to be. I don't worry about the future. If I've got six months' work in front of me, that's the most I need. Six months, strewth! Look how many miles we travel in six months. That's my philosophy. Why plan further?

Sandy's flying out on Monday. He likes flying because it takes his mind out of gear. He reads motoring magazines, watches the films, listens to music, doesn't have to worry about anything. He makes life as simple as possible, that's the secret of his success.

I'm sure he will come up with something this year. He always does, doesn't he? Last year he was the only man to win on both sides of the Atlantic, the TPC in Florida in March and the German Masters in Stuttgart in October. By his standards his position in Europe may not have been very good. He came twelfth with winnings of £116,713. But remember, he finished thirty-fourth with nearly $300,000 in the US as well. I caddied for him in thirty-four tournaments when he won $760,000 in all. I'd say 1987 was pretty good.

I'm sure Sandy will do well this year, too. When I see him in San Diego on Tuesday he'll be all fresh and rarin' to go. He might have found a new club somewhere or a new idea about his swing. We shall see, shan't we? We shall see.

2

10 January–7 February

Caddies' meeting – Desert patrol – Victory in
Phoenix – McCord clouts me in the eye

MONY Tournament of Champions, La Costa CC, Carlsbad, California

Sunday 10 January 1988

Flew to San Diego via Los Angeles. Arrived 3.15 p.m. Pete Coleman was going to come with me but he rang just before I left to say that his girlfriend wasn't well and so he couldn't make it.

It's straightforward and no fun arriving at immigration in the US now. We're legal now, you see. I've got a letter from McCormack (Mark McCormack's International Management Group manage the affairs of Sandy Lyle) saying I'm a caddie for Sandy Lyle. If you're a caddie for a foreign golfer you just get a B1 stamp on your passport. Before, we used to pitch up at immigration and say we were on vacation. They'd ask us how much money we had, where were we going to stay, did we have a return ticket and all this. Now you just hand in the passport, they look at it and say:

'You're on business are you? What do you do?'

'I'm a caddie for a professional golfer. I caddie for Sandy Lyle, actually.'

'Do you? Well, good luck.'

And that's it. No fun at all.

An immigration fellow Sandy played with in the pro-am before the 1986 Tournament Players' Championship sends me a Christmas card and $20 each year. Neville Cramer he's called and he's a senior special agent in the US Department of Justice. In 1987 we were playing a practice round and I had gone forward on one hole when this great big fellow came and clapped me on the shoulder and said: 'Can you remember me? I played with Sandy last year.' Then Sandy proceeded to hit it under a bush and take six and so Neville felt guilty. Every so often he turns up and gives me ten dollars and takes Sandy out.

I rented a car because that came with the air ticket, and went and got somewhere to stay. I knew where to go – the Econo Lodge at Carlsbad. The rooms are pretty good. You get a continental breakfast and there's a cable channel for films, Showtime I think it's called. We pay about $40 a night for two of us. I found it by asking the fellow who worked in the bag-room at La Costa where to stay. Then I returned to the airport to pick up Andy Prodger.

Monday 11 January

Went to the course where they had what is known as an Epson stats match. Epson, the computer makers, do weekly analyses of the competitors' play in each tournament – the ten longest drivers, the ten players who hit the most number of greens in regulation figures, the ten players who get out of a bunker and one-putt most often, the ten best putters. The results of these statistics are known as the Epson stats. Sandy doesn't do very well in these categories because he doesn't play long enough. You have to play nearly all year to do any good.

The winners out of each category play a shoot-out over nine holes. There were ten of them and Dan Pohl won it and got $75,000 for his trouble . . . $75,000 for nine holes, and he had a hole in one as well.

Who should turn up but Ken Brown? He never used to do very well on Sundays, which to us is the last day of the tournament and pay day. So we christened him the Vicar. Because Pete Coleman hadn't arrived to caddie for Ken I caddied for him for nine holes instead. Gil Morgan's caddie, Harry Brown, is a computer expert and he worked out at the Tallahassee Open last year, the last tournament Gil Morgan played in, that Gil had to hit a certain number of greens and miss the cut and then he couldn't get beaten in the statistics. So

Gil Morgan hit the statutory number of greens, missed the cut and won the greens in regulation category.

I did nine holes with the Vicar and then nine holes with Faldo and Prodge. Ken Brown said to me: 'Seeing a new golf course is like being given a new toy to play with.' Ken can't wait for the Masters. He's never played in it, you see, so he's going to miss the Greater Greensboro Open, the last tournament before the Masters, and go straight there. He'll be the first there in the morning and the last to leave at night.

You can't emphasize enough how difficult it has been for Ken and what a helluva job he's done to come over here and get his card through the qualifying school. He earned enough money to be exempt after that, though twice it was virtually the last week of the year when he did so. Finally, he won a tournament, the Southern Open in September 1987. That was a great achievement.

Ken likes playing in Europe, so every so often he goes to something like the French Open under his own steam. When he gets there he finds three or four American golfers he has just been playing with in the US and they're all getting paid their expenses and appearance money and he's not. So he gets a bit choked about it. It doesn't seem fair, really.

Returned to the airport to pick up Terry Holt. It was the first time I had seen him since Wentworth. He looked and sounded very well, considering his girlfriend had been killed three months ago. Terry was carrying for Bill Casper whom he calls the Hook because he's worse than Bobby Locke used to be at hitting the ball out to the right and watching it hook back in. Bumped into Sandy at the airport. He had just flown in with Jolande.

Tuesday 12 January
Practice round. Good weather – about 65 degrees. La Costa was always said to be owned by the Mafia who last year spent $70 million on it, building more rooms and restaurants and everything. But now it has just been sold to the Japanese for $250 million. Crime's not paying much any more, obviously.

Had a good example of the hazards of the caddying game today. Terry was told by Casper that he had withdrawn from the Bob Hope tournament next week to go to South Africa. So Terry tried to fix up some work with his second string, Bob Lohr, for next week but Lohr had already got somebody. If they pull out you haven't got a job. Too bad. And you can be miles away from home. If you're caddying for a regular player you'll get advance warning that they've changed their minds. It's very rare that you're at a tournament and you hear that your man is not coming. But if it's somebody you've just fixed up with for a week and they pull out, then you're stood up. Now and again you might get a week's wages but usually it's hard lines.

Watched Mac O'Grady hitting drivers left-handed further than most people can hit them right-handed. He's a piece of work, he is. He gets through caddies faster than anyone. Last week he had three. Andy Prodger used to be his weekend man. Mac used to fire a couple in the first two rounds and then Andy would take over at the weekend. That was when Andy caddied for Chi-Chi Rodriguez who invariably missed the cut. I hold a unique record. Four straight years with Seve and four straight weeks with Mac O'Grady.

Mac looks for somebody to blame every time he hits the shot, like one or two players do. That's why Curtis Strange has a dance card. He has a different caddie every week. A lot of them do, specially over here because so many of them are Jekyll and Hyde: the moment they step on the golf course they change. A lot of sportsmen change, I think. It could be adrenalin or aggressiveness, and in golf you have the perfect scapegoat – the caddie. You get blamed all the time. Whatever you say you're wrong and if you don't say anything you're wrong.

The shortest I've caddied for someone is one hole, for Manuel Pinero in Switzerland last year. I was standing by the putting green thinking to myself that I ought to go and do a bit of measuring when Pinero asked if I'd seen Jimmy Cousins, his regular caddie, and I said I hadn't. 'I'll come with you,' I said. So I caddied for one hole and then the caddie master brought a little lad with a trolley. Manuel birdied the hole, the first, and I said: 'There you are, one hole and I'm fired.' And he said: 'Yeah, you're not good enough.'

A week is the shortest arrangement I've ever had. I've worked a lot for players out here for a week. I used to go to the States before the European season started and carry ostensibly for Andy North who didn't play every week. So I had to try and fill in. And I did. You can still do it now but I wouldn't like to try it. There's at least twenty caddies what we call roasting this week. Roasting means without work. They go from car park to car park looking for work.

It's the first two weeks in America. Everybody's saying: 'Happy new year' and asking where you've been for the winter. They're asking one another: 'What was your winter like?' I say: 'It's still going on.'

Sandy turned up with a brand new set of clubs. This is nothing like as bad as it sounds because they're bespoke, made to measure, by Mizuno. The lofts and lies, weights, shafts are just as he wants them. The grips are the thickness he wants. Tape had been wound round the shaft under the grip to get the correct thickness. On the back of the grip there's a reminder, a little ridge. You can feel it running down the back of the grip. That has to be put on so that when he grips the club the clubface is open to square. Sandy's got fairly big hands. Joey Sindelar has got tiny little hands. The grips of Sandy's clubs are thick but not as thick as Andy North's. His are so thick you can hardly get your hands round them. Sandy had had the shaft on his driver lengthened by an inch, which helps him keep the ball down. In practice with this club he was hitting the ball lower – not a mile up in the air.

On the first tee they read out the tournaments each player has won as he is introduced. So the announcer says: 'On the tee Don January, winner of the MONY Senior Tournament of Champions.' There's applause, January steps up, hits his drive and there's more applause.

January is playing with Chi-Chi. 'On the tee Chi-Chi Rodriguez,' says the announcer and Chi-Chi walks forward. 'Winner of the Gerald Ford PGA Seniors Championship, the Dominion, United States Hospitals Senior Championship . . .' By this time Chi-Chi's fed up and goes and sits in the grandstand to wait until the announcer has finished. Everybody was killing themselves laughing.

The local pro is called Carl Welty and he took videos of the players on the practice ground. I said to Sandy: 'Why don't we go and have a look at this? Let him film you from different sides and then see what's what.' We did that and then Sandy went and had his putting filmed in slow motion using a ball with a red band painted on it. It's not apparent to the naked eye but when filmed in slow motion you can see that when the ball is not hit properly it bounces at first and then rolls; when it is hit properly it skids before it starts rolling. Welty reflected a laser beam onto the face of Sandy's putter. He noticed the ball was coming off the putter too high and so he suggested less loft. Sandy had one good putting round after that and then he couldn't hole anything so he put the loft back on again.

Welty also had a machine that tells you how fast your clubhead is moving at impact. Tom Kite was 108 m.p.h., Sandy Lyle 114 m.p.h., Joey Sindelar 117 m.p.h., Dave Musgrove was 90 m.p.h. – and ruptured. A fellow called Greg Twiggs holds the record on that machine of 127 m.p.h. but he lost his card if that's anything to go by.

What came out of the films that Welty took was how many golfers finished their swings with their bodies shaped like a back-to-front C. For instance, Greg Norman gives me the impression that he's trying to put his back out. It's frightening watching him. Sandy doesn't do that and that's one of the reasons why he doesn't get so much backache.

Sandy shot 72, 72. And he birdied the first hole the first day, so the year's first birdie came on the first hole he played. Before the third round he was standing on the practice ground and saying: 'I can't hit this ball anywhere. I'm playing terrible.' Then he went out and shot 68. That put him in joint 16th place.

Sunday 17 January

A very bad storm and it was cold. We didn't start on time. Sandy had taken some Adidas waterproofs with him. When he put the jacket on he found it was too tight. He couldn't swing in it. So we had to change jackets. I had the Adidas one and he had my Ryder Cup jacket. It was a case of first up, best dressed.

It was slashing down in the morning and I'm saying to Sandy: 'We're lying in sixteenth place, the money's not bad. If we get rained off, it's not been a bad week. We haven't got wet.' And Andy, who's caddying for Faldo, who is lying second or third, is saying: 'Come on, let's get out there. We want a win, we want a win.' After nine holes Sandy is up on the leader board in the top ten, only about three shots behind, and Faldo started off double bogey and then bogied another one so the positions were completely reversed. I wanted to keep playing and Andy wanted to call it off.

We were playing with Fred Couples and we finished up only playing nine holes. They abandoned it after that because there were trees being blown down and one fellow got hit with a branch. The trees just kept falling down like they did at Wentworth in the October hurricane. The tournament was cut back to fifty-four holes and Steve Pate won it.

Five tournaments have been affected by wind and rain in the last six months. The Open and the German Masters; there was the hurricane during the World Match-play; it rained almost all day the last day of the World Cup in Hawaii, and then we were rained off in Japan in the pro-am.

The wind in San Diego wasn't bad but it got very cold for Southern California, and there was a lot of rain. In fact it was sleeting at one time. We might have played on in Europe but the fairways and the greens were very wet and the forecast was for it to get worse. We drove to Palm Springs over the mountains that night and it was terrifying. They had three-quarters of an inch of rain in one day.

Bob Hope Chrysler Classic, Palm Springs, California

Monday 18 January
In the Bob Hope Chrysler Classic, to give the tournament its proper name, you play four courses and each pro has three different amateur partners each day. It might sound the slowest tournament we play in but the Crosby is even slower. The reason is the courses there are tough. Some of these here are straightforward apart from the ones they have started to introduce. There's one new course – Arnold Palmer's course at PGA West. This is the tough one.

Members of any of the host courses pay $2500, which nets down to $1000 dollars because they get $1000 tax relief for charity. Anybody else must pay $3000 plus.

Tuesday 19 January
Practice round at La Quinta where the starter is Tony Ecclestone, a friend of Sandy's, who comes from Shropshire. He used to court one of Sandy's sisters.

Wednesday 20 January
Sandy's first round was at Indian Wells. There's a big arrow in the ground saying Indian Wells on it and the lavatories don't say ladies and gents, they say squaws and braves. He shot 64. Got round very fast, in $4\frac{1}{4}$ hours. Had his first eagle of the year – a drive and a three-iron to five feet. A 227-yard three iron.

Last year we had a fellow who'd had a heart transplant in our team. A friend of his turned up and he'd had a heart transplant as well. One of the amateurs this year had actually had polio but he played all right. When he walked he was shaking but when he got over the ball he seemed to steady himself and he struck it fairly well. He was a good putter.

Thursday 21 January
A 71 at La Quinta.

Friday 22 January
A 73 with thirty-three putts at PGA West, Palmer course. That course is another one that's laid out just to sell property. Too much walking between holes. You can get lost. One of the television people asked me: 'What do you think of our American courses?' I said: 'They're all right but there's too much walking between holes.'

'But that's why we have carts,' he said.

Every other advertisement that comes on television they say to you: 'Diet this, cholesterol-free that, get some exercise, go jogging.' And then they don't allow you to walk around the golf course. I thought Ireland was the land of paradox, not America.

As the sun goes down in the Coachella Valley the mountains

on the opposite side change colour. They start off yellow, then go red, then grey and finish up black. It can be very hot there – in the summer as high as 120 degrees – but the moment the sun drops behind the mountains the temperature drops, too, and it gets quite cold. That's when you ought to put a cap on or something, unless you want to catch a chill.

Saturday 23 January
Finished up shooting 71 at Bermuda Dunes. The cut was four under par, seventy players on four under par.

Sunday 24 January
Sandy had a 70 at Indian Wells. He only had one three-putt in ninety holes but he averaged thirty to thirty-one putts which is astronomic by their standards. Sandy won $7200.

Me and Andy had checked-in our car the night before at Palm Springs airport and so we all piled into Harry's van for the drive to Phoenix. Harry Brown drives from tournament to tournament in a big Dodge van. He's always looking for riders and he charges five cents a mile. He sometimes takes Sandy's clubs for him and as he's the same size Sandy gives him his old golf shoes. Harry doesn't allow smoking in the van, which is very civilized, and you can go to sleep because they're comfortable vans. They'll easily hold four or so with all the luggage.

Harry always does all the driving. He has a fuzz buster (a detector that warns him of radar checks by police) and he used to blast away and hope for the best. I don't know how fast he drives because his speedometer doesn't work.

Stopped for dinner at Elmer's at Indio on the way. It was 250 miles and after allowing for an hour change to Arizona time we checked in at 10.30 at night. There's an agricultural check on the border between California and Arizona when they ask you if you've got any oranges or apples, plants or vegetables. But as there was nobody there to ask us I managed to smuggle a load of California oranges into Arizona.

Phoenix Open, Scottsdale, Arizona

Monday 25 January

The new Tournament Players' Course is at Scottsdale. It's built in the middle of the desert with a real big high-class hotel, huge thing, called the Scottsdale Princess.

Believe it or not, Sandy played in a shotgun pro-am. A group of players start from each tee and at the allotted time you all start playing. If it's Japan they let fireworks off when it's time to start. Sometimes they shoot a gun, hence its name, sometimes they sound a siren. You can get more than eighteen groups on by having two groups on the par fives. So around twenty-two groups played in the shotgun. They have Monday pro-ams and two pro-ams on a Wednesday to draw the money. It doubles for a practice round as well and so Sandy didn't play on the Tuesday.

Tuesday 26 January

In Phoenix Sandy always stays with a fellow called Richie Alimo, and as they played golf together I had a day off.

The (US) Professional Tour Caddies' Association booked us into the Holiday Inn at Scottsdale at 50 per cent off. It was in downtown Scottsdale about ten miles from the course. Shared a room with Prodge. We finished up paying about $60 per night between us, which is good. It was an expensive week but you have to average it all out. Temperature was approximately 70 degrees all week, which was not bad for January. Had my hair cut and then bought some ear-rings and a bracelet for Hilary. This turquoise jewellery was like the Red Indian jewellery which you can only buy in Arizona.

This is the only tournament apart from the major championships without a large sponsor. It's run by the Thunderbirds, an organization about fifty years old, similar to the Round Table. It consists of fifty-five active members, mostly professional men, and they spend most of their spare time getting this tournament ready. They don't have time for anything else. They get their money from sponsorship deals and tv fees and concession stands selling beer, hot dogs, coffee and the like. It's a charity organization. You know what they say: 'Charity is the number one winner on the PGA Tour.' I felt like saying: 'Have a nice day.'

Before we went I thought to myself that of the four tournaments we were going to play on this trip his best chance was at Phoenix because he liked the course and he's also had two weeks warming up. He hit the ball terrific at the Bob Hope. He just couldn't putt. As I said, he had thirty, thirty-one putts every day and you're not going to do anything doing that over there. The air's thin in the desert and the ball goes further when it's warm.

Wednesday 27 January
Pro-am day, and the organizers had a fancy trouser day. I don't know who judges it; one of the Thunderbirds I suppose. You don't hang around on pro-am days. After you've finished you bugger off as quickly as you can. You couldn't believe the number of spectators today. There was a load of celebrities, you see. Bob Hope, Glenn Campbell and football and baseball players.

In the pro-am last week's winner, Jay Haas, was not included. That's not unusual over here. Nothing over here surprises me, nothing at all. The field is chosen from last year's order of merit and local favourites.

Last year Sandy made the cut on the line and then shot 68, 68 on Saturday and Sunday. In the pro-am today he shot 68. Then he shot 68, 68 and 68 in the first three rounds.

This tournament attracts huge numbers of people. They had 71,000 on the Saturday alone, and a quarter of a million for the week. Sunday was Superbowl Sunday (the Superbowl, the American football final, is roughly equivalent in importance to our Cup final) which reduced the attendance. Even so there were a quarter of a million spectators for the week. God knows how many they'd get if it wasn't the Superbowl.

Over here something happens that never happens in Europe. You get representatives from tournaments down the line coming out punting for players. There were men from the GGO (Greater Greensboro Open, to be held in April). Duke Butler from Houston was there. So were men from Hawaii offering 75 per cent off air fares from California to Hawaii to wherever you wanted to go. This was because United Airlines were a sponsor. 75 per cent off! Begging people to go. To

Hawaii in February! You get this every week, men saying: 'Where do you want to stay?' 'What arrangements can I make for you?' and 'Do you need a car?' Sandy had a brand new car at Phoenix. He gets one each week and after the tournament the cars get sold off as secondhand. There is some sort of tax write-off involved for the car companies, probably because they're advertising for charity.

In the first two rounds we were playing with Fred Couples who we had played with on the Sunday of the Tournament of Champions and the Sunday of the Bob Hope. It was like a right double act. After about two rounds Freddie was about two shots in front of us and so we said: 'See you on Sunday, Fred.'

Thursday 28 January
A US Caddies' Association meeting. I paid $75 to join the Association again. The first bloke that jumps up at the meeting is the White Russian. That's his nickname because his real name is Brad Krosnoff. He's in charge of loans to caddies. He says: 'I'm on the loans committee. It's not really a committee, it's a dictatorship. If you want $100 and you've got a good case I'll lend you $100 dollars but I'll take ten off the top. So actually you get $90 and you've got to pay $100 back. That ten goes into a fund for future loans'.

Andy Davidson, who carries for Bobby Wadkins, does motel reservations. Gypsy Joe Grillo had got married and said he was retiring from running the motor home but luckily for us he changed his mind about the motor home. He cooks meals for the caddies and is paid $1000 each week by the Association for doing this. He's a good cook.

E. T. Fernandez, a lawyer from Jacksonville, was there, too. He had negotiated the deal this year for caddies to wear Nabisco visors for twenty-three tournaments for $100,000.

And then there was the trial of a caddie whom I will call D.B. He is a bit of a sharp operator, and in a motel in Tucson at the end of last year he'd run up a phone bill for a week of $657 which he hadn't paid. The reason it was so high was that he rang this porno number somewhere at three dollars a minute. He gave the number out but by the time I realized what he was on about I had missed the chance to write it down. Purely for research, of course. I just wanted to pass the number on.

He put his case and then several people stood up and said how many tricks he'd pulled over the years and so it was decided he had to repay the money to the Association. Mike Carrick, Tom Kite's caddie, is the driving force behind the Association. He runs it. I don't know how he sticks it. It's a real thankless task. The first meeting was at Greensboro in 1981. I was there. In fact, I am a founder member of both the US Caddies' Association and its European equivalent. The CA got underway properly at Jacksonville early in 1982.

The Association paid the bill. D.B. refused to honour it and was thrown out.

Friday 29 January
The cut was made at 141, one under par. Again there were seventy players exactly on the line, which is a real coincidence two weeks on the trot. Sandy shot 68.

Saturday 30 January
The 15th was a shortish par five with an island green and Citibank had put up $15,000 for whoever was nearest the flag in two shots at the weekend. Sandy hit a driver and a three-iron to the back of the green and when we got up there we saw a big board up saying Gary Koch was nearest with seven feet. I paced Sandy's putt out and it measured twelve paces and there was an official behind the green, one of the Thunderbirds, measuring who's nearest.

So I said to him: 'We're obviously nearest, aren't we? We're a lot nearer than seven feet.'

He started laughing. 'Why don't you let me measure it? I'll probably make it six feet eleven. That's what it looks like to me.'

I thought I'd have a bit of fun. We weren't in a winning position, we were just plodding along. Sandy holed this putt for an eagle and shot 68 again, his sixth in a row.

Sunday 31 January
Davis Love is leading and we are seven shots behind him. I saw Davis come out of the car park looking real down in the mouth. I think his wife hadn't been well. It's like race horses.

You can sometimes spot the winner from the way they're walking in the paddock.

Our official starting time is 11.05. So we've practised and Sandy's taking his time walking slowly along from the putting green to the first tee. This course is spread out and everything seems like a mile. Courses like this one aren't designed to be walked round; they're designed to drive around in carts and people don't realize how long it takes to walk from one place to another.

I know we're first off in our group of three because you get a different vest to wear each day. The vests are red, white and blue, shaped like waistcoats, and have the player's name on the back to identify the players to the spectators. My vest was red which meant that we were first to tee off. I go to get the pin positions (a sheet showing the position of the pins on the greens). Caddies used to have to get this information themselves. But can you imagine dozens of caddies tramping around, getting in the way of the play and the effect that had on the greens? They stopped us doing that and now the measurements are given to us on a sheet at the start of each round.

So I get to the tent by the first tee and Chip Beck and the other lad we're playing with, Jim Carter, are on the tee looking down the fairway, all intent. I said to the starter: 'How much time have we got?'

I got the impression he thought I was Sandy, probably because of my accent, and so he said to me: 'You've got plenty of time. You've got two minutes.' Sandy ain't in sight. I dive out of the tent and there's Sandy ambling over this hill about 200 yards away. I wave frantically at him and shout: 'Come on, come on, we're on the tee.'

Eventually he arrives and the starter is about to shout his name. I give him a one iron and say: 'It's downwind, it's a one iron and the pin's so and so.' Then the starter calls out: 'On the tee, Sandy Lyle.' Sandy hasn't got his card or anything. He thinks he's still got four minutes. He thought he was off at 11.05 when actually it was 11.01.

So he gets up there, takes a swipe at it and hits it 200 yards into the right rough. Then he says: 'Give me some tees, give me a pencil, give me a card.' All the way up the fairway I was saying to him: 'Take your time, take deep breaths.' We get to the ball and we've got 189 yards to the flag on a downhill lie out the rough. So we decide on a seven iron. He whacks this on the green about fifteen feet away and then he holes it for a three. So that was a result.

The next hole he hits a good drive. The green is level with the first tee and it's a nasty-shaped green with a deep bunker on the right, which you mustn't go in. If you do you'll find that the green runs away from you. The pin was back right but he never looked where the pin position was so he didn't know it was very close to this bunker. It was a toss up between a seven and a six. He said: 'I'll hit a six and make sure I get it back there.' That wasn't very good thinking because if you hit it a bit too strong it's a five on your card. I didn't say anything and he hits a six and it comes down six inches from the flag. He holes that and says: 'That was a difficult pin position.'

Normally, he'd have noticed where the pin was because he'd have seen it as he stood on the first tee as the green is just to the left of the tee. That's what he's done on that hole every day so far. But today he was in too much of a hurry to do that. If he'd have known where that pin was he wouldn't have hit a six iron, he'd have hit a seven and he probably would have got a four instead of a three.

The next hole is a par five. After a huge drive he can get on in two. If this was a fairy story he'd eagle the hole and go on to win the tournament. But he didn't. He missed the green, parred the hole and I thought: 'That's the end of that.'

Chip and a putt on the par three 4th. On the fifth hole, a long par four, he took a drive and seven iron to eight feet. Thought to myself: 'This is like a shot and a half if he holes this.' He didn't. Putt for a three on the 6th, a drive and a wedge hole. Missed that. Had to struggle to get a par on the 7th, a very long par three. He hit a four iron 226 yards, chipped to four feet and holed it. On the 8th, he made a good par. On the 9th, drive and eight iron to fifteen feet and holed it. So we're out in 32, three under par. That's all right. Top ten or so.

On the 10th, a birdie chance but missed it. The 11th is a tough par four with water all the way up the left and the green sits out in the lake. He hit a real good drive and he'd got 200 yards which is a five iron because the ball goes one club further in the desert. He drew it in to the flag, *drew* it. The flag's on the left and he's drawing the ball in to the pin towards the water! Goes about twenty feet past. He holes it and punches the air. This is the most aggressive golf I've ever seen him play.

The 12th is a long par three, and the green is a peninsula into a lake. You don't play for the back of the green because the further you hit it the narrower the green is. There is water on three sides. Par. The 13th is a par five. Drive and a four iron landed short of the green and ran over the back. Chip and a putt, birdie.

Now where are we? Where do we stand? All the electronic scoreboards have broken down. He's had five birdies in thirteen holes. At the 14th hole he's got a putt for a three. Drive and a seven iron to eight foot and he misses it. Behind the green Steve Melnyk is up the tv tower commentating for television. So I went to the bottom of the steps and shouted up: 'How are we doing?'

'One behind Couples,' Melnyk replied.

That's the first we knew of the leader board situation. We had seen Davis Love drive into the ditch on one hole and the lake on another so we thought he was out of it. The two players with us aren't going to win – Chip Beck, whose wife has just left him or so he told Sandy on the way round, and Jim Carter, the young lad from Phoenix playing his first tournament.

Then there's that par five, the measuring hole, with the $15,000 at stake. So Sandy hits a drive and a four iron there and gets a four and I'm still trying to persuade this bloke that we were nearest the flag the day before and he's killing himself with laughter. He thinks I'm joking.

The 16th is a par three and he hit a seven iron to about six feet. Missed that. The 17th is a short par four that sometimes you can drive. The hole is 345 yards long but from the back of the back tee it's 324 yards to drive it, which he can do. It has been done. But there's water on the left and there's a bunker which is in play. It's 274 yards to get into it and 283 to carry. So we walk through the crowd and I'm behind Sandy and by now we know we've got a chance to win. Instead of turning right to go to the tee he turned left. They've moved the pots forward from the back tee to a forward tee to encourage the players to have a go at driving the green. I walk to the back of the back tee and measure how much nearer we are. All I'm bothered about is that fairway bunker. It's nearer now and that concerns me.

Sandy says: 'What about a two iron?'

I said: 'A two iron will land in that bunker.'

He thinks I mean a bunker a lot nearer. 'No it won't,' he says. 'I'll get over it easily.'

I said: 'No, you'll land straight in it. The tee is thirty-four yards nearer to the green than it was yesterday. It's either a four iron short or a one iron.' I never thought about Sandy driving the green. After a bit he pulls a driver out and the crowd go wild. 'All right,' they shout. 'All right.' He smashes it on the green. The group in front were still putting but it didn't disturb them because it's a big undulating green rather like ones at St Andrews, and the pin is at the back. Sandy two putts from thirty yards for a good birdie.

The last is a huge dogleg over the lake, similar to the 18th at the Tournament Players' Club at Sawgrass except you're going over the lake instead of up the side of it. He hit a good drive and had 170 yards left. That's a seven iron and he didn't want to be big because it's a difficult chip back, so he tried to hit an easy one but it finished short and in a bunker. He needs a four for a 64 and Richie Alimo, who Sandy always stays with during the Phoenix, said he would shave his beard off if he does it. He's behind the green worrying. Sandy proceeds to make five for a 65 so Richie is relieved on one hand and disappointed on the other.

Behind us, all Fred Couples wants to do is make a four to win. It sounds straightforward enough but it's a very long par four, 447 yards. His plan is to hit the ball over the lake and cut it back onto the fairway. But he didn't, he pulled it and the ball actually landed on the other side of the lake where all the spectators are, and went bouncing along the other bank. It looked perfect. The pin is back right and he's got a straight-forward shot in. But then the ball hits a woman spectator in the back and rebounds into the lake. So he took five.

So we are playing with Fred for the third Sunday in succession in a play-off. They both got fours on the 10th. On the 17th (the second hole of the play-off) they both hit drivers to the right. Sandy finished up missing a four footer for a three to win. On the 18th Sandy drove out to the right again, this time into the semi-rough, perfectly safe. Fred hits it straight in the water. Finish. He drops out, hits his second shot to the downslope of a bunker, which is the worst place in the world, so he is unlikely to make five. All Sandy's got to do is miss the right, greenside, bunker. So he hit it left just off the green and behind a mound and chipped over. Fred is at the back of the green and missed the putt. Sandy is left with two putts from six feet to win. They always say if you've got two for it, take them.

I still can't work out quite why Sandy was so aggressive and why he played so well. It was a bit Switzerlandish, if you see what I mean, where the ball takes off easily because of the thin, warm air. He's fit and happy. And the putts dropped. He got off to a flying start without realizing it.

That night we flew up to San José, Northern California, hired a car and drove to Monterey to start again the next day.

AT&T Pebble Beach National Pro-Am, Pebble Beach, California

Monday 1 February
Nine holes practice at Spyglass Hill. Sandy and Jolande were staying with Chuck Van Linge. Chuck is a successful business-man in San Francisco and a very keen amateur golfer who plays as often as he can. He's in his middle fifties but still plays to about four handicap. He grew up with Tony Lema, played golf with him, and has been Sandy's partner for several years in the AT&T (Associated Telephone and Telegraph) or what used to be the Bing Crosby tournament. He and his wife Lorna have a weekend house on the course at Pebble Beach.

It's a real get-together each year. The old-fashioned atmos-phere of the Crosby comes across in this house, the spirit of Bing's friends and good golfers. One of Chuck's friends is named Bob Rouse and he and his wife Shirley always stay in the house. This year Bob was inaugurated into the California Golf Association Hall of Fame for his services to Californian golf. One year he ran the US Open when it was held in California. Sandy has always stayed at Chuck's house. Nathaniel Crosby used to stay there, too.

Tuesday 2 February

We were mucking about with Mac O'Grady and Gary McCord on the practice ground. McCord used to play on the tour and is said to be the man who originally suggested that there should be an all-exempt tour. He is now a commentator for CBS. The pros are hitting balls and their bags are lined up behind them. If you're behind the bags then you're safe. I saw Pete Coleman over the way and I moved towards him. Mac gave Gary McCord a left-handed club and as I walked behind him he swung it back.

I saw it coming and I dived but it clouted me in the corner of the left eye. I hit the ground, finishing up on one knee. I never felt anything. They fetched some ice and stuff and said it's cut. It certainly was. There was blood everywhere. I thought it had hit me on the side of the head. Got taken to the Monterey hospital with a swab over the eye. I went into the emergency section and the lady behind the desk asked: 'What's wrong with you?' I said: 'You must need your eyes tested.'

I had three nurses, a Dr Kildare and five X-rays and they stitched it up for me. The anaesthetic hurt. It felt like nettles stinging the eye. After that I went straight back to the course with a patch over my eye.

Alan Shepard, the astronaut, was playing in the Crosby and Sandy played with him one day and asked him what it was like on the moon. Shepard told a story about what happened one night. It seemed they were woken by a clanging noise. Some hydraulic thing had come off and it reverberated throughout the capsule. One astronaut whispered to the other: 'Did you hear that?' And the other replied: 'Yeah, what do you think it was?' The first one said: 'I don't know why we're whispering. The nearest human being is a quarter of a million miles away. I don't think they're going to hear us.'

In 1986 Sandy was playing a practice round with Chuck Van Linge and another amateur bloke who was competing in the tournament for the first time. This fellow has a caddie, a big pro bag and he was whacking away, really looking the part. They came to a par five and Sandy hit a driver and a one iron as hard as he could into the middle of the green so you can tell how far the par five was. He finished up holing the putt for an eagle.

The bloke turned to Sandy and asked: 'Are you a pro?'

Sandy replied: 'As a matter of fact I'm the British Open champion.'

The amateur said: 'I thought I recognized the accent.'

Thursday 4 February

The first round of the tournament was at Pebble Beach and Sandy got to the 18th two over par. He needed a birdie four to get a reasonable score. The 18th is a par five but you can get on in two with a good drive up the left, so it's worth going for it. Sandy hit a good drive but he drew it just a bit and it landed on the rocks. These rocks slope towards the sea but not only did his ball kick off the rocks and back to the fairway, but it went forward as well so he gained quite a few yards. When we got up there I set off to work out how far we've got left to the green. It's 230 yards I reckon, and when I get back to Sandy he's cursing and swearing about his bad luck because he had a bad lie and couldn't hit the club he wanted to.

This is typical of golfers, and so I said to him: 'Where has that ball just been?'

Sandy made par on the hole and shot a 74.

Friday 5 February

We started on the 10th tee at Cypress Point. The back 9th is the tough 9 and if you get off there first you've got a result because the wind gets up in the afternoon and makes it harder. He played reasonably well and chipped and putted OK and did the first nine in level par.

On the 1st hole, which is our 10th, he chipped in for a birdie from the rough, as he'd done in a practice round. So we never touched that green at all. On the second he chipped to four feet and one-putted for a birdie. He birdied the 4th, a par five. On the 6th he pitches in from forty-five yards. On the 7th his tee shot ended on the edge of the green and he bladed a sand iron second shot that hit the pin and stayed out. On the 8th he hit a one-iron and then a nine-iron to eight yards and holed it. On the 9th he took a four. He'd come back in 30, gone round in 65 and passed about fifty men in the process.

Saturday 6 February
He actually got to eight under par for the tournament after eleven holes but then it finally got through to him. It was the second pro-am in three weeks and Mark Wiebe, the other pro in Sandy's group, was taking a helluva long time. Took a 73 at Spyglass Hill, Sandy's favourite course of the three. Cut was two under par, which is low.

Sunday 7 February
There are 180 pros and each had an amateur partner. They all play one round each day on three different courses and after that the top sixty pros and the top twenty-five teams make the cut. Chuck Van Linge made it for the third year on the trot and we played with Tom Watson and his partner, bloke called Tatum. His first name is Sandy so there were two Sandys. (Sandy Tatum is a past President of the United States Golf Association and a long-time friend of Watson's. His downswing is slower than his backswing.)

He's a good fellow, Tom is. He gets on with the game, no fuss, no fidgeting. And he doesn't make excuses when things go wrong. He was telling us a story about when he was at Wentworth last year before the Open. He was playing a practice round and after driving on the fourth he waited for the green to clear. Two lady golfers were playing behind him and they couldn't see him as he waited. All of a sudden a ball came bouncing past Watson, a ball that this lady had hit. She came down the hill, realized what had happened and apologized.

Watson replied: 'That's quite all right. There's no need to apologize. It was a good shot.'

It took Wiebe a long while to work out what he had to do every time it was his turn to play, but Watson was always ready. That's my definition of slow play – not being ready to hit when it's your turn; and it's Sandy's, too, as it happens.

Tom's coming back to form all right. Sandy played with him at Muirfield in the Open in 1987 and he was playing well enough to win.

Greg Norman said something striking to me at Stuttgart last year. We played the third round of the German Masters with Seve and in the locker-room Norman asked me: 'What scores did you do?' I said they were both good scores. He said: 'So you had a good game, then?'

That's just what you expect to hear at a golf club. You come in, someone asks you who you played with and says you had a good game, then. That's Tom Watson's attitude as well – you go out and play the game. All very refreshing.

Steve Jones beat Bob Tway in a play-off for the tournament; Sandy shot 73 and won $15,000 for a top-20 finish.

The last round, at Pebble Beach, had taken five and a half hours, which meant we finished at 2.30 p.m. – and I had made reservations for the 3.30 p.m. flight from Monterey (five miles away) to San Francisco. What with one thing and another it called for some fast moving. Sandy had fixed up his own lift to the airport, but Terry and Andy were at the hotel with my luggage already loaded into our car. In something like a Le Mans start we roared off and got to the airport in thirty minutes. Not bad, eh? Got to 'Frisco for four o'clock. I caught a Pam-Am flight home and Sandy caught British Airways.

3

9 February–27 March

Mowing in February – Outdriven by Nicklaus –
A night at the races – Poor defence at TPC

At Home

Tuesday 9 to Saturday 27 February

Decided it was time we changed the car. We'd had a BMW 320 for some time and as we say it owed us nothing. It had run pretty good but it was getting to the point where it needed money spending on it. It was six years old. So we thought, while it's still worth something let's trade it in. Had no clue what to have.

We went to a big Ford dealer near us and George Hoy, a salesman who is a member at Sherwood Forest golf club, recognized me and asked me how my eye was. I still had a black eye from my accident in Pebble Beach. We had a few cars out to test drive and finished up with this Escort XR3i. It suited us very well. It's like buying a house: when you walk into a house you either know whether you want it or not. He gave us a good price for the BMW.

Up at Coxmoor they're refurbishing the interior of the clubhouse at a cost of £35,000. Played quite a bit of golf. There were flurries of snow but not enough to stop us from playing. In general the weather was very mild, so mild I even cut the grass – in February, in Kirkby!

Hilary is going to come with me to the US for the three weeks starting at the end of the month and so I bought our two tickets together. I rented a car at the same time, only £85 for the three weeks because we had British Airways Poundstretcher tickets. We have to have a car. It means that we are independent.

Sunday 28 February
We met Sandy and Jolande at Terminal Four at Heathrow and all flew together to Miami. Sandy and Jolande stayed at Doral Country Club where the tournament is being held and Hilary and I checked into the La Quinta motel on 36th Street booked for us by the Caddies' Association. Statutory wake-up at 3 a.m. because of the time change.

Doral Ryder Open, Doral CC, Miami, Florida

Monday 29 February
Went to the practice ground at Doral and heard that Jimmy Ballard was expecting Sandy. Jimmy Ballard's golf workshop is at the other end of the practice ground. Went up there, met Jimmy. Sandy put a ball down and stone-cold shanked it. This was what he has been complaining about for some time. He has been addressing the ball with a closed stance and been unable to use his full power. This hitting the ball out of the heel was to plague him for some time.

Had a good session with Jimmy Ballard and Artie McNichol who used to play the US tour. Sandy was using the Ballard connector. (A connector is the harness that Ballard uses as a coaching aid.) Other pros working there with Jimmy included Leonard Thompson, Hubert Green, Curtis Strange, Peter Jacobsen and Billy Kratzert.

Sandy and Jimmy went through the old instruction and then Jimmy began to film Sandy. He had kept last year's video of Sandy. It's like gold dust to a teacher to have all these pros come so that he can take pictures of them and then show his amateur pupils. The only similarity between this year's video of Sandy and last year's was that Sandy had got on the same pair of light blue tartan trousers.

Leonard Thompson had been practising in the winter with the connector on under his sweater. So this made Sandy think: did he play better when it's raining because he's trussed up with waterproofs? I've said for years that when it rains Sandy plays better. This seems to confirm it.

Wednesday 2 March

Sandy shot 68 in the pro-am, 31 and 37. He got $300 for his own score and his team were 14 under par and he got $300 for that as well.

Thursday 3 and Friday 4 March

Played with Jack Nicklaus and Paul Azinger. Sandy made the cut with two good scores – 70 and 71 – and it was a very good cut to make. You can go to America, have a few days' practice, play the tournament and miss the cut. Then you have to start again the next week. But if you make the cut it gets you going. Gives your confidence a boost.

There's always a lot of wind in Florida at this time of the year. Example: at the 1st hole, 533 yards downwind, he hit a driver and a seven iron second shot and it landed on the green and ran over the back. And that was the hole where Nicklaus outdrove Sandy using a metal wood. He finished ten yards in front of Sandy and that was what got Sandy on to the idea of using metal woods.

Nicklaus shot 68, 69 and putted superbly. He still has that big putter he used to win the US Masters, but he said he had changed his stance the week before after watching an old Shell Wonderful World of Golf film of himself playing Sam Snead at Pebble Beach in 1962. I remember seeing that film. On the last hole Snead chipped in and Jack had to hole a real good putt down the hill for a half.

Nicklaus said he has to stoop over and make sure that his right forearm is parallel to the ground and acts as a piston behind the ball. 'There are a lot of things you can forget about golf,' he said.

He's a good fellow to play with, Nicklaus. There's no frills, no showmanship. He's there for a game of golf. He's always considerate to his playing partners. The last time Sandy had played with Nicklaus was the last round of the 1986 Masters, which Nicklaus won, and we mentioned that and the 8th hole where he was in the trees. Jack said that he hit his second shot through a gap smaller than the one he was aiming at. He was aiming at a gap about six feet wide and he hit it through a gap about two feet wide. That was when he came out laughing on to the fairway and told us. He didn't birdie the hole but it built up his confidence and he started making birdies after that. That was the turning point of the tournament.

Saturday 5 and Sunday 6 March
Sandy played very well in the third round – a 67. That moved him right up and we were with McCumber in the next-to-last group out on the Sunday. McCumber played well. Shot a 68 in the last round. Sandy had a 72.

The Americans have followed the European example of playing in pairs rather than in threes at the weekend, which is very refreshing. They say it makes for better tv coverage and it's certainly better to play.

We had the usual caddie harassment here. I took a short cut across some grass and a guard called out to me: 'If you do that again I'll call the police and arrest you.' There were no signs saying don't cross here. I don't know why we have trouble here but we do. It's their attitude. Nick DePaul was escorted off the premises for doing the same as I had done and two other caddies were threatened with arrest for having their players' clubs with them. They were accused of trying to steal them. They're into that at Doral. It's their way of saying, 'We don't want you here' I suppose; but it's only once a year.

Drove up to Fort Lauderdale, less than an hour away, on the Sunday night ready for the Honda Classic at Eagle Trace. Stayed at the Hampton Inn. At different times we have stayed in a lot of dives in Florida. It's a very flat part of the country and there's a lot of bugs, spiders and ants about. But La Quinta and the Hampton Inn were very comfortable.

Somebody said that the population of Florida increases by one thousand people each day. A lot of golfers have moved down there to live because there's no state tax and the weather is so good. Because the local government is struggling to pay for the amenities needed to cope with the extra people moving in, they've had to introduce a lottery. Petrol is less than one dollar a gallon. Don't know why they don't give it away.

Honda Classic, Eagle Trace, Florida

Monday 7 March

Sandy had to go up to Jacksonville for a press day because he was defending champion for the Tournament Players' Championship. We did the washing and had lunch on the beach.

Eagle Trace is on the edge of the Everglades and always windy. It's one of those courses that is built for selling real estate. There are new houses every time I go there.

Many of the top players missed it this year. You have to miss one. You can't play in them all. Doral is a million dollars. Eagle Trace is a tough course and not as much money. Next week is Bay Hill, which is a good tournament to play in, and the week after that is the TPC, so the logical one to miss is Eagle Trace.

Tuesday 8 March

In the shoot-out Sandy finished third. He bogied the 8th and Gene Sauers and Paul Azinger parred it. Sandy got $1000 for his efforts. Sauers went on to beat Azinger on the last hole.

Gary McCord did the commentary. He called Fred Couples Boom-boom because he booms the ball so far, and Ed Fiori is known as Grip because he has a double-handed grip. Curtis Strange was playing, too. He has a reputation for being careful with his money. When McCord introduced Strange and described him as having won a million dollars last season someone shouted out: 'Yeah, and he's still got them all.' McCord kept on about Strange and money, continually referring to Strange as the leading money-winner. Finally Curtis got his own back on a green where everyone had marked their ball with coins. Strange went round the green peering at the coins and added them all up. 'There's one dollar and 75 cents on this green,' he said.

That night the four of us went to have dinner with Tony Sher and his wife, Dodie West, the singer. He is entertainments director on cruise liners. They live at Boca Raton and he's golf mad and always turns up to watch Sandy when he can. Had a barbecue and then he showed us a tape of him entertaining on a boat, telling jokes. Then Dodie showed us her audition tape where she sings the beginning and end of different songs. We had a good sing-song.

She was on a lot of tv shows but the only one I can remember was an old Stars and Garter show when she followed Kathy Kirby.

Thursday 10 and Friday 11 March

Sandy didn't do very well. It was a grinding round on a relentless course. Water is in play on sixteen holes and on almost all of them it's very close. Hit in the water on a par three and took five. Ended up with a 74. So we needed a good score on Friday morning to beat the cut and he shot 64 with nine birdies. Sandy was playing with Dan Forsman and Ray Floyd and they had nineteen birdies between them in the second round. Floyd had a 69 and Forsman a 67.

Sandy needed a four at the last for a 63, for a new course record. The 18th hole is a long par four and there is a big bunker on the left of the landing zone from the tee. If you're in the bunker you're all right because you get a flat lie, but his ball finished on the bank at the side of the bunker. He had to stand in the bunker with the ball above his feet, which is when you tend to pull it. He didn't want to do that and so he pushed it slightly into another bunker and made five.

That night we went to the trotting races at Pompano Beach. One of the caddies, Russ Steib, gave us tickets and off we went to the top of the grandstand. Brilliant view. Couple of drinks. You bet by going to the Tote just as in England. They didn't start racing until half-past seven and they had thirteen races. It was only a short course, one mile, and you could see it all from the grandstand. Nine horses in each race each pulling a small cart containing a jockey lying on his back and looking as if he was doing the splits.

The betting was very complicated. If you want to win a lot of money you have to back so many horses in a certain order. If you back a winner it's a win, obviously. A place is if it finishes second. And show betting is if it finishes third. I thought the way to do it is to back it each way as we call it in England.

I put $10 on two favourites in one race and thought I must have a chance that one of them would finish in the top three. I walked up to the Tote and said I wanted $10 win, show and place on these two horses. It came to $60 total. I thought to myself: 'Go on, have a go. Don't back down now.' I put my

$60 on and returned to my seat, thinking: 'I'd better not tell Hilary how much I've put on a couple of nags with three legs.'

We had an expert at our side, the Al Read figure, Johnny-Know-It-All. 'These races are bent,' he was saying. 'They get summonsed every week at this track for bent racing.' My heart sank.

Off they went. One horse of mine finished second and one finished third so I went belting up to the tote and got my winnings – $125; then I had to confess. We finished up $30 in front and left. It was a good night.

Saturday 12 and Sunday 13 March
Sandy shot a 70 in the third round which put him two shots behind Joey Sindelar and Ken Brown. So we had a good chance of winning. He played very well on the Sunday. Another 70. Came to the last hole only one shot behind Joey. Sandy drove towards the same bunker again, landed on the fairway, hit the bank, ran through the bunker on to the far lip. He's got one foot down in the bunker and one on the lip, the ball neither in the bunker nor out of it and a three iron in his hand. Automatic bogey, so that bunker cost him the tournament.

The tournament was scheduled to finish at 6 p.m. but this was one of the few times when playing in pairs on the last two days didn't speed up play. The par fives were within range in two shots and they put the pin positions in bad places on some of the par threes and that contributed to the field backing up. It was getting so dark Joey couldn't see his ball finish after he had played his second shot to the last hole. Just as well there wasn't a play-off.

Sandy finished joint second. That means that in the course of a year he has won $180,000 at Sawgrass, $117,000 at Phoenix and $52,000 here. So in three tournaments on TPC courses he has won $350,000 – on courses he doesn't like because there's so much water! He'd have won $25,000 more with a four on the last hole here.

That night Hilary and I drove 200 miles to Orlando where Sandy was to play in the Hertz Bay Hill Classic at Arnold Palmer's club. It slashed down with rain all the way.

People come from all over the US, Canada and the rest of the world at this time of the year – spring break – to go to

Epcot Centre, Sea World, Disneyworld and everything else in Orlando. The main hotels are on International Drive. It's like a zoo. You have to queue up to eat. We rented a condominium at the International Resort Club and Pete Coleman and Andy Prodger stayed with us. Do your own cooking. Best apartment I've ever stayed in, no question. The other caddies had an apartment next door. Bernhard and Vikki Langer stayed there as well. Saw him on the tennis court one day: he's a good player.

Hertz Bay Hill Classic, Bay Hill Club and Lodge, Orlando, Florida

Monday 14 March
Went to Epcot Centre. I've been before but Hilary wanted to go. There were long queues. It was high season. I paid $56 for the day and we went on most of the rides. It's the same sort of thing as Disneyland but bigger and more educational.

The organization was superb, even to get you in and out. You can't believe the size of the car parks. The only drawback was after Hilary had bought some cuddly toys for her nieces we noticed it said 'Made in Korea' on them.

Tuesday 15 March
Day off. It was cold and Sandy decided not to practice.

Big Brian Bellenger came over from England to caddie for Ken Brown, and Andy Prodger was supposed to caddie for Faldo. But Faldo pulled out and so Andy hadn't got a bag. He decided there and then he was going to have a week off and avoid work. Big Brian said he wished he had known about Faldo because he'd have let Andy caddie for Ken and he could have stayed another week in England. Then he wouldn't have missed the race meeting at Cheltenham. Brian spent the rest of the week trying to get the results.

Thursday 17 and Friday 18 March
Sandy played with Dan Forsman again and David Peoples, who lives at Bay Hill. Hal Sutton withdrew and so Peoples was the

alternate. He was in bed when the phone rang telling him he was due on the tee in three-quarters of an hour.

Des Smyth, Ove Sellberg and Woosnam all turned up to play. Sandy was 68 and coasting in the first round. A 73 the second day.

Usual mistake of putting too much sand in the bunkers. It's not generally appreciated that if you have a lot of sand in the bunkers it's no good at all. The ball buries and you get a lot of bad if not impossible lies. You can't put backspin on a ball played from a plugged lie.

Dave Eichelberger, a previous winner, was doing well for a change. He's a Texan. He walks about saying: 'Gol damn' (God damn) every five minutes and gripping and ungripping an imaginary club because five years ago he found the perfect grip. One of these days it's going to come back to him. Creamy Carolan was caddying for him. Their ages came to 117. Eichelberger is forty-four and Creamy is nearly seventy-three.

Creamy, who caddied for Palmer for years, used to say: 'Arnie and I have the perfect partnership. We share everything. He gets all the credit and I take all the blame.'

Saturday 19 March
Irish Dave [McNeilly] was carrying for Nick Price for the first time since falling down and injuring his leg during the winter. He managed the first two rounds all right but only by carrying the bag on his other shoulder to ease the weight on his injured leg.

Trouble was this was hurting his back and in the car driving to the course this morning he sneezed and damaged his back so badly Nick Price had to help him out of the car. Clearly he couldn't caddie and so Andy was pressed into service carrying for Pricey for the last two days.

Bernard Bissonnett is one of the old timers and a friend of Creamy's. We call him Frenchie because he is a French-Canadian teaching pro from Montreal. He can't play in the winter in Canada because of the snow so he caddies on the pro tour in the US from January until the Masters. He's been in the car park since half-past seven each morning trying to get a bag. It's specially difficult to get one at Bay Hill because it's only a

120-man field instead of 144. So Frenchie's been standing out there all week trying to get a bag and Prodger's been hiding all week and he gets the job, not Frenchie. Frenchie did get a job in the end because somebody got fired on Friday but it took him all week to do it.

Sandy double bogied the last for a 70, one under par. We're still in the top ten.

Mac O'Grady, who by this time is on his third caddie of the week, offered me or Pete Coleman $1000 a week and 10 per cent of what he won to caddie for him. But you never know how long you're going to last with Mac. He offered me this money and I said: 'Mac, who's got the best job on this tour?'

'You have.'

And I said: 'Well, there you are, then.'

Sandy had just made his double bogey on the last, and I said to Mac: 'If you had done that the caddie would be lying on the green with an iron through his chest and you'd be swimming across the lake trying to find an alligator to fight.'

'Yeah, yeah, I would,' he said.

Sunday 20 March
Sandy had a disappointing final round of 73 and finished joint 15th. He won $12,000, making it a respectable week's work.

The Players' Championship, Jacksonville, Florida

Wednesday 23 March
Sandy played in the shoot-out before the Players' Championship and performed miracles time and again to stay in it until the 17th. He was trying out a new metal driver.

Metal drivers are like solid balls – an unbelievable advantage for handicap golfers because you've only got to touch the ball and it's gone. You flick at the ball and it takes off and goes miles. That's all right for an amateur but the feeling of flicking a ball is not what a pro wants. A pro wants to feel the ball on the club face as long as possible.

Greg Norman never uses a metal wood, nor does Seve, nor does Watson. All right, Nicklaus is using one now but his career is coming to an end and he wants length. That's why Trevino is using one as well.

Sandy had got to the point where he was smothering the ball and tapping it instead of hitting it. He lasted until the 17th in the shoot-out, but then Payne Stewart and Fred Couples both birdied it and Sandy didn't and so he was out. He won a thousand dollars.

After the shoot-out Greg Larsen wrote in the *Florida Times-Union* newspaper: 'Who'd have believed for instance that defending Players' Championship winner Sandy Lyle would have been spraying shots with his new metal driver everywhere but the fairway.

'After Lyle hooked another drive into the trees on number 16 his caddie David Musgrove said in disgust: "This is the first time he's really used it and it's going into the lake in a moment because I'm going to throw it in." Yet Lyle recovered with the same kind of recoveries he had made at last year's Players' Championship until losing to birdies of Stewart and Couples on number 17.'

Thursday 24 March
They've done away with the pro-am because somebody pointed out that it can't be a major championship if it has a pro-am. The debate goes on. The traditionalists will only have the four majors.

What makes the US PGA the fourth major? Tradition? How long is tradition going on for? The US PGA can't be more of a major championship than the TPC. The TPC is held on a stadium course, a course built specially to play a major championship on. The field is selected on merit over the previous twelve months apart from two invitations. It's the strongest field of the year. There are no club pros and no amateurs. This championship is always held on the same course every year, which gives you continuity like the Match-play at Wentworth and the US Masters at Augusta. And it's played on a course built to accommodate spectators. PGA National in Florida where the 1987 PGA championship was held isn't. It was played on a course that was designed solely to sell houses. There was so much walking in between holes you got lost.

The TPC is good fun for caddies. As far as we're concerned, the players and caddies I mean, we get looked after in the best possible way. There's a committee tent where all the volunteers go and eat and we can go in there as well at very reasonable prices. Halfway round there's a snack hut for players and caddies where we get bars of chocolate, fruit, drinks, peanut butter sandwiches, crisps. Nibbles, I call them. There's a nibbles tent between the 5th and the 6th and another between the 15th and 16th.

First round, Sandy shot 79, one under par after five. He pushed his second shot into the trees on the 6th and the second shot out landed up a palm tree. We couldn't find it, although we knew it was up there somewhere, so it was a lost ball. In the circumstances he did well to chip and a putt for a six.

Then he got a load of terrible lies. He didn't play particularly well but those lies were awful. But, only twenty-eight putts. He was mad with himself a lot of times but he didn't lose his temper as far as the next shot was concerned. He didn't give up.

You've got to have a bad round every now and then and it's just unfortunate it was here. He wasn't using his metal wood, oh no! Certainly not.

Friday 25 March
Finished with a 72 but if a couple of putts had dropped on the 2nd and 3rd, the 11th and 12th as we played them, he would have had a chance of playing at the weekend. That was the end of his defence. Sandy has now played four times in the TPC, missed the cut three times and on the other occasion he won. This gives him an average of $45,000 dollars a week prize money.

He wasn't as self-conscious as he was when he was defending Open champion at Turnberry in 1986. He kept trying, and then Woosnam pointed out about his standing too closed. He wanted to hold on more with his left hand because he felt that his right hand was dominating. Those were the changes he made for the next week.

So, a weekend off, a rest. He'd played five weeks in a row. If you make the cut every week, which is tough for anybody to do on the US tour, you don't get much time off. The last time he missed a cut in the US was at Hilton Head after the 1987 Masters and the last time in Europe was in the Lawrence Batley International last August.

Saturday 26 March
Five of us caddies shared a flat on the beach, which had been arranged by Terry Holt. The five were Andy, Big Brian, Pete and Paul Stephens. I spent the day by the sea. Sandy did some practice at the TPC.

Sunday 27 March
I returned my hired car and got a lift back to our flat with the lady who had driven Sandy to the airport.

4

28 March–30 April

*Sandy wins Greensboro – Augusta under the microscope –
Lyle the 1988 Master*

K-Mart Greater Greensboro Open, Forest Oaks CC, Greensboro, North Carolina

Monday 28 March
An eight and a half hour drive up to Greensboro, North Carolina, in Harry's van. It can be cold there. Last year it snowed on the Saturday morning and this delayed play for an hour. T. C. Chen had never seen snow before and he dashed out to see what it was like. What he didn't realize was how cold it had to be for it to snow, and he couldn't play in the cold. He couldn't hold his club. As it happened this year the warm wind from Florida followed us up the east coast to Greensboro so we had a warm week.

Tuesday 29 March
There was a pro-am at Sedgefield, where they used to play the Greater Greensboro Open. It took the form of a nine-hole Texas scramble to mark the 50th anniversary of the GGO. All five players drive and the captain, the pro, picks the best-positioned tee shot and everybody plays from there. Then you take the best-positioned second shot and all play from there, and so on. Only one score counts. They add all the handicaps up, take a tenth of the total and deduct that from the gross score. They invited all the past winners and they all showed up, bar Seve.

   In the afternoon there was a shoot-out and we played the wrong ball. I walked up to a ball in the rough on the 15th and

Sandy played it without really looking at it. So he was disqualified. In a tournament he'd have gone back and found his ball and played it and so he'd have been penalized stroke and distance, not disqualified.

This week we are staying in Greensboro, half an hour from the club, with Neil and Bridget Macpherson and their three children, Mark, Kathy and Nicholas. Neil is the son of Jeffrey Macpherson, who used to be the chairman of Notts Forest football club. I sometimes caddied for him at Hollinwell when I was still at school. I used to play with Neil at Coxmoor.

When Sandy first played at Greensboro three or four years ago, Neil made himself known to us, took us out to dinner and said: 'Next year you come and stay with us.' And so we did. They have a big beautiful house with two acres of land.

Neil's company buys Japanese machinery that embroiders logos onto shirts and sweaters and sells it to the Americans. The company was doing all right until about two years ago when the yen started getting very strong against the dollar, so he's on the point of selling out and doing something else because it's not the fun that it used to be.

It's a good week. They know some Scottish people who live on the next street and we went round there one night. Quite a homely atmosphere. Good cups of tea all the time, and they're difficult to get in the States. It makes a big difference for Sandy because he feels at home. He cuts the grass, plays with the children, watches the telly, relaxes. He's won the GGO two of the three years he's stayed there.

Sandy likes his home comforts. He always does all right when he's staying with friends like the Macphersons, and at Pebble Beach where he stays with the Van Linges. At Phoenix he stays with Richie Alimo. You can't relax in a hotel like you can in a house. People think it's a treat to stay in a hotel but when you've done it a few times you soon discover it's a bind. You never know when you're well off, do you?

They call the GGO 'A Celebration of Spring' because it's a sign that summer's coming to North Carolina. It's a big event for Greensboro. There's tents full of sandwiches and drinks for caddies and players at the 1st, 9th, 10th and 18th, so we make good use of them.

The tournament organizers asked for a better date and the PGA Tour said: 'If you put the prize money up to one million dollars you can have a better date.' So they did. They have tried to improve their image as well. For instance on that 17th hole they used to have bleachers (stands) full of people who got drunk and made a helluva noise. So they cut the stands and the beer stall out this year.

They're real friendly people in Greensboro, especially after Florida which I find artificial, full of people who have moved down there recently or retired there or are on holiday; after four weeks there I must say I find them rather pretentious.

Thursday 31 March
Sandy used a stronger grip with his left hand, lined up better and shot a 68, no trouble at all.

Friday 1 April
A 63. Holed a 20-yard bunker shot for an eagle at the second and off he went. Only 27 putts. I won't say it could have been lower but he hit the ball so far and straight he made the course look silly.

Played with Chip Beck again, whom we had played with at Phoenix. Got on to one tee and there was a load of Chip's family there come to watch. They lived nearby.

I said: 'How many are there in your family?'

'I'm one of ten children,' he replied.

Sandy says: 'Are they all singles or there any doubles among them?'

'They're all singles. My mother had two miscarriages as well.'

Sandy said: 'Didn't your Dad ever find out what caused them?'

Saturday 2 April
Another 68. He was so good that at one point I was thinking of offering to pay somebody admission. Fancy being paid to watch Sandy Lyle play golf! This much entertainment can't be free, I thought.

The Macphersons were talking about going out somewhere

tonight but they couldn't find a baby sitter and so I volunteered. Neil and Bridget had said that the children must be in bed at half-past nine. We were all watching tv and I was wondering how I was going to get them off to bed at the prescribed time? There's bound to be an argument.

It gets to twenty-five past nine and so I said: 'Soon be your bedtime. Half-past nine is coming.' They said: 'Do you think so? Oh all right,' and they went to bed. Couldn't believe it. What a shock!

Sunday 3 April

Easter Sunday. We got cakes and cards and we gave the family presents. The children are nine, eight and four. They're good fun actually. They play on their own nicely. It was also Neil and Bridget's wedding anniversary and she took the children to church. She sings in the choir. Bridget explained that they got to know more people in Greensboro by going to church than by any other way.

Neil drove us up to the course in the Mercedes. They've also got a Ferrari, a Jeep for Bridget which says Hers on the front, and one of those vans like a mini bus. Jolande followed later with the luggage in the car provided by the tournament.

Played with Ken Green and Jeff Sluman. Ken turned up on the first tee with a green glove, white and green shoes and flashes of green in his trousers. Do you think he's superstitious?

After nine holes Sandy had a three-shot lead. On the tenth Sluman drove in to a bunker and couldn't reach the green. I told Sandy: 'He's not the threat, Green is the threat.' Ken Green at that point had a healthy complexion, ruddy-faced. He birdied the 10th, 11th and 13th where Sandy bogied. So Sandy was level with Green and Sluman was one behind. We looked on the board and saw that the three of us were well clear of the rest of the field. Whatever happens we're going to finish in the top three. This doesn't sound very ambitious but that's a good position to be in, believe me. Don't let anybody tell you anything else.

By now Ken Green's red face had started to go a little pale and at the 16th hole he hit an eight iron to three feet. Next man to play is Sluman. He goes in the left-hand bunker. Sandy played a nine iron. He didn't want to go over the back so he eased off on it and it came up on the front of the green, sixteen yards short of the flag.

He had a go at the putt and holed it. Sluman comes out of the bunker and goes in the hole for another birdie. So this three-footer of Green's has grown a bit. But he holed it, bravely.

Green birdied the 17th from outside Sluman and Sandy. Sandy parred the hole and Sluman bogied it. Ken Green's colour now is white. He has a one-stroke lead. On the 18th, Green putts up to three feet, Sandy is just over the back. His chip hit the hole and stayed out. I was attending the pin and he said if it hadn't been attended his ball might have hit it and gone in. Anyway, it didn't. By now we've all had a good meaningful look at Ken Green's three-foot putt and thought to ourselves: 'That's not quite dead' without saying anything. He proceeded to miss it. He'd gone round in 67, Sandy in 72 and Sluman in 71.

Now Ken Green's complexion is grey.

For the play-off they put us in buggies and drove us across the practice ground to the designated hole, the 16th. It was all well coordinated between the PGA and the tv people. PGA officials are in touch via walkie-talkies with a man named Paul Spangler, a friend of Chuck Van Linge. Spangler is the producer of ESPN's television broadcast. (ESPN stands for Entirely Sports Promotion Network.) And the television tells them when they can start playing.

The hole is 408 yards into the wind. Green hit a drive and a poor six iron left and short of the left-hand bunker behind which the pin is tucked in. Sandy hit a big drive and then a 117-yard wedge shot to six feet. That shows you what a long drive he had hit down there. He had been inhibited during the round because he was protecting his lead but now in the play-off it was match-play, all or nothing, and he let one rip.

Sandy said: 'Green's in a tough spot to make a four.' I said to him: 'Don't be expecting him to make five and give it to you. Make your mind up that you've got to hole it.' Green chipped to four feet and then Sandy holed his putt to win $180,000. Thank you very much.

So Sandy became the first European ever to lead the US

money list. In the seven-odd years I've been caddying for him that was the best I've ever seen him play over four rounds. There were no weaknesses at all in his game.

The getting away from a tournament is very important for caddies. We don't want to be held up by all the traffic. We want to nip off smartly and get on the road to our next event. I'd arranged a lift to Augusta (for the Masters) with Harry Brown. Harry was caddying for Gil Morgan who finished fifth. This meant that out of the six tournaments he'd played this year Morgan's worst finish was eighth.

Harry came off the course a group in front of us and went to fetch his van. We'd come off the course, won the play-off hole, come back to the car park and I was still ten minutes waiting for Harry to turn up, so our being in the play-off didn't lose us any time, as it happened.

Then a four-hour drive through the Carolinas to Augusta, Georgia. On Sunday night when you've had a good week and there are several caddies and their gear in the car or van and you're heading down the road – that's the best feeling we get. You haven't got to go back. You're leaving one place and going to another. You're not worrying about money. The stuff's in the van and you can stop when you like. It's the freedom of the road. It's like it says in that song by Lee Marvin: 'I was born under a wandering star.'

Just outside Charlotte, North Carolina, Pete Coleman said: 'They've just renamed that street.' It said: 'Dave Lyle Boulevard exit one mile.'

Checked into the Motel 6 in Augusta. We had reservations from last year and on the spot we made reservations for next year. Vital move, that is. You pay for one night and they reserve it for eight. The rate is $20 plus tax. Two hundred dollars for eight nights, all in. They don't put the rates up in Masters week like they do in other places round here. It is a paid reservation and so a room will be held automatically. If you don't have a paid reservation they let the room go at six o'clock.

The caddies found this motel three or four years ago, soon after it had been built. It had plenty of vacancies, which is very unusual for Masters week. There must be nearly fifty of us here this year. Andy North's dad, Stuart, always stays here as well.

We call him the Professor because he teaches at a university in Florida. What could be better than this? Plenty of restaurants nearby. Only a twenty-minute walk to the course. It's perfect.

US Masters, Augusta National GC, Augusta, Georgia

Monday 4 April

Up to the course to register. You go to gate number one and explain who you're caddying for. The guard asks you your name and then checks it on a list before sending you to the security trailer. Then the same thing happens again and you have your picture taken. Then you go to the caddie shack to get your uniform and you're given a green cap, shoes and socks, which you keep, a white overall, towel, soap and a locker. You give the bloke two dollars and he gives you a key so you can lock the locker. The two dollars is supposed to be a deposit but you give it to him anyway. You can eat in there, chicken or pork chops between two slices of bread, have a drink, watch the telly.

Sandy didn't play today. He went to the course to check in, show his face, do a bit of press, but he had no intention of playing. In fact he didn't even take his golf shoes with him. He needed to rest after Greensboro. His parents arrived in the evening – Alex and Agnes Lyle. The first three days of this week are very hard. They can tire you out, especially when you've had a hard week the week before, so you have to plan very carefully.

The Caddies' Association has made an unbelievable difference to our lives. We have credentials to get into each tournament. It used to be a Catch-22 situation. You couldn't get in without a ticket and you couldn't get a ticket until you'd got in. Now we arrive at the gate, show our credentials and in we go. Brilliant. Some of the boys get parking stickers, some get guest badges. Then there's the Nabisco deal, which is quite lucrative for doing nothing. What happens is that the names of a certain number of Association members are drawn out of a hat each week and they get a turn to wear the Nabisco visor. You wear it Thursday and Friday and that's $50. If you make the cut that's another $50. If you get in the last four groups on Saturday it's more money and it's more money still if you're in the last group on Sunday. And if you get in the last four groups and your name has not been drawn out of the hat that week you still get paid for it. In the Kapalua tournament last year they asked me if I would wear a Nabisco visor and they gave me $200 for doing so. Beats working, doesn't it? I wanted to wear a visor anyway.

Then there's Gypsy Joe's caddie trailer, motor home if you like, where we get our food. Mike Carrick has been behind all this and these improvements have made our life more pleasant.

Mike went skiing in February and twisted his knee and now it's in plaster. He can't work for the biggest part of this year. I thought the thing to do was to have a collection for him, not only because he can't work but also because he stuck his neck out for so long regarding the Association and got results. Up to date I've collected $950. I got Bridget Macpherson to type a letter and I'm going to get a card for everybody to sign. I'll carry on collecting this week and try and catch a few more next week at Hilton Head. Then Big Brian will take the card and the money to New Orleans to give to Gypsy who will either carry on the collection or send the money to Mike.

Tuesday 5 April

Sandy and his parents came to collect me and we drove to the course in Sandy's big white Cadillac. All the golfers are given one for the week. The first thing you do when you get the car is to steal the key ring because it has a little Masters insignia on it. I've got one, of course. Nothing loose must be left, that's the old caddie rule. Joke, joke.

A practice round, the only one Sandy played as it happens. He turned up, hit some balls and made up a four-ball on the practice ground like you do at your own club. Sandy and Ian Woosnam for Shropshire played Seve Ballesteros and Greg Norman for the rest of the world. Ninety-two degrees it was, and you had to fight your way between each hole there were that many people there.

Anybody can get in early in the week just by paying at the gate – $10 Monday, $20 Tuesday and $30 Wednesday. The best value is Tuesday. You're guaranteed everybody being there and it's ten dollars cheaper than Wednesday. The match ended all square but Sandy and Woosie paid out $20 to the other two because of side bets.

Seve didn't seem to be in a very good mood at the start but he finished up asking how I was going on at home, and was I still in my mother's house? He remembers everything. Greg was all right, too. There's no point in having airs and graces with me.

As we were going up the 18th fairway Sandy asked Seve why he didn't play more in the US. 'This is the first division,' Sandy said. 'No, it's not,' replied Seve. 'The first division is in Europe. They're the better golfers. You've won three times in the last year over here but you haven't won in Europe.'

Sandy thrives over here because of the facilities. They have good weather and the courses have a lot of money spent on them. I still think many American courses are a bit artificial compared with the Old Course at Sunningdale, say, or a linksland course in Britain which in top condition can't be beaten.

This was when Seve made the point to Sandy that his success can't be put down to Jimmy Ballard or anybody else. 'You're winning because you've got the talent to win,' Seve told Sandy. Seve said he didn't like Jimmy Ballard because he spoke to you as if you didn't know anything about the game. I didn't get that impression from what I saw and heard of him when I was with Sandy, but there you are. One man's meat is another man's poison. But Seve did win the Open at St Andrews in 1984 after seeing Ballard earlier in the year.

Ballard said you could say anything to Sandy and he'd go out there and try it. 'I don't know how he does it,' Jimmy says. 'He'll change his grip, stance, anything. And then he'll go and hit balls. You try and tell an amateur golfer that.' Sandy listens to them all and takes a little from each.

Wednesday 6 April
He didn't want to play today. He still hasn't recovered from Greensboro. As I said, this course is too tiring. There's a drop of 100 feet from the 10th tee to the 12th green. Watching on

television you get no idea how tough it is to walk on, and the atmosphere generated by the people that want to see it is wearing as well.

We played with Billy Casper and Gay Brewer in the par three competition on the adjoining par three course, just finishing before the rain started. This competition is always held on the Wednesday afternoon preceding the opening day of the Masters. Seve and Jack Nicklaus never play in it, perhaps because its too much hassle. It takes their mind off the serious business. It's a fact that the winner of the par three has never gone on to win the US Masters as well. It's a good show for the crowd, though. I'd like to play that course. They've got eleven holes now they've put two more in. The first and second used to be very short and few spectators could see the players. So they've built two new holes over the other lake so more people can watch what's happening.

What I can't understand is why the papers always predict Seve and Norman to win the Masters. No mention of Larry Nelson or Lanny Wadkins or people like that. These pundits ought to make a living competing against such blokes as that. When you're out here every week you realize how good they are. Larry Nelson has got a good record in majors. He's had three chances and he's won three, but he's never mentioned. The forecasts seem very predictable to me even though Seve will probably show. He always does at Augusta.

It says in the paper that Hord Hardin (the Chairman of the US Masters) is worried about the rising prize money at other US tournaments. He's worried that this will devalue the importance of the Masters. The caddies' attitude is: 'The bloke is a retired banker. He's made his money. How much would he pay caddies?'

I come from a mining town and when I was growing up the local shopkeepers had a very narrow-minded attitude. So long as the miners and the railway men kept going to work and spending money in their shops, that was all right. If there was a strike for a better standard of living the shopkeepers didn't like it. They were losing trade in the short term and they couldn't bear to think of anyone getting ahead. Hardin's attitude sounds to me a bit like Ashfield shopkeepers.

When you go through the gate at Augusta it's like Fort Knox, there are so many men with guns. I asked an Augusta policeman, who was wearing the black uniform, how many of them are here each day. He said twenty-five. And there's 125 Pinkerton men and about thirty from the Sheriff's office, mainly dealing with the traffic. At first it struck me there were far too many, but those numbers aren't excessive.

When you've got through this initial barrier of security most people at the course are very friendly and helpful. Bill Thibodeau, the old boy that sits outside the players' locker room, for instance, and the gentleman on the practice ground, name of Ed Jones. I asked him if he was a member. There are two or three of them that are in charge of the lads on the practice ground, giving the balls out, collecting them in. He said: 'No, I'm not a member. I do a lot of business with the club and every year I come and do this job.' They take it in shifts. They're real old southern gentlemen. And the staff in the pro's shop and the caddie shack, they're real friendly.

It can give the impression of being very officious and regimented. But really inside it's just a laid-back, sleepy old place like it is the rest of the year. People do pester you all the time. I suppose that's only reasonable. Must be hell for the golfers, specially if they're doing well. But you can't have one without the other. That practice round for example. You had to fight your way through all the time even though there were security guards helping you.

The only people inside the ropes are golfers and caddies. No scorers, journalists, photographers. So there are only four people in each group and if you're one of them you can't help but feel the eyes of the people boring into you even though you're used to being in the public eye.

Another thing that isn't appreciated is that there's hardly anything called a flat lie on this course. The ball's either above the feet or below the feet. The fairways this year have got more grass on than I've ever seen. Usually they're bare and it's a helluva job to get the ball up in the air. These are the best fairways I've seen here.

1983 was my first year at the Masters, the year white men were allowed to caddie for the first time, the year players were allowed to bring their own caddies. In 1983 Nick DePaul was the first white man to caddie for the winner (Seve Ballesteros). Until then, Greensboro was usually my last tournament. I used to go home after that except for 1982 when I caddied for Faldo when he played at Hattiesburg (a tournament in Mississippi that is staged at the same time as the Masters). 1982 was the year Craig Stadler won. I remember that because Pete Coleman and I were watching him on television and betting whether he would hole putts or not. He kept on holing them. That event used to be called the Magnolia Classic. In the Hattiesburg papers they refer to this tournament (the Masters) as 'the other tournament'.

Thursday 7 April
First round. A cold windy day. Sandy had five birdies in his 71, a good workmanlike round. Played with Raymond Floyd who shot 80. He played some tripe and his caddie 'Golf' Ball seemed under the weather. Floyd fired him later.

The first few scores of the first round set the standard. When you know what they are you can tell whether the course is playing easy or tough. You can play as many practice rounds as you like but when you go out on the first day it's a different course. It's like sitting an examination paper; you can do as much revising as you like but all of a sudden you've got the questions in front of you. That's how I think of major championships.

We were off at 2.00. There were only a few groups behind us. Sandy doesn't like going out so late, nobody does. You want to get out there and do it. You don't want to sit around watching other people watching the scoreboard. If it's good scores you know you've got to do a good score, and if the scores are high you know what you're in for. Also the course is usually better in the mornings. The greens are not as hard. In the morning you usually get calm weather. This time we got the best weather.

Friday 8 April
Second round, 67. One bogey and that was the 1st hole. The birdie on the 9th, which was only about three feet, took Sandy

into the lead. If the ball had missed it would have been off the green. He only just started it rolling. Nine golfers out of ninety four-putted the 9th – one tenth of the field. Most of the rest three-putted it.

We literally sat down on the tenth tee and it's rather like living in a glasshouse with just your underpants on. You know everybody in the world is looking at you and at everything you do. You're under a microscope and there's a long way to go. You can't avoid the feeling of being scrutinized. Everybody knows what the stakes are and where the pitfalls are. You get used to it after a bit but I said to myself: 'It's going to be bloody hard for the rest of the week.'

The greens by this time were almost unplayable. We were very late out again and the 9th, 11th, 14th, 16th and 18th had turned blue because of the heat and the lack of watering. That course has to have a defence and its defence is the hard, fast greens. There is a fine line between them being a real good test of nerve and skill and being impossible. Sandy says the course is at least one shot harder in the afternoon, when it is dry and the greens have got bumpy, than it is in the morning. And he has played in the afternoon both days so far.

Sandy putted out very well. He read some grain into the putts. In the afternoon when the sun was very strong the grain affected the ball. That was it: 138, six under par and in the lead.

Putting is the tiring part, the nerve required to keep holing these putts. This is true at almost any championship but it's specially true at Augusta. You have to strike them 100 per cent on the line and at the pace you've already worked out. You have to commit yourself to every putt. You can't just shovel them forward with any old stroke and hope they'll finish somewhere near. They won't.

Sandy putted well in Greensboro, too. He's said over the last couple of years: 'I've had trouble hitting the ball over the line I intended to.' But he never mentioned it at Greensboro. That's why I say there was no weakness in his game when he came here.

But this afternoon he said on the 10th: 'I'll be glad when this is over.' And I said to him: 'I know you will, but there's a long way to go.' Fatigue is the biggest enemy. Sandy has played for six weeks. TPC was a week off, really. Lot of travelling. Four on the west coast and this is the sixth this side. That's ten and in nine of them at some stage he has been in the frame, if not leading. That in itself is very tiring.

The last round at Greensboro was like playing two men at once. If you think of it as an athletics race, they were chasing him. Sandy's supposed to be a good front-runner but he's not in the same class as Lanny Wadkins and Ian Woosnam. Sandy's biggest winning margin while I've caddied for him was in the 1984 Italian Open at Monza when he birdied the last four holes to win by four shots.

We spent the evening with Bob Cunningham and family – myself, Dave McNeilly (an Ulsterman who used to caddie for Nick Faldo before joining Nick Price), Andy and Pete. Bob was born in Belfast, moved to London to find work and finished up in Augusta thirty-six years ago. He's an 11-handicap golfer and works for the Columbia Nitrogen Corporation selling fertilizers, and has been a captain of stewards on number five hole for twenty-five years. McNeilly, being Irish, got to know him. His sons Bob and Jeff help, along with their wives, at the crossings. They each get paid $6 a day and they give it to charity.

We go round to the Cunninghams each year. They live just over the border in South Carolina. Their house is what we'd call a bungalow, but a big one. They cooked us steaks on a barbecue and salads. Big pieces of cake and gateau which Coleman ate an immense amount of, and a drop of Jameson's Irish whiskey to finish it off, thank you very much.

Saturday 9 April

Sandy hit one bad shot – on the 13th; and he got one bad break – on the 16th. And he got bogies on both. On the 13th tee he was held up for so long you could see that his concentration or his patience gave way and he just hammered it. He'd been there for ever, it seemed. On the 10th, 11th, 12th and 13th we just stood on the tees doing absolutely nothing. Yesterday the pile-up came at the end of the round. The reason was that Seve took a double bogey on the 11th and he and Mark McNulty lost a lot of ground on the group in front. Today the congestion came in the middle of the round.

When we were on the practice ground yesterday Gary McCord and some of the other tv commentators were talking to the players and McCord, who commentates on the 14th, told us that the only way to play the hole was to land the ball up on the left of the green and let it roll all the way down. Sandy played his ball to the left, expecting it to roll down, but it didn't. The green was a bit softer than it had been yesterday. Sandy's ball pitched and stayed up there. Left him a putt of fifteen yards and it pulled up about nine feet past. He had to make a good second putt to save par. That 14th is a difficult green, shaped like a hog's back. Michael Bonallack, secretary of the Royal and Ancient, saw two people five-putt it.

Gary McCord also told me that since he hit me in the eye with his club at Pebble Beach he hadn't been able to play because he'd had a sore shoulder and a sore wrist. We think he brought it up in case I was going to sue him and he could have a counter-suit.

Another thing about the Masters – the number of R & A officials who come over to help officiate. They have every hole covered. You don't have to send for a ruling, they're there all the time. It seems as though there are four rules officials on each hole. And this year there's David Eger from the US PGA also assisting.

Now then, about the 16th where Sandy had his other bogey of the day. The pin was back right and his ball landed between the hole and the bunker and hopped onto the apron of the green. If his tee shot had pitched six inches further left it would have run down to the pin. Sandy thought it had gone in the bunker. That would have been very bad news because it's practically impossible to make par from that bunker unless you hit the pin. You're pitching out from above the hole and trying to stop the ball on a downslope. Might as well try and stop a ball on a tabletop.

There was a foot of fringe grass to go through and the grass is like wire wool. Chip and it's down the bottom of the green. The only chance is to take the putter and dribble it through the grass with enough pace to get it out of the fringe, on to the apron of the green so that it will roll down to the hole. You can't do it any other way. It went to within one roll of being perfect. Somebody who didn't know the course would think it was a terrible shot but one more roll and it would have got on to the putting surface and down to the hole.

Sandy had a 72 – two birdies on the front nine and two bogies on the second nine. Finished the day on 210, two strokes clear as he had been at the start. In the third round all the names you never want to see if you're leading came on to the scoreboard – Crenshaw, Norman, Ballesteros, Stadler, Watson. Six of the eight past champions are within six shots of the lead – Zoeller, Crenshaw, Stadler, Watson, Norman and Seve.

Now Sandy's led for twenty-seven holes. We'll be playing with Crenshaw tomorrow. That's good for Sandy because Ben gets on with it and is very good company. He and Sandy get on well together. It'll be like Sandy and Christy O'Connor Jnr on the last day of the Open at St George's in 1985.

Sunday 10 April
What are my thoughts this morning? You've got to stay calm. There's no point in getting all excited about the outcome. Tomorrow morning is going to come whatever happens. I know we're going to be very, very tired when we're finished today. And I do worry about the mistakes I might make. I know what they are because I've made most of them at some time or other. Getting your figures wrong, leaving a club out of the bag, taking one club too many.

I left the eight iron out of Sandy's bag at Phoenix last year. Guess how many times he wanted an eight iron in the round? He shot a 71. Went out the next day with the eight iron safely in place and he shot seventy-bloody-one. That's a lot better than having one club too many in the bag. I've nearly done that, too. I can't forget the clubs because they're in Sandy's locker. I've never overslept. That's the game, to be there on time.

We'll be all right for golf balls. We'll have nine, maybe a dozen. Sandy rarely uses more than three in a round. I sometimes have to beg him to change his ball. He seems to want to see how long he can make it last. Not like Langer. He'll use fifteen or sixteen in a round. He did that in the Ryder Cup last year. In the foursomes on Saturday morning we had eighteen balls and we used nearly all of them. Sandy played his next two matches with balls that Langer had rejected.

The balls will be marked with a sign so I know they're Sandy's. Since the Open at Muirfield in 1987 Sandy has been playing Dunlop balls world-wide but before that he used both Dunlop and Titleist. If they were Titleists there was a pencil dot above and below the number. With Dunlops I put the dots on either side of the number. The thing about playing Titleists in the States was the pool. If you finished in the top twenty Titleist players you got money for it. Sandy got $25,000 at the 1987 Tournament Players' Championship just for using a Titleist, plus $5000 for finishing top Titleist player and $20,000 for winning the tournament. It was double money in majors.

The Titleist ball flies higher than the Dunlop. So in warm countries with tight fairways and hard greens where you have to hit it precise distances over bunkers and water, the Titleist is superior. But it's not a very versatile ball. It moves a lot in the wind. The Dunlop DDH stays on line better.

There'll be two towels in the bag, one in the pocket to keep the clubs dry in case it rains and one hanging on the outside for cleaning the clubs. I always carry a gadget for tightening up studs, and several pencils. Sam Torrance always keeps his pencil above his right ear. This is because he once put his hand into his pocket to get his pencil and the tip of it jammed into his thumbnail.

At every golf club I've been to in America they've got boxes of pencils in the pro's shop or on the first tee. Pencils with rubbers on are what I go for. They're very useful for doing the crossword. And I'll have masses of tees, all wooden so they won't damage the face of the club. I try to select white tees because they don't mark the club's sole plate the way red and green tees do. Sometimes the colour of the tee peg comes off on the ball. A white peg never shows.

I'll put Sandy's watch in a drawstring bag. He's contracted to Ebel the Swiss watch manufacturer so he has one to play in, a slim one like the ones that Boris Becker, Bernhard Langer and Greg Norman wear, and a diver's watch, a big one, for dress. I've got my yardage book, the car keys, the locker key.

Sandy's got a pitchmark repairer that he has had for years. We have to keep track of that because it's a good big one and it has a bottle-opener on the end. I carry tape for him to put on the fourth finger of his right hand, which tends to split. In the past I have even carried medicine in case his stomach got upset. I don't think we'll need that today. I have some small coins with me to use as markers, nickels and dimes, the currency of the week. In Germany the fifty pfennig piece is very good. They are the right size, little silver things with a nice pattern on them of a fellow kneeling down.

Sandy never worries about anything until he's out on the course, by which time it's too late. My aim is have everything he could ask me for.

In the old days I'd worry about the results we were going to get and how much money I would make, but not now. It's like Fuzzy Zoeller says: 'Why should Sandy worry? He's won $400,000 this year and he's on a high. Just play.' As I said on Friday, fatigue's his biggest worry.

Whatever happens Sandy has never looked fitter, happier, more content, and he has never played better. He does a lot of exercises. He has a rowing machine and a static bike at home. He watches what he eats and drinks. There are certain things on the course he won't drink because he gets too pumped up – Coca-Cola and Sprite, for instance.

Sandy's tee times for the week have been 2.00 first day, 2.25 second day, last off at 1.45 third day and last off at 2.55 today. So we've had all morning each day to think about it and do nothing and think about it and do nothing again. It's totally alien to the times we have been playing at over here – 7.00, 7.30, 8.00. Also every round has been very slow. It's been nothing to have three groups on that second tee.

When I got to the club this morning I had to do some interviews with Steve Rider for the BBC. I was telling him about my wind chart.

The first thing I do each day is to get a starting sheet. I draw the direction of the wind on the first tee on it and from that I can work out where the wind is going to be blowing from for the rest of the round. As it happens the wind changed today from what it had been all week. When we arrived the first hole was downwind and the second hole was into the wind. But by the time we got to the second the wind had dropped. Actually, it's not a wind so much as an air movement.

While I waited for Sandy to arrive I lounged about on the wooden benches outside the players' locker-room. It's very peaceful there and it's in the shade. All the crowds are the other side of the clubhouse. I don't like it before a late round like this. The longer the day goes on the less I like it. I'm used to being out early. You get up, have your breakfast, get to the course and play, so you're not thinking of what to do all the time. But leading is a big responsibility.

Sandy pitched up about quarter past one and said he'd be ready to play about two o'clock. He went inside to take his nasty pills. Hate, hate, hate. He seemed a lot calmer today than he had been yesterday. He knew it would be over tonight one way or the other.

On the practice ground he didn't look very good. He had a few low hooks. But by the time he left the practice ground he was hitting the ball well.

On the first tee Ben Crenshaw came over to me to check what sort of ball Sandy was using. He plays with a Titleist and Sandy plays with Dunlops. Crenshaw is a real gentleman to play with. He always makes a point of getting to know the caddies. Some players won't speak to us at all.

Sandy hit a superb drive up the first hole and that was a great relief. He'd been under pressure for a long time, what with being in the lead and everybody wanting to talk about it all the time, the newspapers, the tv. We've had all day doing absolutely nothing. Then all of a sudden he can go. To hit a huge drive over the hill and on the fairway gives you a terrific boost. The tension has gone. Off we go!

The driver is the club that wins the money. It builds up confidence. If you're putting the ball in play all the time from the tee you're not under such pressure, but if you're saving your score on the green you're making life very difficult for yourself. When you hit good drives, specially at Augusta, you're dominating the course. Roberto de Vicenzo, arguably the best striker of a golf ball ever to tread shoe leather, used to say that, and he was the best with a driver.

Sandy took a driver on the first hole because it's nearly 250 yards to carry that bunker on the right. He hit a great nine iron second shot and took two putts and I thought to myself: 'That's good.' When you've got the first hole out of the way successfully you're in a better frame of mind to hit a good drive down the next hole, which you've got to do to get on in two. He reached the green with a drive and a seven iron. Had a putt for an eagle but had to settle for a birdie.

The 3rd hole is 360 yards but played shorter than that. Sandy drove with a one iron, then hit a sand iron that had no intention of stopping on the green. He played a good chip and got a four. Crenshaw holed his chip for a birdie.

As we walked up the 3rd we looked at the big scoreboard to the left of the fairway. I remember Arnold Palmer saying when he won the Masters that he had his visor on and he tilted his head so that he could see the scores but not the names of the players chasing him. When you're leading a tournament like the Masters it's easy to understand why. It's depressing to see all the big names coming on to the board. The first time Sandy won at Greensboro, in 1986, on the last day there was Isao Aoki, Lanny Wadkins, Craig Stadler and Andy Bean all breathing down his neck. You don't want to know that. It was the same here. You're not going to get any shop eggs chasing you on the last day of the Masters.

That scoreboard showed that Norman had finished the 9th and was five under for the day and level par for the tournament. I said: 'He's got the back nine to play with the par fives downwind so he's going to get some more birdies.' Even so Sandy or whoever is leading had to play badly to let Greg in.

Somebody always comes from the back on the last day at the Masters. There are two reasons for this. The first is there is no pressure on him; the second, and more important, is that the course plays easier early on because the wind and the sun haven't dried out the greens as they have for the later players. Sandy says it's always one shot harder later in the day.

The 4th was playing a lot shorter than normal – 210 yards to the hole. Crenshaw hit a crappy four iron, which didn't get to the flag, so Sandy thought he wanted a big five iron. He hit it well and it cleared the green. When we got there we found it wasn't lying in a very good spot. It was twenty yards from the flag in a tiny furrow. Sandy took his sand iron. It's good and heavy with a sharp leading edge. You can chip and hit the ball first and the club's own momentum will take it through the grass. Sandy holed the chip, for a two. Nick Royds from the R & A said to Sandy: 'You deserved to hole that because that's the only ball the crowd have allowed to go through this afternoon.'

On the next hole Sandy tried to force an eight iron second shot and left it on the front edge of the green. The required shot is a seven iron to the right of the flag. But if it goes left it can run over the back of the green, which is worse than being short because the green slopes from back to front and you can't stop the ball on it. It was good to two-putt from the front, up the bank, for a par.

So far Crenshaw looked as he always does. He gave the impression he could hole anything. If you've never seen him play before it's frightening, but when you've played with him a lot you get used to it. You expect him to hole everything from everywhere.

Sandy used an eight iron on the 6th. The pin was top right and the air caused the ball to drift a little left so it hit the top of the green and rolled all the way down the bottom. He was forty feet from the flag and, not surprisingly, he three-putted it. That was his first bogey since the 16th the previous day. Sandy knew the line of his second putt but he said it was too easy and he didn't make himself concentrate enough. Crenshaw chipped past on the same line and missed the putt back.

Sandy stood on the 7th tee with a one iron in his hand and pulled the shot into the trees. You must be straight off the tee on this hole. It is probably the narrowest fairway and is certainly the smallest green. He was a bit quick. He should have taken a little longer to settle down after three-putting the 6th. When he got to his ball he found he had a shot, though I couldn't see it. It looked to me as though he was blocked by trees. He said there was a gap he could get through. The pin was front and left of the green, 100 yards away. His ball was lying in some fluffy grass and he asked me if I thought a sand iron was enough club. His shot came up short, in a bunker.

Came out to ten or twelve feet and holed the putt. That was a really important putt. Crenshaw bogied the hole, taking three from the edge of the green and went back to three under par. As we were playing the hole Stadler eagled the 8th to go to five under.

'They're going to be making charges all day,' I said to Sandy. 'You just have to live with it. There are six former champions behind you and they all know they can win.'

The 8th was downwind and Sandy hit a good drive. It was 260 yards to carry the bunker on the right and he cleared it comfortably. I know because I was standing level with the bunker on the left of the fairway. That left 230 yards to the front of the green. He pulled a one iron behind a big mound on the left of the green. Played a good pitch and then his putt lipped out for a birdie.

The 9th, a dog leg left, was a tough hole because the pin was in a difficult position. You must hit a good drive. Sandy didn't. He hit one out of the neck. Its only saving grace was that it went down the right-hand side of the fairway, opening the green up a bit. So far this week the flag has been on the middle tier but today it's on the front tier. You don't want a downhill putt because it's easy to end up off the green.

I had gone forward on that hole and so I got to the ball first. When Sandy arrived he asked: 'How far is it?'

'173 yards,' I replied.

'It's a seven iron, then.' He hit it on to the top tier of the green and it rolled back to about two feet from the flag. It was a break for us that Sandy could play so quickly. Had the group in front been on the green, Sandy would have had time to think about the shot and it might not have worked out so well. As I've said many times before, he's one that wants to get on with it.

I think that was a turning point of the tournament. Crenshaw's second shot came up short and right and his chip went right up to the hole, had a good look and sort of wobbled back a quarter of an inch. He remained on three under par; Sandy moved to eight under par.

Sandy had a straightforward four on the 10th, a drive and a six iron. He hit a good drive down number 11 but it landed and stopped by its pitch mark on the right of the fairway where the grass was cut towards the tee. I've said before about how grass is shiny one way and dark the other. The shiny grass means the grass is growing with you and it's easier to make good contact with the ball. There's no such thing as a lucky shot at Augusta. Every shot has to be precise.

He had exactly the same distance to the flag as he'd had on the 10th – 180 yards – but more downhill. You don't want to go left and risk ending in the water so he hit the ball out to the right and with a little mud on it it drifted further right. It ended on the fringe of the green. I couldn't clean it. The mud was still on the ball. That green was totally different to what it had been on the Saturday when it was very slick and hard and shiny and had turned purple. Now it was back to a reasonable speed.

Sandy was that interested in watching what Langer and Calcavecchia were doing on the 12th, the key hole on the back nine, he hadn't got his mind 100 per cent on the 11th. He left the putt short and missed the next one.

When you're playing in the Masters you're also watching it as well. It's like being on the 7th, 8th, 9th, 10th and 11th at St Andrews where you can always see someone else playing. You're very aware of what the other golfers are doing all the time. In most other tournaments you only see the numbers on the board but in the Masters you're watching it as you're playing in it.

On the 12th tee Crenshaw hit a seven iron into the back bunker. Sandy had already had the eight iron in his hand. If he hits a solid eight iron he could go straight at the pin but he was worried that he might turn it a little and send it into the bunker at the back as Crenshaw has just done. Normally when the pin is on the right you don't go for it. You play for the middle of the green. Today there was no wind at all. It was a perfect length for an eight iron – 160 yards.

He came off his tee shot a bit, hit it thin. It sounded a little bony to me and I didn't like its left-to-right shape so I was urging it on. 'Go on, get over the water,' I shouted at it. The ball landed a few feet short of the putting surface and rolled slowly back into the water.

As we were walking forward from the tee Sandy started

cursing himself for not thinking properly. 'That was a shit shot,' he kept muttering. My only thought was: 'I hope we make five.' I had no thoughts of a four because I know how difficult the next shot is. I was trying to measure from the tee to wherever he was going to drop but at the same time I'm trying to calm him down. I'm doing two jobs at once. I had to keep stopping, remember the number I'd reached and say to him: 'Let's just play the shot,' and then start counting again. It's times like this when you've got to keep calm. This is when I earn my money. Sandy's got to play again. Where from, and how far is it? I've got to keep a cool head, otherwise we'll make another mistake. I told him: 'Don't worry about what's happened. That's done, ancient history. Just make sure you make a five.'

The rules officials on duty on this hole included Michael Bonallack. It was Bonallack who had officiated the previous day when Sandy hooked it into the trees on the 13th and had to take a drop. They told Sandy the line he could drop his ball on. Many American players simply tell their caddies: 'Give me 100 yards.' I've heard Jay Haas and Lanny Wadkins do that before now. So the caddie paces out 100 yards.

But in this case I didn't know what length Sandy wanted and I couldn't ask him because I was busy counting and calming him down. He went back sixty yards from the flag and then he moved five yards nearer. I thought he would be better off going further back, making it a shot of 100 yards to help him stop the ball easier. The hardest shot in the world is the third shot to that green. But no, he played it from there. The ball landed between the front edge of the green and the pin and rolled just off the back. It was a brilliant shot. A few feet less and it would have been down in the water again. Two putts for a five. It's a terrible green, like baked clay.

We got on to the 13th tee. What most people don't know is how far away this tee is from the spectators. It's miles. At any other course after you've made a double bogey you can hear the buzz in the crowd, people saying one to another: 'He's just double bogied', or 'He's just dropped two shots', or 'He's lost his lead.' But when you stand on the 13th it's like being on the stage of an empty theatre. You can't hear anything down there. You could be playing in a private two-ball. It's a great chance to regroup.

It was getting cooler by then, too. It must have been about five o'clock. The crowd were like a backdrop somebody had painted. That gave him the best chance in the world to collect his thoughts as we had to watch Calcavecchia hammering out of the trees on the right.

As we stood waiting on the tee Sandy was still muttering at himself. 'What have I done? I've chucked it all away,' he kept saying.

'Look, we've got six holes left,' I said. 'And you're still playing well. There's time. Get on with it.'

We considered which club Sandy should use from the tee.

'A driver up the right of the fairway will go too far. You'll end up in the trees,' I said. 'That's where Calcavecchia has gone. Langer drew his ball round the corner.'

Sandy had already got his shot worked out in his own mind. He took his driver and hit a huge shot across the corner. It was brave even though it was always on for him with a slight wind assistance.

It left him with a second shot of 170 yards, a seven iron. Incidentally, he played seven seven-iron second shots during this round. He pulled it a little bit because he was conscious of the creek on the right and it hit the top of the green near that ridiculous swale (a sort of marshy dip) which somebody whose name escapes me [Jack Nicklaus] designed.

I don't like the swale because you can hit the green, run down the swale and up the other side and stay there, so although you've hit the green you've got a downhill lie for a chip shot on to a green that's like concrete and running away from you. I don't think it's very clever. You're better off missing the green wide, hitting the swale and running back in to the bottom of it.

Anyhow, Sandy's ball ends up in a bunker. I thought to myself: 'That's all right. If it's in a good lie it's a straightforward shot. Land it on the top tier of the green and let it run down to the bottom.'

But he didn't have a very good lie. There was a great lump of sand behind the ball. 'I've got a lot to do to stop this on the green,' he said as he lined up the shot. He did it though, and got a five. That's like half a shot dropped. And by not birdieing it Sandy had lost the lead for the first time since the ninth hole on the second day.

The 14th is one of Augusta's lesser known holes. It's a slight dog leg left and the adverse camber of the fairway throws the ball to the right. Sandy always hits a one iron because he can shape his shot better with this club. If you overdo it and hit the left-hand trees you're dead. He hit his one iron up the middle to run to the right hand side of the fairway. From there you're perfectly positioned with the pin back left of the green. He had 170 yards again and hit a great seven iron that ran ten feet past the flag. He hit a real pure putt but it just stayed on the lip.

Sandy hit a good tee shot on the 15th and was left with 197 yards to the front of the green. We had a pretty good idea what club to take because in a practice round he'd had 191 yards for his second shot and he'd hit a five iron which stayed on the green.

While we were waiting to play I made casual conversation. 'What a great view this is, Sandy.' Standing in the middle of the fairway – not on one side or the other – you've got an uninterrupted view of the slope, the water, the green, the water behind, the spectators all around and the trees behind them. It's a fantastic view. Then I thought it was time to talk seriously. I said: 'You've lost the lead and you're chasing now. A weight's been taken off your shoulders. Put that to your advantage. Let somebody else do the work for a change and we'll chase them.'

We watched Calcavecchia chipping from the back of the green and we both knew he was struggling to make five, though he did get his par. We both noticed that the bounce had gone from his walk as he was conscious of leading the tournament. He misjudged both these holes. On the 16th he hit a six iron, far too much club. It went over the back. He didn't realize how much the air was helping.

While we were waiting in the middle of the 15th fairway Sandy looked at the 17th green. 'Where that pin is I've got a real good chance of making a birdie there,' he said.

'Let's just play one hole at a time,' I said. 'Concentrate on this hole. We haven't reached the 16th yet, never mind the 17th. We'll get there eventually'.

Sandy was talking very aggressively. 'Shall we get an eagle here?' he asked. 'Go on and do it', I replied.

He hit a five iron. He didn't want to hit it too hard nor did he want to do what Seve did in 1986 and get too cute with it and dump it into the water. He turned it a little and with the green sloping right to left and his ball drawing it landed on the green and went three or four yards over the back. His chip shot hit the hole and he under-read the putt. That's a shot gone.

The 16th was playing short. We had seen as much from watching Calcavecchia, who made another good putt for par. I could feel the movement of the air in the direction of the green. Sandy hit a good seven iron to fifteen feet above the hole. Now he's got a dicey putt down the slope. When you're putting downhill there's more borrow than there is when you're putting uphill. I read the putt to have a one-foot break. As the putt went in it was accelerating. It wasn't exactly a slam-dunk but it was going quick. That chuffed him no end. He punched the air at least four times.

Now he was all pumped up and he drew his tee shot on the 17th. It hit a spectator. It wasn't too far off the fairway. It was just up the left side which is OK when the flag is back right. He fancied his chances of a birdie there because he knew he'd be hitting a wedge or a nine iron into the green. He'd hit good drives there all week but this time I think he was trying a little too hard. He had 122 yards to the flag on a 400-yard hole so he'd not hit his best drive.

'That's just right for the pitching wedge,' he said when I told him the yardage to the flag. He hit his shot slightly heavy and the ball didn't carry all the way to the flag. It screwed back down just off the front of the green. Two putts.

I thought about giving him a three iron on the 18th tee but if he had hit a three iron that would have given him a longer club to play into the green and therefore less chance of getting the ball close enough to get a birdie. He suspected he needed a birdie to win, though he wasn't sure. He could have hit a driver and cleared the bunkers but then he'd have had a difficult place to approach the green from. You're at a bad angle to the flag if you do that. You're coming in across the green and there's not much landing area.

He used a one iron instead and it started off perfect but drifted a fraction left and ran into the bunker. Having hit it, he started hopping from one foot to the other in annoyance. He knew it was heading for the bunker. As we walked up the hill he said: 'If it's in that first bunker I've had it. I can't get on the green. I should have hit a driver.'

The first thing he did when he got to his ball was ask someone how Calcavecchia stood. I said there had been no cheers so we must assume he's got a four, and the tv man on the fairway confirmed this.

I noticed the ball lay clean in the bunker but I thought it was too close for comfort to the front lip. Sandy had 142 yards to the front. The pin was eight yards on so that made it 150. Obviously the eight iron for distance but coming out of sand from an uphill lie and going uphill meant one extra club. So he played his seven iron.

As soon as he'd hit the bunker shot he came charging out really quickly, jumping in excitement à la Seve. This is not the old phlegmatic Lyle. Then the visor was thrown down. 'Your man's throwing tantrums,' someone joked to me. 'I wouldn't like to work for him. He's dangerous.'

My prime concern was for the ball to miss the lip. When I saw that it had, I wanted to rake the bunker as quickly as possible. The crowd started to cheer after the ball had landed so I knew it was rolling back towards the hole. He'd gone. He wanted to get there and see where the ball was. I chased after him up the slope as fast as I could. The caddie's job is to be organized and to keep up with his player. It's hard work going up that slope. You never realize how steep the 18th is until you're going up it.

Crenshaw had played his tee shot left, come up left of the green on his second shot and pitched inside Sandy. 'Would it be better for you to putt out?' Sandy asked Crenshaw. 'Whatever you like, Sandy' Crenshaw replied. 'What's the line, Carl?' he asked his caddie. 'I like the left lip,' Carl replied, and Crenshaw holed it.

I can remember very clearly what I was thinking at the time. I had started to get backache on the last three holes and I didn't want to go down that bloody tenth hole in a bloody play-off, not for anyone. I'd had enough. Apparently somebody said to Calcavecchia, 'What do you think about a play-off?' And he said: 'I don't want one.'

We both walked round Sandy's putt and he said it looked straight. What struck me was that the grass was pretty green round there and if there was going to be any grain it would influence the putt left-to-right. I then moved to the left of the green, halfway between him and the hole. Apparently the line is right-to-left normally but it was held up by the grain so it ended up a straight putt. As I stood there watching, I thought it was going to miss on the right but it dropped in.

Sandy went running away waving his arms in the air and I picked the ball out of the hole. He didn't need telling he'd won. I gave the ball to Jolande. I took home the ball he won the TPC with and the dog chewed it up, so I thought I won't do that again.

While Sandy signed his card I waited outside the tent so I could give him his wallet, his watch and his ring. Someone from the R & A asked if he could have a ball for the R & A museum. I said Jolande had got the one he won with, but here's one he played with.

An Irishman who was captain of Warrenpoint golf club in Northern Ireland when we went there for a pro-am asked me for a ball and so I gave him a new one. And then they all started shouting for balls and gloves. 'The rest of it is going back to England,' I said. Then a little lad wanted a towel and so I gave it to him. 'Thank God for that,' I said, 'that's something less to carry.' And I put the headcover on the bag.

Sandy was taking a long time checking his card, which is as it should be. It's like getting out of bed in the morning. You've only got to do it once. Eventually he appeared looking drained. They all started milling around him and so I thought: 'I'm out of here.' I started to fight my way through the crowd and I kept asking people: 'How do you get a drink of beer here?' They were going to send inside for it but then Malcolm Needs (of North Western, the golf club manufacturers) showed up and he went to fetch me one from the clubhouse.

While I was waiting I looked up at the balcony and there's Sandy's mother and father, Steve Rider, Tony Jacklin and Nick Faldo standing up there with the BBC-TV crowd. I shouted to them: 'Did you get all that? Did you have enough film in your camera?'

They shouted back: 'Come up here, come up here.' I said to the security bloke: 'When that man comes out with a beer tell him where I am and send him up.' I took Sandy's clubs up to the balcony and talked to the BBC about Sandy's last few holes. Steve Rider asked: 'Will it change Sandy?' 'No. How you gonna change him?' I replied. Then Steve asked: 'Will it change you?' I said: 'I don't know.' I ought to have said something like, 'I can stop sending the missus out to work on a Saturday night,' but I wasn't quick enough. Faldo helped me by asking how many pockets I'd got in my overalls 'to put your money in'. I said: 'I've just sold the ball five times walking from the 18th green to the clubhouse.'

Then Sandy appeared and I gave him what was left of the beer and I buggered off to get another one. I got collared by one reporter after another including one from the *Sunday Times*. John something, he said he was. Can't remember his surname.

The spectators weren't 100 per cent for Sandy like they were for Jack Nicklaus in 1986. I remember that Norman and Nick Price were the last off two years ago and as they were playing the 13th the crowd had left them to watch Jack Nicklaus. Nevertheless there was plenty of cheering for Sandy today. When we walked from one green to the next tee a lot of English and Scottish people walked up to him and personally gave him support.

I'm sure Sandy had learned something from playing with Nicklaus in 1986. It's a coincidence that in 1978, two years before Seve won the Masters for the first time, he played with Gary Player when Player shot 64 to win. It was the same with Sandy. He played with Jack two years earlier and Jack shot 65 to win.

I didn't enjoy caddying for Sandy as much as I had enjoyed myself when Jack won in 1986. There was too much pressure this time. It's the difference between a supporting actor and the starring role. However, I did enjoy it more than the last round of the Open in 1985. That was hard work all the way round because Sandy was never in front.

Fewer and fewer people see the last two holes of the Masters because there are no grandstands as there are at the Open. The

17th and 18th are fairly narrow holes and there are a few spectator mounds which a limited number of people can use. In fact I was barely aware of anybody watching the last two holes. It's a great occasion but for the players it's an intimate evening's golf at the same time. The occasion is seen all over the world but on those last two holes the numbers of spectators are very little compared with the 17th and 18th at Royal Lytham, say.

I didn't see Sandy again that night but we had decided what we were going to do tomorrow. We'd agreed to pick up a Cadillac this morning ready to drive it down to Hilton Head island. A vital move. All our worries about transportation were put to one side.

When there's a chance to win a tournament or when we are going to leave town immediately after play has finished, I make arrangements with Sandy that morning or the evening before. You don't leave it until play is over for the day. In this case Sandy had said: 'There are four of us in our car (himself plus his parents and Jolande) and we haven't enough room for the cases and the clubs, so I want you to take the clubs and some bags to Hilton Head for us. Come round to my hotel tomorrow morning.'

So having fought my way through all the newspapermen I got rid of my overalls and gave the boys (the staff) a drink in the caddie shack. I tipped them $100 between them. They got me into the locker-room where I put all the extra golf clubs in the bag with spare balls, and left all the stuff I didn't want, like visors and gloves, for Sandy and off we went. We went to celebrate and the Lyles did, too, I suppose. Somebody said: 'Aren't you going to the prize-giving?' and I said: 'They're not going to give me anything. I don't want to listen to a load of bloody speeches.'

A quick shower back at the motel and then the official boozing started. When you're going to have a drinking session you must remember to set your alarm clock before you go out. So I did that last thing before I left my room to meet Andy, Peter and later Dai Davies of the *Guardian* and Patricia his wife. Dai, being a crafty old bugger, wrote down all the banter there was that night and put it in the *Guardian* the next day.

Went to a Mexican restaurant and began drinking hot

margueritas on the rocks. In Georgia they shut the bars at midnight. We found one or two of the American caddies having a drink and we had time for one more with them before we were chucked out.

Monday 11 April
I woke up with a headache so it must have been a successful night. Pete, Andy and I went round to Sandy's hotel about nine o'clock and found Sandy still having breakfast. He insisted on paying for our breakfast. So Coleman got the knife and fork out and so did Prodge, neither of whom was hungry before we got there.

We filled the Cadillac with petrol and had to go back to Augusta National to pick up his green jacket. Peter drove up to the gate of the club first and said to the guard: 'This is Sandy Lyle's caddie and we've come to pick the green jacket up.'

'That's all right,' said the guard, waving us on.

'By the way,' Peter called to the guard as we drove on, 'in the car behind is a person trying to impersonate Sandy Lyle. Don't let him in.'

At the club Langer and his little girl were having their picture taken by some Japanese. Sandy got his green jacket and had a lot of pictures with his mother and father. Then I had to have the jacket on of course. I didn't think it was the right thing to do but he insisted. More photographs.

Drove down to Hilton Head, got rid of all the gear in Sandy's house, checked in at the tournament headquarters. All the while we kept our Cadillac well hidden in case anybody wanted it. Went to the agency to pay for the house, went to the house, dumped our stuff and then went to the supermarket to get a couple of days' groceries. Then I started attacking the travel agent to book my flights home.

In the house this week we have six caddies – Coleman, Prodger, Nick DePaul, Big Brian, Harry Parker-Brown and myself. Three of us have won the Masters in the last six years – Coleman with Langer in 1985 and Nick with Seve two years before that.

We call ourselves the American International Personnel Services or AIPS for short. So if any aspiring caddie wants a 50

1. A four-bagger. If you think it's hard carrying one bag
then try it with four, as this Japanese lady caddie is doing.

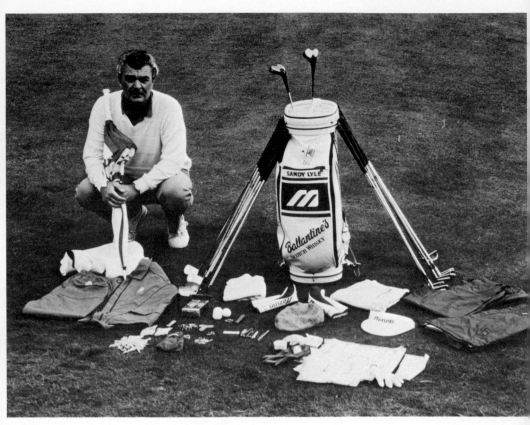

2. This is how it turns out.
It all adds up to 33 lb. – at least.

3. (*right*) 'What's on the menu, Gypsy Joe?' The caddies' cook,
'Gypsy Joe' Grillo, in front of the caddies' caravan.

5. 'Could you flog this in Watford, Andy?'
Pete Coleman and Andy Prodger with the Cadillac they drove
from the US Masters to Hilton Head island.

4. (*left*) I surrender. He's asking me the line of a putt.
Sandy preparing to putt on the 15th green during the 1988 US Masters at Augusta.

6. How blind can you be? Sandy hones his putting at Royal Lytham by aiming at a 2-in. diameter hole on the putting green during the 1988 Open.

7. On the tee our immaculate starter, Ivor Robson.
A popular figure on the European tour and a great supporter of Sandy.

8. Best flasher in the business. Photographer Phil Sheldon
(and appropriate sign) poses with the author and Hilary
at the Volvo Masters in Sotogrande, Spain.

per cent chance of winning the Masters all he has to do is join AIPS. Nick DePaul and Brian Bellenger started AIPS mainly so that if any American player was coming to Britain for the world match-play, say, one of the AIPS could caddie for him.

MCI Heritage Classic, Harbour Town GL, Hilton Head Island, South Carolina

Tuesday 12 April
Sauntered down for the shoot-out in the Heritage tournament. It was raining, of course. We got rid of the Americans after eight holes. Chip Beck was the last to survive. Both Sandy and Langer made four on the 18th. Then they had a chip off from a bunker at the back of the green. Sandy put it close, 8½ inches, and then Langer put his inside Sandy's, 6½ inches away. So Sandy's not invincible after all.

Pete returned the Cadillac we had driven down from Augusta. The attitude of the transportation people was that we could have kept it all week. Nobody would have said anything, apparently. That will be borne in mind, don't worry. That's vital information.

Wednesday 13 April
Coleman's birthday. Somebody asked if I got him breakfast in bed. No I bloody didn't! I had to get up at half-past six this morning. He can get his own breakfast. He was up as well. The Masters champion was drawn in the pro-am at 7.54. Actually, that's a good time. You get round half an hour faster. Andy, whose tee time was 1.45, set his alarm for 7 a.m. to get all the grub ready for this evening.

When we were warming up on the practice ground something happened to prove that Sandy's the same fellow this week after winning the Masters as he was last week. An amateur who turned out to be in our group had a go at this ball with a seven iron and the clubhead flew about fifty yards down the practice ground. It's a funny experience. It happened to me once and the worst of it is that every time you hit an iron after that you expect it to happen again. This amateur finished practising and

— 121 —

left. Sandy asked his caddie: 'Hasn't he fetched his club?' His caddie said he hadn't. So Sandy stops Jeff Sluman and Denis Watson practising and goes and picks up this bloke's club and gives it back to him on the first tee. This bloke could dine out on this story for the rest of his life – the man who won the Masters three days before is still fetching and carrying.

On the third hole today Sandy hit a tee shot left and so I went forward to find it. One of the marshals who had spotted the ball said to me: 'That's Mark's ball, over there. I saw it land.'

'Mark who?' I asked and he could tell from my tone that something was wrong.

'I've not looked in my programme,' he says. 'Isn't it Mark Lye?'

'No, it's Sandy Lyle,' I said.

I discovered how tired I was during this round. Sandy must have been the same. My legs felt weak after about eight holes. Good job it's a flat course. The amateurs couldn't believe the Masters champion would play with them. Even though he didn't do a decent score they all said what a privilege it had been.

It's traditional for AIPS men to buy dinner for the other caddies after their player has won a tournament. So all the other caddies staying here – Nick, Andy, Big Brian, Harry Brown and Pete – took it for granted they would have dinner at my expense. After all, I was the winning caddie at the last two tournaments. And we decided to invite the British journalists who had travelled down from Augusta to join us here at our rented house. You get fed up with eating out. When you're away from home you do it often enough as it is.

There were seven of them: Raymond Jacobs (*Glasgow Herald*), John Hopkins (*Sunday Times*), Tim Glover (*The Independent*), Michael McDonnell (*Daily Mail*), Martin Hardy (*Daily Express*), Bill Blighton (*Today*) and Mitchell Platts (*The Times*). Big Brian and Andy did the cooking as they usually do. One of the pressmen said it was the best meal he'd had on this side of the Atlantic. Alec and Agnes Lyle were there as well and Sandy and Jolande, of course.

Dinner is communal. At the beginning of the week two or

three of us will buy enough food for everyone and the cost is shared. But breakfast is up to you. You buy what you think you need. I eat raisin bran with half a banana in, orange juice and two cups of coffee.

When I rang Hilary she told me there had been loads of telephone calls offering congratulations. My cousin's daughter rang from Australia where she had watched it all on television. The Walkers rang in the middle of the night, paralytic. Pam Meadows, who came to Tenerife with us at Christmas, telephoned Hilary and asked: 'Who was that comedian we saw on television last night?'

Thursday 14 and Friday 15 April

Sandy played all right in the first round – a 70 – and then got to four under par after nine in his second round. But he hit two bad five irons coming back and hit two shots into the water on the 14th and 16th holes.

He didn't seem too tired. This is a nice quiet place and there's not a lot of pressure. He's staying on the course and he just walks down to the first hole every morning from where he stays to the practice ground, hits a few balls. There's not much walking between holes. Perfect temperature for playing.

Everywhere Sandy has gone this week people have stopped him, congratulated him, asked to shake his hand and have their picture taken with him. A lot of the experienced players have mentioned certain shots to him, like his second to the 14th. The old pros Andy North, Hubert Green (who knows what it's like to win three on the trot), Lanny Wadkins and Curtis Strange have all sincerely congratulated him.

Strange was bouncing up and down the other morning when we were talking. I haven't seen him like that before. 'I've never known anything as exciting as that finish,' he said to me. Paul Azinger was like a little kid. On the buggy ride from the 18th green to the clubhouse Azinger was describing Sandy's shots in detail. He rattled through the round as if he and not Sandy had been playing the shots.

Sandy must have had dozens of telegrams. If he was at home it would have been absolute murder but nobody knows where he is. Nobody knows what flight he's on going home, either.

That's what Michael Williams wrote in the *Daily Telegraph* when Sandy won the Open: 'He walked off the 15th green after the two birdies and into a lifestyle that will take him a long time to become accustomed to.'

Saturday 16 April
Sandy had a 67, a good score. His father said he fought well. He took only twenty-four putts today in his 67. You've got to remember these are tiny greens, so you're going to get fewer putts this week than anywhere else. He still hasn't given up hope of winning this and making it three in a row, but it's going to be a very tall order. The whole thing is becoming a marathon for Sandy. Interestingly, both Ken Green and Mark Calcavecchia have withdrawn.

Harry Brown, Gil Morgan's caddie, has written to Hord Hardin offering his personal views about the way the Masters can be improved. He wrote last year and got a nice acknowledgement and so has written again this year. He suggests how the Masters can be made better for caddies. For instance, the only toilets on the course are behind the 11th tee and that is the only tee where there are drinks. The trouble is that on this hole 90 per cent of the caddies go forward to watch their player's drive and to save walking back to the tee. Short cuts have priority with caddies. I go forward and after Sandy has driven I usually go into the bushes on the left of the fairway. Sandy brings me a can of something soft to drink. If you're in the last few matches all the good stuff has gone so you end up with Coca-Cola or something similar.

It's a fight to get from the putting green to the first tee every day, and Harry has suggested the roping should be improved there.

I've booked my flight from Dallas to Las Vegas return ready for the next trip, which is early next month. I've already got my flight from London to Dallas. I went to Stan Smith's travel agency here on the island – Stan Smith, the former Wimbledon champion. He was down at the course the other day competing in the pro-celebrity long driving contest.

I've done my washing. Watched some films on television. Played cards – crib and solo – every night with Andy, Peter, and Brian. It's a hard school. Coleman makes you keep on playing until he's won. I'm looking forward to getting home. You shouldn't wish your life away but I've had enough now. Strewth! I feel as if all my affairs are scattered across the face of the earth. I'm still very tired. I never relax until I've had a week at home.

We moved around quickly today, just three and a quarter hours. That's how it should be, even though we had Bobby Clampett in front of us.

Tonight there's a dinner at Primo's given by the seven British journalists for Sandy and Jolande plus Alec and Agnes, and me. It's the same complement as had dinner here at this house on Wednesday night. We'll have seen enough of each other by the end of the week.

Sunday 17 April

Greg Norman won the Heritage, and dedicated it to Jamie Hutton, a seventeen-year-old from Madison, Wisconsin. Jamie had recently been diagnosed as having leukaemia and been granted one wish when he entered hospital – to see Greg Norman play golf. Jamie's flight from Madison to Hilton Head was sponsored by Thursday's Child, the group that helps youngsters that face long confinements in hospital. He should have returned to Madison yesterday but Greg arranged a private jet so that Jamie could stay for today and walk with him.

This is what the *Savannah Morning News* wrote about Norman: 'Norman has long been associated with children's causes. He works extensively with the Ronald McDonald house program for ill children and does a one-day benefit in Orlando, Florida, for their children's hospital. Last year, that one day was worth $250,000 to the hospital.'

Norman has children of his own. At the end of the tournament, he gave Jamie Hutton the trophy to keep. It was very moving. The lad wasn't very big for seventeen and he was very pasty-faced. It was obvious he had something seriously wrong with him.

The end of the tournament, thank God. I came off the 18th green virtually on my hands and knees. Sandy finished joint 13th after a respectable round of 70. If I'm honest I realized he wasn't going to win three tournaments in a row when he went in the water twice on the back nine on Friday.

Monday 18 April
Pete, Andy and myself drove a car to Atlanta. They flew from there to Gatwick but I flew to New York. Got on the flight at Atlanta and the pilot gave us the kiss of death by saying: 'We expect to land early at JFK.' The next thing he says is: 'We're now going to turn back.' We were over Boston at this stage. We circled for an hour before landing and then had to wait forty minutes for another plane to leave. So now I've got half an hour to get from the TWA terminal to the BA terminal to catch my connection to London.

The terminals at JFK are all in a circle and you get a bus that calls at all of them. Outside the TWA terminal there was a traffic jam. I ran to the next terminal, got on the bus to BA, sprinted through there and bumped into Mr Lyle. But my luggage was on a plane two hours behind. We were late taking off from New York and so I didn't have much time to kill in London while I waited for my luggage.

While I was waiting I rang Hilary and told her I'd be on the next plane to East Midlands. I went to Terminal One to find out that not only was the next plane full but there were already seven standing-by.

I got the tube to central London and saw there was a train going to Derby in five minutes. I rang the East Midlands airport and got them to put a message on the tannoy to say that I'd be on the train arriving at Derby. The fellow who took my message knew what he was doing and so when I got in, there was Hilary. What a miracle that was.

Got home and the first thing we did was put the video on and there's Musgrove D. with a pot of beer in his hand, pontificating. The BBC people told me the satellite had broken down and so I didn't think the cameras were on. But they were. I didn't swear, though. I'm quite proud of that.

Faldo was excellent doing the commentary. The BBC had grabbed him to commentate on the closing stages of Lyle's round after he had finished his own round. He called all the right shots. I congratulated him later. He's not out of his element, admittedly. He's talking about his job. He knew how to think in any given position.

When players find themselves in with a chance to win, their minds can go sometimes. It's a different situation. You can still be playing good but you have to think. You're going to be pumped up so you have to know how the other fellows are thinking and reacting. When you're coming down the last nine holes of a tournament with a chance to win, what separates the wheat from the chaff is knowing how to handle yourself at the death. You'll see no end of players blow it because they don't know how to cope. Faldo does because he's been in similar situations himself. For instance on the 12th hole he said: 'Sandy's got to take his medicine here. He's got to take a five, get off the hole and start to regroup. He musn't try and make a four and so rush the first putt past the hole.' He was dead right.

Also when he was talking about Calcavecchia on 15 and 16 he said players have to learn how to control their adrenalin flow while they're in contention. At 15 Calcavecchia had taken too much club and his ball had gone way over the back of the green. He was lucky not to go into the water on the 16th. There was a little rough growing between the trees and his ball got caught up in that. At 16 he overclubbed and did very well to make three.

When I got home there was a phone call from Mark McCormack's IMG saying they wanted me to appear on the tv programme *People* with Derek Jameson. I immediately thought it was a chat show which I hate watching anyway and which takes me out of my own environment. I thought to myself: 'That's a pain in the arse. I don't want to put my best suit on, go to London and answer a lot of questions in front of a studio audience.' You don't know what they're going to ask you anyway. I'd rather stay at home and scrub the floor. So I declined.

At Home

Wednesday 20 April to Saturday 30 April
It seemed that no sooner had I got home than it was time to

leave again. The time went too fast. We went to Sandy's mother and father at Hawkestone Park one day. And as soon as we got there four of the members came in to congratulate them with a bottle of champagne. We had lunch in the hotel. It was a great day out, a marvellous place.

I didn't get fed up with telling everyone about Augusta, people like my friend Billy Betteridge, his wife Pauline and their two sons, one a pro and one a very good amateur golfer. They said they scared the older boy's girlfriend to death just after Sandy played out of the bunker on the 18th because everyone dived at the tv to push the ball back down the green. Lots of people told me, 'We were jumping on the television set' or 'We were behind it trying to blow the ball down the hill.'

5

1 May–31 May

Life in Las Vegas – Questions in Lymm –
On safari in Windsor – 55° drop in temperature

Panasonic Las Vegas Invitational, Las Vegas, Nevada

Sunday 1 May
I flew to Washington, Dallas and then Las Vegas on my way to
the Panasonic Las Vegas Invitational. The caddies and golfers
who had been at the Houston tournament were on the same
flight from Dallas including Curtis Strange who had won it
beating Greg Norman in a play-off, and Mike Harmon who
caddied for him. So I got to know all about the tournament
itself. Some of them had heard about Jacklin's wife Vivien, who
had died of a brain haemorrhage in Spain, and some hadn't.
Lanny Wadkins was in a state of shock when he found out. He's
a nice bloke, Lanny. He might be the same as Faldo, the sort
who can't bear fools gladly.

I stayed at a place called Circus-Circus, on the strip in Las
Vegas, Nevada. Huge place. Thirty-three hundred employees.
It's open twenty-four hours a day. The casino is shaped like a
big tent with the hotel behind, and while you're playing the
gambling machines in the casino the trapeze artists are up above
doing their acts. All sorts of different acts – people on mini
bikes, dog trainers and the like. The bottom floor is the casino,
the mezzanine floor the fun-fair stalls. Amazing place it is.

They have a buffet breakfast, which you've never seen
anything like in your life. You pay to go in and then you take a
tray down one of four lines and help yourself. They give you
twelve-inch diameter plates. Each line must be fifty yards long,

lines of things to help yourself off the self-service. There's everything, fruit, cakes, scrambled eggs and sausages and that stuff that's halfway between bacon and ham. And all you can drink, coffee, freshly-squeezed orange juice. And you can go back as many times as you like: $2 and 98 cents. They are open from half-past six in the morning and they're snowed under with people.

When you come out of the restaurant they give you a load of coupons for free goes on certain slot machines. You find a machine, give the lady your coupon and you get two free punts on the machine. I found my machine, started to work it and all of a sudden, tick, tick, tick, tick. All four signs had shown – and this is to win a car. I didn't win a car, I won a key ring, which is on display at home for anybody willing to pay half a crown to see it.

One of the prizes was a van, one a small helicopter. The lady there said they give away five or six cars a year from this one machine and there were four machines doing the same thing.

Next door was a place called Slot City and it had a sign saying, 'We pay out half a million dollars a day'. Pay out! What do they take in? And that's only one place. The strip goes along for ever.

The Hilton in Vegas is the biggest hotel in the world at present with 3,500 rooms, though a new hotel currently being built is going to be bigger – 3,800 rooms. You can't get a room at the weekend at any of them. They're absolutely chokker. Most punters are middle-aged women putting their money into not one but two bandits at once, and pulling both handles. Twenty-four hours a day, non-stop. There are no clocks and no windows in these casinos and they pump in oxygen to keep the people awake.

The first round of the Panasonic was at Spanish Trail. Then we had to play Las Vegas Country Club, the Desert Inn, and then there should have been a cut and the pros would play two more rounds at the Las Vegas Country Club, the host course. The best course of the three was Desert Inn but we only played one round there unfortunately. I don't suppose they've got enough room.

Spanish Trail was a new course a little way out of town,

designed by Robert Trent Jones. Old Sarge, who used to caddie for Chi-Chi Rodriguez, is living there now. He married a rich lady who owns several 7–11 shops. They're open twenty-four hours a day and sell mainly drinks, and snacks, cups of coffee and newpapers. At least one rat has retired in style.

Tuesday 3 May

Practice day at Desert Inn. We played from carts today because it was so hot. Just drove the cart around as fast as we could.

There are 156 pros and each day they have four amateur partners so there's 156 times four amateurs who are paying between $3000 and $5000 each. We worked that out to be over two million dollars.

Wednesday 4 May

First round and we were off at 7.30. That's a good time. Might as well get on with it. You've got to get up some time. Sandy shot 71 but he three-putted four times on the huge greens. He hasn't got down to it yet after Augusta. He's still up on cloud nine.

There were lovely views all around of the desert and the mountains. That's what always strikes me in Arizona and Nevada and New Mexico. You tell people about the desert but you can't explain to them about the mountains you can see all the time as well.

When we got to the 17th we suddenly noticed this huge cloud going up rather like after an atomic bomb had been dropped. It got a helluva height in the air and then there was a bang, boom! Bloody hell! we all thought, what's going off over there. 'I tell you what,' said one bloke. 'It ain't natural.' Then another cloud goes up. Someone timed it between the cloud going up and the boom – thirty-four seconds.

What had happened was that a chemical plant had blown up. The American Pacific company make rocket fuel and a fire had started at their plant at Henderson. They evacuated everybody and then there were these two explosions. An amateur photographer who had been driving past stopped to take some video shots and the blast knocked him over. One person was killed and school windows were blown out several miles away. The clouds had acid in them but they blew past Las Vegas and away into the desert.

Thursday 5 May
We played eleven holes at Las Vegas Country Club and then play was called off because of the strong winds, which were worse at Spanish Trail where dust was blowing across the course and nobody could see. Greg Norman drove the 1st hole, 420 yards, the wind was so strong. So then the tournament was down from five days to four days and the next morning we went back and played the last seven holes.

Friday 6 May and Saturday 7 May
Shot 76 and then at Desert Inn he shot 71 and missed the cut with the greatest of ease.

Sunday 8 May
Took the opportunity to spend as much time as possible going from one casino to another. Some machines you can play poker on. I can make five dollars last me an hour and a half. In fact the last three nights I finished up a few dollars in front. The shows are brilliant – illusionists, follies, singers. You name it, they've got it.

It's fascinating when you see the performance that goes on twenty-four hours a day and the money that changes hands. They don't have a jackpot prize on one bandit. They have a circle of jackpot prizes and in the middle is one with a big neon sign. This is an accumulative jackpot and one of them at Caesar's Palace is a million dollars. The money's there in a glass case in $100 bills. One million dollars right in front of you. I've got an illegal photograph of it.

I'm not a gambler. I like to have a go on the bandits every now and then, but that's all. These aren't complicated things like the ones we have in England. They're very simple. You just put your money in and pull. You haven't got all these holds and feature holds and stuff like that.

There's static electricity everywhere. You go back to your room and hold your key up to the lock and a spark flies across between the key and the lock. I like Las Vegas. You're like a little child that's gone to the fair for the first time. You have a good time. You know — the shows, the meals, the buffets, the gambling. But you don't need a lot of time there. Three or four days and that's it.

GTE Byron Nelson Golf Classic, Las Colinas, Irving, Texas

Monday 9 May
Flew from Las Vegas to Dallas, going through a two-hour time change. When we got there it was very, very hot, 90 degrees all week. Nick DePaul and Big Brian and I stayed in a small apartment in a place called Irving, which is a dry county. They're only allowed to sell liquor in bars. No liquor stores, no beer in supermarkets. When we wanted beer we had to drive to the next county. Nick and Brian hired a car because the next tournament, the Colonial, is only twenty-five miles away so it was an economic deal.

The Tournament Players' Championship course at Las Colinas in Irving, Texas, is a very good course and great for spectators. The holes are laid out between huge mounds ideal for watching from. And they get an incredible number of spectators. There's a sports complex, an indoor running track and a swimming pool and every facility you can imagine. Sandy stayed at the Four Seasons hotel at the club.

Tuesday 10 May
We only played twelve holes of a practice round in order to get back for the shoot-out. By the time they got to the 16th the starting field of ten had been narrowed down to Sandy, Ben Crenshaw and Payne Stewart. Trevino had gone out at the 1st hole. He doesn't like shoot-outs. Sandy birdied the 16th, 17th and 18th and won. Crenshaw bogied the 17th and Stewart parred the 18th. Stewart had already had four birdies in nine holes, more than anybody else, and so he got an extra $1000. Sandy got $3000 for winning it. Stewart got $2000 for coming second.

This put Sandy at the top of the Merrill Lynch shoot-out

order of merit. The leaders play for about $250,000 the Monday and Tuesday of the week of the Seiko Tucson Open, 3–6 November. I don't think that Sandy can make it. If he's going to play in the Volvo Masters in Sotogrande, he can't possibly get to Tucson in time.

While Sandy was at home he got his driver serviced – regripped with cord grips, the shaft was refitted into the head and rewhipped. The Japanese had put some tape under the whipping and it had come loose. So that was fixed. Also the insert had come loose.

Wednesday 11 May

Pro-am. Started at the statutory 7.09. Who should be off ahead of us but Mark Calcavecchia, who was announced as the runner up in the 1998 US Masters over a tannoy that carried all over the course? Is this an example of advance information?

We were invited to a barbecue this evening at David and Linda Frost's house – me, Nick and Brian because Nick caddies for David. David is like Mark McNulty, a very polite, straight sort of bloke who gets on with it.

Lee Trevino was saying that the scores David's done to finish second in all those tournaments were phenomenal. At Bay Hill last year he had an incredible total when Payne Stewart won. And this year at the Memorial tournament he deserved to win. He's doing all these good scores and somebody's doing something daft to beat him each time. He doesn't choke. It can't last, all these good scores and coming second. He's bound to win one sometime soon if he carries on playing so well.

Payne Stewart went through a similar thing. He always did a good score and somebody beat him. Then eventually he won. There's a lot of golfers that can't play anything like as well as David Frost that win tournaments.

Thursday 12 May to Sunday 15 May

Sandy shot 68, 71, 70, 70 to finish about thirtieth. There was bound to be a reaction to the US Masters and I think he was just beginning to get over it. The last day he teed off at 10.30 with Dick Mast, who's a very good golfer though probably not many people have heard of him.

Left the course at 2.35 p.m. Big Brian took me back to the motel where I showered and finished packing. Time for a beer, even. Then a fifteen-minute drive to Dallas–Fort Worth airport to catch the United Airlines plane to Chicago at 4.50 p.m. to connect with the BA flight to London Heathrow.

When I got there they said the Chicago flight was going to be delayed and probably cancelled and so they'd put me on another. I said I was sure there was a British Caledonian flight straight to Gatwick at this time and asked if we could get on it? She punched her computer for a few moments and then said: 'That'll be all right, sir.' I showed this lady my Executive Club membership and she led me up to the executive lounge where I watched the finish of the golf. I had a whisky as well, of course.

At Home

Monday 16 May
Landed at Gatwick at 8.30 a.m. I quickly cleared customs and got to the South Terminal in time to catch the express to Victoria. Sprinted across Victoria station and arrived on the Underground platform as a King's Cross train was arriving.

I telephoned Hilary last night and told her I'd probably be at Newark around dinner time. She was due to stop work at one o'clock and so I said: 'When you finish go to Newark and if I'm not at the station I'll be in the pub opposite.'

At King's Cross there was an announcement that the next train to Newark would leave at 10.55 and get in at 12.05. Got on the train, had a nod, came out of Newark station. It was a nice sort of day, believe it or not, and I thought to myself: 'Perfect, I've got an hour in the pub.' I was really looking forward to a pint after several weeks in the US. They serve their beer too cold over there. Even the glasses come out of the fridge with frost on them. And it's tasteless, anyway. There's nothing like a nice pint of English beer – specially from north of the Trent. Mansfield and Home Brewery are my two favourite beers – beers with a head on the top. I've got beer mats at home with a picture of President Reagan on the front and they say: 'He might be President of the most powerful nation on earth but he's never had a pint of Mansfield bitter.'

So there I was having travelled thousands of miles to be in a certain pub at a certain time, and guess what – there was a big sign outside saying: 'We are closed due to alterations. We reopen again on Thursday and apologise for any inconvenience.' Naturally, I found another pub around the corner.

Tuesday 17 May
Yesterday was nice and warm, as I said, but today was cold. I had a 55° drop in temperature between Sunday afternoon and this morning.

Thursday 19 May
I made the mistake of trying to go out and play golf, and finished up with the worst backache ever.

It dates back to when I used to drive a lorry. One day I was delivering a load of kerb stones and I strained my back unloading them. I was in a hurry, got in a sweat and then cooled off. Every now and then it comes on again. I don't know what it's called. I ought to go to the doctor, but you know how it is.

I don't want to leave home at the moment. I could stop here for two months to get everything done. I specially like it in the spring when everything's growing. You can see what wants doing. I'm not really a keen gardener but now that the house is ours it's like having a new toy. When you've never had one before it's a novelty.

This is the only house I've ever lived in. My mother was born here and so was I. My grandparents moved into it as tenants in 1908 and before the second world war they had the chance of buying it for £200 but it was unusual for the working man to have a mortgage in those days.

As soon as I started work and earning some money I wanted to buy the house. It's the only thing you can buy that's any good to you, a house. When my mother died I twice went to see the owner to try and buy it but he was adamant he wouldn't sell. But when I came home from Sun City in December 1985, to my surprise I had this letter offering me the house. I sent off a deposit but the old fellow died before he could sign the documents. Neither he nor his father had made a will. Then followed a period of probate and it took until July 1986 until we actually bought it.

The house had a Coal Board subsidence claim on it because there are coal workings running underneath. That's why we had to pay the colossal sum of £7500 for it. I only offered the agent £7000 but he said: 'Being as there's a Coal Board claim on it, if you make it £7500 then I'll recommend acceptance.' We finished up getting £2500 from the Board to cover the repairs caused by the subsidence and did the work ourselves. The whole point of this is that when I went to see the owner four years before we bought it, I offered him £10,000.

Having lived in the house all my life I was delighted to get it. Forty-three years and now it's mine. What an achievement that was! Now I'm the owner I just want to clear everything up and make it neat, specially this time of year – the doors, the windows, do up a load of old furniture. It's a wrench to have to go away.

Friday 20 May
I got up in the middle of the night and my back was so bad I fainted with pain. I felt like staying in bed today but I couldn't. Sandy had to do a day for his sponsors Ballantine's, the whisky people, at Lymm golf club in Cheshire and so I struggled painfully on because I've never yet failed to appear. And there was the chance of some whisky.

When I got to the golf club there was a big banner up at the entrance saying: 'Welcome Sandy Lyle, Masters champion.' As I finished walking the course doing my yardages Sandy was finishing his clinic. Charlie Green, the veteran Scottish amateur international, was there. He works for Ballantine's. We had a very civilized lunch and then played eighteen holes.

During the round the members and guests asked questions of both of us. They wanted to know everything, every mortal thing.

'Why do you stand with the flag at an angle when Sandy is putting?' was one question. The answer is I take it out of the hole to start with and then put it back, not in the base of the cup but leaning backwards so it won't get stuck. I have to remember not only the line the ball is coming from but the line it will continue on if it misses the hole. Imagine three different players aiming at the hole and you have to stand somewhere that misses all three lines. So I stand as far away as possible and the only way I can do that is by holding the flag at an angle.

Another point I made was about carrying the golf bag. I said that if I gave someone a golf bag to carry they would never put it on their back the correct way. They would try and slip it on their shoulder whereas I make sure the bag goes across my back. That way I can't feel it.

I was signing autographs as fast as Sandy was. You can't believe the questions they asked. It brought home to me that golf is all about the club golfer. One of the members, a right insistent one, said to me: 'Do you get any perks in your job?' I said: 'Yes. I thought coming here for the day was one, but now I'm here I've changed my mind.'

They asked that many questions I told them: 'All you've got to do is read my book. Lymm members will be given a special price: twice as much as everyone else.'

Volvo PGA Championship, Wentworth, Surrey

Tuesday 24 May
To stay with the Walkers at Twyford ready for the skins game at Wentworth before the PGA. Graham and Vera Walker are old friends of ours. I call Graham the Lord Mayor of Twyford. He and Vera are newsagents and they've put Carol, their younger daughter, into a travel agent's across the road called Thames Valley Travel. They do all of my travel arrangements to and from the US. They're very good.

We all went to visit Janet, the Walkers' elder daughter. She and Clive live at Bray. Their house is tiny, about a quarter the size of ours and yet it's supposed to be worth £130,000 because of the area. It's near the river Thames and the Waterside Inn which is run by a load of French and where you can't get away with less than £100 for your dinner, which, as you can imagine, is not my style. Instead we had a barbecue in the garden.

I drove to Sandy's house to meet him instead of meeting him

at the course. He's got that net I tried to help him put up just before Christmas and he hits a few balls in that before he leaves his house, which is to the right of the 14th on the East Course as you play the hole. Then he continues his warm-up by walking across to play some wedge shots to the 16th hole and does a bit of putting as well. He plays the 17th, the par three down the hill. Then he drives off on the 18th and if there's not too many people there he'll play his second shot to the green. This brings him to the clubhouse where he goes on to the putting green and then on to the first tee of the West Course and he's away.

When you go to his house you see that every room has got trophies, mementoes and photographs. It brings home to you just what he has achieved. The plaque from the Phoenix Open is still on the floor. You open a cupboard and there's a load of glasses in there saying 1983 Ryder Cup or an ashtray from the 1985 Ryder Cup.

Dave Cannon, a photographer specializing in golf, had sent Sandy a load of pictures from the Masters. There's a brilliant one of Sandy and myself walking to the 12th green, with our reflections in the water. It's taken from 100 yards away. My favourite photo is the one of Larry Mize handing the green jacket over to Sandy. Larry is looking a bit down in the mouth and Sandy's got his chest puffed out and pointing to the badge on the jacket like a schoolboy.

Thursday 26 May

What struck me about the skins game today (between Seve Ballesteros, Bernhard Langer, Nick Faldo, Sandy and Ian Woosnam) was how chuffed Ken Schofield, boss of the European tour, was that he had the best European tour players competing in this match. I hadn't realized that until I got there. I took it all for granted. It was a showcase. There's no need to pay the Americans to come any more because our best players are so good.

The first thing they did today was give me a pair of overalls, then separate bibs and then they wanted us to wear sweatshirts as well. You stand on the first tee and every two minutes somebody gives you something else to wear. I hate the sight of overalls so I was all steamed up about them for five hours. What do you do if you're wearing overalls and it rains? I keep asking people this and nobody gives me the answer. So what *do* we do when it rains? We put the water proof jacket on top of the overalls and this covers the advertising, the players' names, so bugger 'em. This defeats the object of the exercise.

So when I came off the course I was hungry, and angry and frustrated and this sturdy, tweedily-dressed girl I've never seen before in my life came up to me and said: 'I'm so-and-so from such-and-such and we're doing an article on caddies. Can I interview you, please?'

In a bad mood, I said, 'He's got to go and practice,' gesticulating at Sandy.

'What about after he's finished his practice?'

'I'm going to have my dinner.'

'Do you consider it an imposition?' she asked.

'It's not only an imposition, it's a pain in the arse. Pete Coleman is over there. He'll tell you what you like.' And I sent her over to see Coleman.

It only turned out that the girl was Maggie Thatcher's daughter, didn't it? Good job I didn't know who she was or it would have been even worse. We've always been staunch Labour in Kirkby. She wrote a good story, though.

Friday 27 May to Monday 30 May
Sandy shot 70 and 76 and made the cut on the line by birdie-ing the 17th. This meant that he was out at 8.14 on the Sunday. He shot 68, which pulled him up quite a lot because the weather got worse as the day wore on.

Hilary had flown down and she followed us in the third round. I wanted her to walk round Wentworth once so that she could imagine what it's like to play twice in one day as we do in the matchplay. After we had finished we went to Windsor Safari Park and had a brilliant time.

Fantastic isn't it? The size of the paws on the lions is frightening. We drove through the monkey enclosure and although they were climbing all over buses, vans and lorries they didn't climb over our car. I was dead disappointed. Then the emu got in our way and wouldn't move. All of a sudden this lioness walked across in front of us as if we weren't there. She never looked at the car at all. A magnificent animal.

Sandy shot 66 in the last round. He finished with two birdies and an eagle – 3, 4, 3, – and tied seventh with Langer. At one stage he was 14 shots behind Langer, which Pete Coleman noted.

Guess what Langer did at the start of the third round? He was 11 under par and leading the tournament, and on the first tee he said to Pete: 'Go and fetch another putter.' If Sandy had asked me to do that I wouldn't have. Langer then took a load of putts and said later it was the biggest mistake he'd ever made in his life.

Ivor Robson was on the first tee. He was acting as a starter as he does at a number of tournaments throughout the season. There used to be three starters, one in the north, one in the midlands and one in the south but they got rid of the other two. I think they were all Accles and Pollock representatives. Ivor, who used to be a pro, is now the landlord of the Bonnington Hotel in Moffat, south-west of Glasgow. He's a great fan of Sandy's and always gives him a pep talk. 'What are you doing here at this time in the morning?' is the sort of thing he'll say. 'You should be up at the head of the field. This is not good enough.'

'Do you know,' he said to Sandy after we had returned from Augusta earlier this year, 'watching you win the Masters nearly made me an alcoholic.'

At the 1985 Open at Sandwich big Ivor was looking over the crowd when he saw Sandy and waved him over. 'Come here, you,' he says. 'Now then, you can win this. I want you to go out there and give it a good show.'

Home on the Monday night.

Dunhill British Masters, Woburn G & CC, Bedfordshire

Tuesday 31 May
Down to Woburn for the pro-am before the Dunhill British Masters. We played with Brucie-baby (Bruce Forsyth) and our team won. We can't seem to do anything wrong at present. Brucie's a great admirer of Sandy's. He's good to play with because he's very experienced in pro-ams. When somebody's

played in a lot they know how to score, when to pick up if they're out of the hole, and they know how to encourage the other amateurs in their group and get them together as a team. They are not intimidated by playing with Sandy; they know the others in the group are nervous so they are a big help to the pro. I'm thinking of such as Brucie, Sean Connery, Jimmy Tarbuck, Henry Cooper, Bobby Charlton, the ones that play in pro-ams regularly.

The pro-am took the form of a Texas scramble. Everyone drives and then you all play from where the best drive finishes and the two best scores count. Because it was a scramble Sandy dared to hit his driver a lot and he only missed two fairways.

Sandy's very good with amateurs – if they'll listen to him. He'll try and give them a lesson. If they won't listen he gets a bit worked up. And he always tries to explain the format to them. Once, after he'd explained that it was the best score on every hole, one fellow was still convinced it was an individual stableford.

The amateurs can be generous to us. Pete Coleman got the world record tip after a pro-am in Switzerland one year.

He caddied for Seve and he knew the team of amateurs was good because they were the Rolex team. He ran up and down all the hills giving everyone exact yardages to the flag and a load of bull as well. When it was over they didn't give Pete anything. So he said: 'I am never ever going to try for amateurs again.' The next morning he was still on about it. Then Seve came into the locker-room and said: 'By the way they gave me this to give to you.' He handed over a thousand Swiss franc note, about £400. Pete is convinced Seve made a mistake and gave him the wrong note.

My rule of thumb in pro-ams is that it's our practice round. First and foremost I'm working with Sandy, checking yardages and so on, but if you've got decent company you help them. You just have to make the round as pleasant as possible. The amateurs are petrified so you've got to try and overcome that so they all have a good day. You have a joke with them, talk to them. Don't tell them too much because once they get it in to their head they ought to know how far it is then it's a bit of a bugbear – 18-handicappers asking you for the yardage every time. You can tell them anything between two feet and a hundred miles and it wouldn't make any difference because they're going to duff it anyway.

In the States, you get tipped almost automatically there and you can get tipped pretty good – bung, we call it, because they bung it at you. Sometimes they'll take you out to dinner as well.

The best crawling I've ever done to amateurs in a pro-am was in Las Vegas. The manager of the Tropicana Hotel was in our group and he had several hangers-on including a girl who was about thirty years younger than he was.

I asked: 'Is that your daughter?' I knew that she had about as much chance of being his daughter as flying to the moon.

'No, it's my girlfriend. She's in the front line of the Follies.'

'What's the Follies?' I asked, all innocence.

'It's a show at the Tropicana.'

'Is it?' I replied. 'Do they have shows? We've never been here before.'

'Would you like to go to one? Leave it to me. I'll fix you up with a couple of tickets. When you get there you'll see this big queue. Ignore it. You go to the front and the tickets will be waiting there. It's all on the house.'

The queue was half the length of the first hole at St Andrews and about ten wide, but we went to the front and were shown to a booth about thirty feet from the stage and we had all we could eat and drink. At one stage we were even prepared to pay for it, it was so good.

I got voted the crawler of the year by the other caddies for that.

One year at Hilton Head island I was caddying for Andy North who always used to ask for an early tee time. They're the best. Sandy always get early times in the US. He is averaging a quarter past seven in tee-off times in pro-ams this year. It might sound horrendous to anyone else but you're going to get round in an hour less than it will take in the afternoon and also you've finished by dinner time.

Andy North was first off at 7.00 and we've got these four amateurs who all looked like death warmed up. They didn't say anything for nine holes. On the second nine they started talking a little. What had happened was they'd travelled in from some way away the previous evening and stopped at this hotel for a drink. It got to midnight and they had a few more drinks and it got to 1 a.m. and then they realized they had got to get up at 5.30 so they said: 'We might as well keep going.' They hadn't been to bed at all. Not a good idea.

6

1 June–2 July

Winning at Woburn – Home at the Country Club – A hex on Andy – Back early from Paris

Wednesday 1 June
Gave Sandy the day off and he and Jolande took his two boys to the Windsor Safari Park.

Thursday 2 June
First round of the Dunhill. Played with Trevino and Barry Lane. Trevino is like Watson and Nicklaus and other great players. They're ready to play when it's their turn. They've thought about their shot by the time they've got to their ball. That's what they're there for, to play golf. It's second nature to them. They aren't there to pose and they're not self-conscious of crowds. On the green Trevino has half weighed up his putt before it's his turn.

Sandy likes to move quickly too, to establish a rhythm. If the ball is the far side of the flag when he comes on to the green he'll look at the line first before he gets near his ball. It all helps the flow. Sandy had a 66 today and Trevino said to me that if Sandy keeps going like this he's going to be unstoppable.

Friday 3 June
Heavy rain. We got in before it became bad and so we weren't interrupted like some of the others. We went through the group in front of us.

On the par-four 7th Sandy drove and missed the fairway left. He missed the fairway every day on this hole and yet still played it in two under par. The pin was on the left today and he went in to the left bunker which you mustn't do. But he came out of there straight into the hole.

Number 8, a par three, he was quite a long way from the flag and he hit the ball that hard it would have gone in the bunker beside the green if it hadn't hit the hole. It jumped into the air and dropped in. And on number nine he hit it nearly thirty feet past and holed that. So in the space of three holes he'd holed out from a bunker and sunk two enormous putts. That was when Trevino put his white cap on the end of his putter and held it up to surrender.

Sandy actually went out of bounds after that – on the 14th. He hit his second shot a little bit left but apparently it hit a tree and bounced onto that bridle path that runs through the course. He hit a provisional and when he got up there and asked if his first had gone out of bounds they told him it had. 'It's in the gorse bush the other side of the fence,' they said. Sandy said: 'I'll leave it there. It was a bad shot anyway.' And he never mentioned it again. Had a 68.

He was having trouble with his game. Seve said years ago that when his game is off he tries to play certain shots like draws or slices or cuts to exaggerate the shot and make sure he concentrates. So the first two days Sandy played a lot of punched shots and half shots and managed to keep it in play off the tee. And he chipped and putted brilliantly and made the scores.

Saturday 4 June
We were down on the practice ground and all of a sudden there was a big storm that turned into a hailstorm followed by thunder and lightning, so we had about two hours' delay. The thunder and lightning passed but you could still see it so of course they wrote it up in the papers that he was practising in it.

It was raining heavily off and on all the way round and at the death it wasn't fit for play. But as there were only three groups on the course and they were playing in two-balls they squeegeed the greens so we could finish. The 18th tee was actually under water.

Sandy wasn't playing very well. He'd hit a lot of heely shots, semi shanks. He put that down to British conditions. Also, he'd had a lot of real bad lies. Both Wentworth last week and Woburn this week are very narrow and Sandy's been hitting his one iron for two weeks. It's claustrophobic and gets to you after a while. Sandy said on television tonight that he had virtually worn out the grooves on his one iron.

Sandy's leading by four strokes. He has played badly but scored well – 66, 68, 68.

Sunday 5 June

There was not much conversation between Sandy and Faldo when they played today. It's not like Sandy and Woosnam who rattle away all the time, laughing and joking. Faldo's very serious, strict, severe. It struck me on Saturday watching him on the practice ground how well he was swinging and how his stance to the ball with a putter looks very comfortable. He is a tall fellow but he doesn't give the impression he is crouching. He looks as though the putter is a real comfortable length for him. And he's nearly in the same class of putter as Crenshaw.

I was trying to dissuade Sandy all day from looking at it as a matchplay situation. I said to him yesterday: 'You've got a four-shot lead. If you go out there and shoot 68 or 69 he ain't going to pass you. Play the course, not the man.' But he played the man not the course for a start. He was watching what Faldo was doing all the time. I kept saying: 'The tournament is up to you, not him.'

We were still four in front of Faldo playing the 6th. Sandy hits a good tee shot, Faldo skies his. Faldo plays up with a long iron, pitches to the green and holes the putt for a four. Sandy hit a bad second shot to the right, can't get to the green and takes six.

So now Sandy's only two shots ahead. But then he hit his famous seven iron to the seventh nearly into the hole and gets a birdie, and birdies the ninth and tenth as well. That's it. Sandy went on to win by two shots. That's the three Masters, German, American and British. The only one he hasn't won is the Australian Masters and he won't play in that.

We're going to Australia at the end of the year. Well, at least I'll be able to say I've been. It's all flies and Fosters lager, I understand.

What with Sandy coming seventh at Wentworth and first here he's won more than £50,000 in the last two weeks. That means I've earned a lot of money this past fortnight as well. No travelling expenses and very few nights in hotels. Friday night I went home. I went through three bad storms on the way but you can't beat being in your own bed. I got some friends to take me down this morning in return for some tickets to get in.

Manufacturers Hanover Westchester Classic, Westchester CC, Rye, Connecticut

Monday 6 June
Met Andy at the airport and we flew to New York, which is only a five-hour time change. We landed at 1.30 p.m. and got to the hotel we were staying at in White Plains, New York, by 5 p.m. When you're used to big time changes, five hours is not hard to cope with. You just wake up a bit earlier, that's all.

Nick Faldo was on our plane and he got off quicker than we did. He was travelling first-class and we were right at the back of the plane and at the back of the queue at immigration. We couldn't catch him to cadge a lift and so we had to go on the subway which is a real adventure, from JFK airport to downtown New York. You'd swear that the subway trains had been decorated in a paint shop but in fact it was graffiti, top to bottom, one end to the other. Very colourful.

There were a load of brothers (blacks) on this subway train. They were only lads, only 15 or so. Every one was Cassius Clay's double in appearance and manual dexterity.

Took a taxi to Grand Central station, which is incredible. If they blindfolded you, took you inside, took the blindfolds off and asked where you were you'd say a cathedral. It's like the biggest nave of the biggest cathedral I've ever seen, magnified by ten. From there we had to catch a train to White Plains where the Westchester Classic is being held. We didn't know which platform our train left from and so we went to the circular information booth. 'When is the next train to White Plains and what platform does it go from?' I asked the lady behind the counter. She just rattled it off, boom, boom, boom, without looking in a book. I only caught half of it and as I started to say 'Pardon' she was dealing with the fellow behind me. So I went round to the other side of the booth, queued up again and got the rest of the details.

We had the players' rate in the White Plains hotel, about $80 a night for two, when we usually aim for 30 or 40. But they're big comfortable rooms with cable television. In my room, I managed to find thirty-eight different tv stations including the news in Japanese and a soap opera in Spanish.

You get a full buffet breakfast, newspaper delivered, happy hour. Happy hour is an American institution, a time in the early evening when drinks are half price and free snacks are served. It's meant to attract people on their way home from work. Naturally for us caddies it's our main target most weeks. The best happy hour I've come across was in the Hyatt Regency hotel in Phoenix where the management spent $100 each night on food.

For us the main advantage of the White Plains hotel is that you get transport to and from the golf course because the players are going all the time. All you need to do this week is to get to the course and back to the hotel because all the bars and restaurants are right there.

You can walk around the corner to the Irish pub called Memories, run by Kieran, who comes from Belfast, and Dennis, a New Yorker mad on baseball. They've got draught Guinness there. There's a Chinese restaurant among others nearby. They're all in walking distance. It's like being in downtown Kirkby there are so many.

Tuesday 7 June

A practice day for us and also a qualifying day for the US Open. There are twelve different qualifying areas throughout the country and only a few spaces available at each venue. Two of them were very close to where we were in White Plains. What you have to do is play thirty-six holes, one round on one course and one on another on the same day. Johnny Miller, a former US Open champion, tried to pre-qualify but failed, and so did Arnold Palmer. They even made Ben Hogan pre-qualify when his exemption status ran out.

Sandy just hit balls and played nine holes. He also changed his one iron. It was a club with square grooves and Ping sent

— 149 —

him one with normal grooves. He had changed to the square groove one iron in Florida earlier in the year.

All Masters' champions receive a letter explaining precisely what they've won. Sandy's going to have a replica of the trophy sent to him and some cut glass and a medal. The green jacket that is presented to them at the prize-giving ceremony is not necessarily the one they will keep. Sandy went back the next morning and was fitted for his. It is his to keep for a year. After that it must be returned to Augusta and hung in his locker in the champions' locker-room for him to wear when he is at the club. Finally they ask each champion to send a club to Augusta, a club that has been instrumental in them winning the title. For instance, all Bobby Jones's clubs are hanging up there. So Sandy sent a one iron.

Wednesday 8 June

Sandy had an 8.26 start in the pro-am but before that he had appeared live on NBC's *Today* show at 7.40 a.m. The car came to pick us up from the hotel and took us halfway down the practice ground where the lights and cameras were all set up. There were trays of coffee and doughnuts, traditional American breakfast, and the fellow in the studio in New York is asking Sandy questions. The amateurs are all warming up and one of them is aiming his shots at our set-up on purpose. I'm keeping one eye on Sandy and the other on this amateur. Sandy did very well. He handled the questions easily.

As anybody will tell you, the moment you come off after a pro-am round you have a complete mental blank as to what you've done, who you've been with and how long it's taken you. We caddies always describe pro-ams as brain damage. Not all are, of course, but if you're trying to will a group of amateurs round a course for five hours it is hard work.

Who should turn up at the practice ground but Jimmy Ballard. He spends the summers up there because the people who own Doral where he teaches in Miami, Florida, own a convention centre and nine-hole golf course in New York State called Arrowwood. It's ten minutes from Westchester. Jimmy has his winters in Florida and then when it gets very hot down there he comes up to New York to teach.

He said that Sandy sold more connectors than he did. It is not going down very well in the States but in England Sandy can sell hundreds. When Sandy wears one on the practice ground the other pros automatically want a go. Every pro that sees Sandy wearing one wants one.

Thursday 9 and Friday 10 June
First round tee-off time 8.18. These tee-off times sound very early but when you've had a five-hours time change it's perfect, it's like the middle of the morning. Cold and wet it was, just like Woburn. Sandy shot 74 and 74 again on the Friday, and missed the cut by three. Three times he took four to get down from just off the green. He wasn't very happy with the way he was hitting the ball. Heely cuts I call the shots that were giving him trouble. Very thin, with no divots. The ball kept going out of the heel of his club. They were very close to shanking. He couldn't get to the back of the ball.

At Westchester there's a lady called Susan Lewis who comes and sets a stall up selling golf books and pictures. Big Brian Bellenger, who has got nearly 500 books on golf and is an avid collector, said we would go round to her apartment in Mamaroneck. Her husband, George Lewis, is the head pro at a place called Leewood golf club and when he was young he had a collection of books given to him. Since then he's built on it and the apartment is packed solid. The sitting-room is full of stuff, books at least fifty years old and every stamp that has ever been issued in the world to do with golf. He has sheet music with all the songs that have ever been written about golf. He's got the Scottish Laws 1537, a book with clasps on it, which outlaws golf.

I picked up a book that took my fancy, a fairly modern one, looked at it and there's a picture of Roberto de Vicenzo and me caddying for him taken in 1971. I said: 'Look who's here!' So they gave me that one and then I bought a book of Bernard Darwin's about golf courses in England, including Hollinwell, that has been reissued in facsimile. Ben Crenshaw has written an afterword to this book. I'm going to get him to sign it, hopefully.

Susan and George keep in touch with other collectors from

around the world. He said that hardly a day goes past without somebody sending stuff over. He said to Brian: 'I'll pay you thousands right now for your collection. Thousands. Right now. Just name your price.' Brian refused the offer because he is collecting as an investment. Brian buys books and is always asking whoever is going to England to take some back for him.

Saturday 11 June
Went to Arrowwood to practice with Jimmy Ballard. We finally got to know the exact history of his connector.

When Babe Ruth, the baseball player, was in his prime in the 1920s he had a room-mate and back-up called Sam Byrd, a young lad. When Byrd was eighteen and going to play in Yankee Stadium for the first time Ruth said to him: 'When you get out there you're going to be very tense and it's going to make you restrict your backswing and thus lose power. What you need to do is practise with a towel under your left arm. That'll make you swing your arms back the right way. If you do it wrong you'll drop the towel.'

Over the years the lad did pretty good and then he started playing golf. Babe Ruth had had golf lessons and tried to swing the orthodox way, keeping his left arm straight at the address and as straight as he could on the backswing and religiously keeping his head still. He was a pitiful golfer. Sam Byrd took the way he hit a baseball on to the golf course and he could hit a five iron past Babe Ruth's drives.

Eventually Byrd turned pro and from 1942 until 1951 he won twenty tournaments and was runner-up to Byron Nelson in the PGA. Ben Hogan came to Byrd and said he didn't think his own swing was good enough for him to become a great player. So Byrd got him to practice with a handkerchief under his left arm. Byrd taught Jimmy Ballard and told him about the towel under the left arm. This is one of Ballard's crucial pieces of instruction: keep the *left* arm close to the chest. Even when Jack Nicklaus was in his prime it looked as though he had a flying right elbow. But he won seventeen majors with that swing, which was never criticized by his bank manager.

US Open, The Country Club, Brookline, Massachusetts

Sunday 12 June
Drove up to Boston in Harry Brown's van and we came through Rhode Island. It's a tiny little state, just like the south of England, Swanage, Bournemouth. You keep seeing these harbours and sailing boats. Apparently Newport, Rhode Island, is really picturesque. It was a nice drive because it gave us an opportunity to see some of the countryside. We can't do this very often because we drive a lot at night or we fly from one tournament to the next.

Got up here, booked into the Comfort Inn, Dedham. There must be fifty of us at least. It's perfect, has a restaurant and a bar. Caddies' Association booked it. We watched the end of the Westchester Classic on tv, the play-off with Seve beating Norman and David Frost and Ken Green, and then went to measure the course. It was a beautiful evening, about 80 degrees. We signed in at the caddies' headquarters down by the putting green and they gave us a book containing yardages done by laser beam. The first person I bumped into was Lanny Wadkins on the putting green. 'This is a great course,' he said. 'You can play it like a links course in Britain. You can play a lot of run shots. It's the best US Open course I've seen.'

Three of us went round measuring: me, Harry Brown and Dave McNeilly, caddie for Nick Price. We got to the 13th and behind the tee there's a big house and this fellow is leaning over the fence saying to us: 'How are you going on?' He and his wife were both working as volunteers in the caddies' tent. His name is David Dowton and he brought us out drinks. He said he used to caddie. The house looks just like a typical caddie's house – 150 yards long with a great big swimming-pool at the end.

Everybody here has been very friendly. It's a big event and they've been planning it for years and years. We've no real comprehension just how much work goes into it.

Monday 13 June
When we checked in at the course we were given some caddies' regulations as laid down by the USGA. Some of them were hilarious. Number six says that caddies will not be permitted to

shag (fetch) balls on the practice ground. That's the last thing we want to do anyway. We've campaigned for years in Europe not to have to do that. It's too dangerous.

Here's another one. The caddie fee shall be posted in the caddie area on the contestants' bulletin board. Caddies shall be paid promptly.

It was extremely hot and muggy today. Everybody was shattered. Even Faldo admitted to being tired. We trudged round eighteen holes and then Sandy made up his mind just to play half a round on Tuesday and half a round on Wednesday and do a bit of practice. You can wear yourself out before you start in major tournaments, specially if you're a fancied player because you're going to get pestered all the time.

The parking lots at the Country Club were well away from the course and shuttle buses ran. One of the lots was on Allendale Farm and the rumour was that the farmer who owned it had been paid more money by the USGA for them to use his land for parking for one week then he would ever make from a year growing vegetables. This was what we called a bumper crop.

Tuesday 14 and Wednesday 15 June
Sandy played ten holes on Tuesday with Mac O'Grady, Seve and Langer. Sandy liked the course straightaway. It's very English-looking. You can see why they called it New England.

I've never been here before and I don't suppose many people have. I saw an article by Jack Nicklaus in *Golf World* about how to play this course. He said the key thing is to work out where the flat parts are on the fairways and hit to them to give yourself as many flat stances as possible. I measured to those targets. I noticed Seve was hitting his tee shots to these flat areas. He'd had one look at the course and worked it out for himself.

Seve was on about the 1979 Open at Lytham that he won. Few people realize what an achievement it is to win the Open, specially with me caddying for him. Mac was saying to Seve that I never get excited. 'How can you win an Open with a bloke that never gets excited?' O'Grady asked Seve.

Seve said: 'When I got to the last green I said I could take four putts here and still win.'

I had replied: 'No you can't. You've got to get down in two because I've got a bet with Brian Barnes's caddie that an under-par total will win the tournament.'

Seve said now: 'You were more interested in the bet than the tournament.'

And I replied: 'I wouldn't want your worries. In any case my claim to fame is that I caddied for you for four straight years and for Mac O'Grady for four straight weeks.'

We played the remaining eight holes on Wednesday with Scott Simpson and Larry Mize. Simpson was DC this week – defending champion.

Sandy had had these sessions with Jimmy Ballard but something still wasn't quite clicking and he bumped into David Leadbetter on the Wednesday afternoon. David said to him: 'Take the top of the club and make it pass over the right knee on the backswing.' That's what he worked on, and all of a sudden it clicked on the Wednesday afternoon.

Thursday 16 June

We played with Andy North and Tom Watson and, as I've said many a time about great players, when it's their turn they're ready. They're good to play with. No crying. You can complain about everything in golf, but they don't. No rushing, but no time wasted either. It was a nice two days of golf, made more enjoyable by the fact that I've known Bruce Edwards, Watson's caddie, and Popeye, who caddies for Andy North, for some time. We call him Popeye because he's got big eyes, not because he's strong. They are both members of the Association and have got the Nabisco visor.

Sandy was a lot happier about his ball-striking today than he had been since the Masters or Hilton Head – twenty-three putts, ten on the back nine. He had a 68, what the pros call a good working round. You've played badly and made a score, the sign of a champion. Henry Longhurst always used to say that. It was one of his favourite expressions.

The Duke (Andy North) is a great fellow. He's got nicknames for everybody. Mark McCumber is 'Tattoo' after the little fellow in *Fantasy Island* [an American tv soap opera]. He calls Jack Renner 'Prince' because Renner sounds like

Rainier. He calls J. C. Snead 'Goose' because there is a J. C. Goosie who plays on the US senior tour. Jerry Pate is 'Bone' as in bonehead.

He calls them these names to their faces. He only does it to the people he likes, mind. I caddied for him for two winters and he was coming out with all these nicknames and so I, as a prolific inventor of names for school teachers and bosses at work, thought we've got to have a name for him. If you listen to his voice he speaks very like John Wayne, so I christened him the Duke. It fits him perfectly.

Today Sandy was over the back of the 11th green in two and holed a chip. Andy North snap hooked his drive into the trees; it ricocheted out and his second shot hit somebody in the grandstand. Then he chipped on the green and holed a long putt for a par. Watson, meanwhile, has split the fairway with his drive, hit his second shot to about ten feet and missed the putt. On the next tee Andy said to Tom: 'You're far too conventional a player to be in this group.'

Sandy was saying that his dad and his business associates have sold Hawkestone Park and also Patshull Park (golf and country clubs in Shropshire). Twenty-three of them bought it originally and some have died off in the meantime and the rest are getting on, so Sandy's dad has been advocating selling it for ages. Now a group of Indian businessmen have taken over. Sandy says: 'At least we'll be able to go and get a good curry.' The old practical thinking, you see.

Friday 17 June

Much cooler today. It's down to just over 70 compared with 100 yesterday. This is a hilly course but nothing like Augusta. He's hitting the shots he wants to, now. On the 11th he was over the back again. At that moment he was leading the tournament by two shots. As Sandy prepared to chip, Andy North came right up to me and said: 'If he holes this he's got my vote.' I nearly burst out laughing. Sandy's drive on the 12th finished just off the fairway and his drive on the 18th finished just in the rough.

Hilary is carrying on organizing the trip at the end of the year. We've got to send a deposit to Hawaii for the hotel and because Sandy's not playing in the Kirin Cup I've got to get myself a bag for it. I'm working on different ones at the moment. I don't want to leave it to the last minute.

The Kirin Cup finishes on 18 December. If he goes and plays there he's halfway round the world, got to come back home for Christmas and then it's straight out again to the US for the Tournament of Champions early the next year. It's not worth going. It's all right for the Australians, and to some extent the Americans, and from Japan to Hawaii is not as bad, but for the Europeans it's a helluva trek.

Our preoccupation is getting to The Country Club in the morning. We're only eight miles away but if you haven't got a lift you spend the whole of the previous day or the week finding out who's got cars. I got a lift from Bruce Edwards this morning and we left at 6.45 a.m., and ate breakfast on the way. Bruce has rented a car this week. I think Scotty who caddies for Larry Mize has rented one as well. You find out who's near your time and work it out that way. Then you give him some gas money or buy him a breakfast just to make sure of getting here.

We have a caddies' tent beyond the putting green where they serve coffee and doughnuts free in the morning and drinks. You get a clean towel every day to clean the clubs, and they're good towels, too. You pay $20 deposit and you get a bib and a baseball hat, the towel, the doughnuts and drinks. The hats are like the green ones you get at the Masters. Nobody's worn them of course. We're all too busy earning money from Nabisco for wearing their visors.

When we sit in the caddies' tent people come and talk to us. There are loads of interesting British people who have just come here to watch this tournament. I met some people from Birkdale yesterday. The US Open is an all-ticket event but they had been successful in the ballot. I asked one of them what he did for a living. 'I work on the railways over here,' he replied.

I met another fellow whose father was Irish. There is a big Irish community in Boston. After we'd been talking for a while he said: 'It's a good job my father doesn't know I'm speaking to an Englishman.'

There's a post office near the caddies' tent and I got some

first-day covers of the Francis Ouimet stamp and sent some letters – to Jim Mehigan, an Irishman in California, the Macphersons, Sandy's friend Neville Cramer, who works for immigration, and Bill Myers, the policeman in Hawaii, who hopefully we're going to stay with for Christmas.

Then there's the dreaded green bibs to wear. They give us bibs made of cheapjack material and they come halfway down your thighs and are tied at the sides. They're Irish bibs – the pockets are on the inside. When we came in after the first day Sandy's bag had changed from white to green. I thought to myself: 'If that's what Sandy's bag looks like, what sort of a state is my shirt going to be in?' Of course that was full of green dye as well.

I had a word with one of the officials sitting in the recorders' tent. 'We've got a proper organization all set up. We're professionals caddying for 35, 40, 45 weeks a year. We know what we're on about. We can help you as much as you can help us. Why don't you try and liaise with us a bit?'

He reckoned he had. He said they'd had a meeting with Mike Carrick. He was very nice about it and said they were trying to make provision to get the bags and clothes cleaned.

The USGA told us to take our stained clothes to the pro's shop and get them replaced. I got a new shirt and some of the boys got new trousers courtesy of the USGA. We hope that the cost to the USGA of buying us these shirts and trousers will prompt them into giving us something reasonable to wear in future.

It has been a good two days for Sandy. He's had rounds of 68 and 71 and at one stage he got to six under par and led the field by two shots.

Saturday 18 June

Sandy had a 75 today, not very good. One reason is that he's tired. He has been backwards and forwards across the Atlantic four times so far this year, and on top of this it was nearly 100 degrees today.

The other reason is that he lost his rhythm. For the first two days we played in three-balls; they were very slow and we got used to that rhythm. A lot of people who play golf will never understand how you become used to that. Then all of a sudden you're off in two-balls and it feels as though you're running round. He was rushing things and I was trying to get him to slow down, but he was tiring.

That 75 ended all the talk about the Grand Slam. That's a load of rubbish. The last man to win the US Masters and the US Open was Jack Nicklaus in 1972, and the last man to win three successive majors in one season was Ben Hogan in 1953. I ask you, what bloody chance have we got? Hogan was an outstanding golfer but the competition can't have been anything like these days. Nor can the media attendance have been similar. The tournaments are still called tournaments, but that's all. Almost everything else has changed. You never had grandstands, television and stuff like that. How many newspapermen have got credentials this week?

It's like going to Mars. Andy North says where they're playing the US PGA they might as well play it in a blast furnace because it's going to be 100 degrees and 40 m.p.h. winds. If Sandy had won three, yes, let's talk about it; but not when he's only won one.

I put the hex on Andy tonight. He said that Nick Faldo was going to play in Monte Carlo and I explained about the hilly course, the fog and the ride up and down from Monte Carlo to the top of the mountain each day. Then we started to talk about catching the plane home and how long it would take to get to the airport because in the centre of Boston you have to go through a tunnel that becomes a bottleneck. I said to Andy: 'You won't be on it anyway because you're going to be in a play-off.' And he was.

That's the worst thing that can happen to anybody. We all hate play-offs, especially those starting at 2.00 like this one. It's all right if you go straight into them, but who wants to wait overnight and all morning as well when you've got a plane to catch to the other side of the world? Everybody wants sudden death. Sandy does. It's matchplay and he's good at matchplay and that's why we win so many.

Sunday 19 June
Sandy shot a 73 and finished twenty-fifth equal. He said it had

been a satisfactory US Open for him because he'd never done any good in it before, whereas at least at one stage this time he led. It was his fourth tournament in a row. He has played Wentworth, Woburn, Westchester and now here.

Woburn took a lot out of him. He wasn't playing very well and he was having to concentrate very hard because it was wet and windy and sludgey. Also he had a tiring drive to and from home each day, even though it was only an hour each way.

Another reason for his tiredness is that he'd been in contention in so many tournaments throughout the winter. The US Open is the fifteenth he has played in the States this year and he has played in the PGA at Wentworth, where he came seventh, and the British Masters two weeks ago, which he won. In the States he has been in contention at some time in twelve of the fifteen he entered.

Monday 20 June
Got home about midday, unpacked and put the barbecue on. I'd had a halfway decent night's sleep on the plane from Boston. I'm not terrific at sleeping on planes but Sandy has bought me an inflatable pillow that you blow up and put around your neck. If you don't use one you feel as though your head's going to fall off and roll around on the floor.

Peugeot French Open, Chantilly, Paris

Tuesday 21 to Friday 24 June
Somebody had told me that Chantilly was only ten minutes north of Charles de Gaulle airport in Paris and so I got a taxi there. A quick £20. There was a big chateau with a lake around it and the hotel was just beyond. Traveleads had been there earlier in the year, sussed it all out and put 50 per cent deposit down on the better rooms. At the last minute the French Golf Federation commandeered them and we were put in inferior ones, which hadn't been refurbished.

The bath in our room was shaped like a hip bath. Two tiers, and the water never rose above my ankles. I used it once and thereafter stuck to the shower. It was a really grotty room. I used to go to reception and say: 'Key for cell so-and-so please' and they never batted an eyelid.

Traveleads played hell over the way they had been treated, bless their hearts. There was a room with television in it for the players and everyone was given a bottle of champagne. I finished up the first night in room 309 drinking with Glenn Ralph and Ross McFarlane and others. Woke up with a headache late the next morning.

It was a typical French Open and it reminded me of the first time I went to Le Touquet in 1976 when I first caddied for Seve. Salvador Balbueno, the Spaniard, who had won in Portugal, led all week. It was about 90 degrees and the starter wore a Maurice Chevalier hat and in between calling out the names of each group he'd sing into the microphone, 'Every little breeze seems to whisper Louise' or some other song to entertain the punters. Vincent Tshabalala, the African player who was as black as coal and had a baseball grip, came to the last green pulling his own trolley and needing two putts for victory. He walked across to his ball and cleaned it with a piece of old rag, two-putted and won the tournament. His tribe back in Africa gave him a cow. It was the highest honour they could bestow. Both he and Balbueno have since died, unfortunately.

Chantilly is a fast-playing course, very long with waist-deep rough, big rolling greens and big bunkers. It was fabulous. Nice little town, good restaurants and half an hour top whack north from the airport. Don't have to go round the périphérique.

Sandy played with Seve and Peter Senior. They had a good time but Sandy was too tired. I remember that Seve made two points. One was it was a mistake to play a tournament after a major championship. He said you put so much into a major it's difficult to build yourself up again the next week. The other was about slow play. He said he'd advocated to Ken Schofield for a long while that the field should be 125 players starting from two tees instead of the usual 150, who in this case were playing from one tee. The answer he got back was: 'It's only for two days.'

This week Sandy added up how many tournaments he had played since he turned pro and it came to thirty-five a year for the last eleven years. Seve said to him: 'Don't you like being at home?' I asked Seve: 'How many do you play?' 'About twenty-five', he replied.

The thing about Seve is that he's in contention in almost all of those twenty-five tournaments. When he heard this Sandy said: 'I've got to try and get down to thirty because the other five I just walk round anyway.' He may yet decide to cut his tournaments back to thirty-one for this year. He was knackered in Paris, shot 77, 73 and missed the cut comfortably.

My return ticket is for a British Midland flight at 9 p.m. on Sunday night. So I've got two more nights to endure here. 'Bugger this,' I thought to myself and rang Hilary and said I was buying a ticket and coming home. My legs ached, I was tired. I didn't want to spend two whole days there doing nothing.

Saturday 25 June

Got up rather late for me – half-past eight – packed, went for breakfast and the first person I saw was Des Smyth who was there with his caddie, John Reilly. They were leaving for the airport in a courtesy car. 'Hang on a minute,' I said and I got my bag, jumped in the car and off we went to the airport at 120 m.p.h.

There's two terminals at Charles de Gaulle and one of them is split in half. Neither of the Irish lads had a clue where to go. We finished up at exactly the right spot. That's the Irish – never worry where they're going or what they're doing, but all of a sudden they're in the right place at the right time. They're always bright and cheerful and great company.

I went to the Air France ticket counter. 'When is the next plane for London?' I asked.

'At 10.30 and it's full,' the girl replied. 'Have you got a ticket?'

'No,' I replied.

'I'll give you one then, and if you don't get on this flight there's a British Airways one at 12.30 and another Air France plane at 2.30. You can definitely get on that.'

The next thing I'm in the stand-by queue, and the *next* thing I'm on the plane back to Heathrow. Got the tube in to London and the 11.30 rattler up to Newark.

The train was packed. It was like the Black Hole of Calcutta. Me and another fellow were jammed against the bar and the barman gave us a couple of pints before we started, on the house. All I did from King's Cross to Newark was pick people's bags up, climb over prams and direct them up and down the train. I didn't mind a bit, of course, because I was going home.

The time change coming back from Paris was my seventeenth of the year.

At Home

Sunday 26 June to Saturday 2 July
Made the statutory visit to the Lincolnshire coast, this time to Cleethorpes. I used to go there on Salvation Army outings and the only thing I can remember about it is that the sand was covered with coal dust from Grimsby, making it black. I hadn't been there for thirty years easily, maybe thirty-five. This time I noticed the sand on the beach looked like the new sand they put in bunkers before a tournament.

The tide comes in fast at Cleethorpes – two or three hours after it has looked to be miles away it's lapping against the promenade wall. Then it starts to go out again and leaves this black coal line that I remembered from my childhood.

The railway line approaching Cleethorpes goes to within twenty-five yards of the promenade. It's a brilliant set-up, being so compact. It looks as though the station is right on the beach. And the pier either burned down or fell down, I can't remember which. It's only about one tenth of its former length. We managed to find a few slot machines. People fishing off the end of the pier. The donkeys all looked very well. Must have been a dozen of them. We had fish and chips and fed the birds. It was cold as hell and slashing with rain but that didn't matter. There was a bus trip in from Kirkby for the day. We bumped into several people we knew. It was great fun.

There were two days of bad weather so I got everything done inside – my accounts and things like that.

7

3 July–2 August

Confrontation about overalls – Drenched at St Mellion –
Supporting role at Lytham

Bell's Scottish Open, Gleneagles Hotel, Auchterarder

Sunday 3 July
Drove up to Gleneagles. Rented this palatial caravan which we
found through a local tourist board brochure. It's in a garden
centre in Auchterarder, a great name to be able to spell.

Got here after five hours driving. Went straight to the course
to do my measurements so I could have Monday off. It was a
nice evening and we were hoping for a fine week in Scotland
for a change.

Monday 4 July
Went the tourist route to Pitlochry, over the mountains. They
have a hydroelectric dam that was built in 1951. The salmon
have to pass the dam to get to their spawning ground so at the
side they've built something that is called a fish ladder, a series
of twenty-five concrete pens, each higher than the previous one,
and the fish swim through pipes to get from one pen to the
next. One pen has a glass side and you can see the salmon
swimming about inside.

The spawning season is from April to October and the
salmon are counted as they go up. There have been 1,600 so far
this year but they expect it to be 5,000 or 6,000 ultimately.

Tuesday 5 July
Here we are in Perthshire and you can see its rolling hills for

miles and miles. There's the glen, Glendevon, opposite the course, the hotel and the Queen's course at the side.

Sandy played in the pro-am of the Bells Scottish Open with Sir Norman McFarlane from Bell's. He was explaining how many bottles of Pimms they supped at Wimbledon and Henley. Typical old Scottish laird. A very fit-looking bloke. Ian St John, the former footballer, was in the group behind us.

Going up the first hole I slipped on to one knee. It's a hilly course but that wasn't why I fell. It had been very dry for months and then came two days of rain. More dry weather followed before it started raining again and so there was a greasy surface to the course. It looked like oil on the surface of the grass and it made the place a skating rink. The caddies were going up and down these hills in flat-soled shoes and falling over like ninepins.

During the pro-am Sandy was telling me about going to Silverstone last week prior to the British Grand Prix. Nigel Mansell drove Sandy around the track in Sandy's 944 turbo Porsche. He gave Sandy two tips – to keep the pressure in his car tyes to that printed on the side of the tyre; and that the best oil you can put in a car engine is Mobil One. That's what they use in racing circles. You can buy it in any garage. It gets to very high temperatures without breaking down. He said it's twice as much money but for a high-performance car it's worth paying extra.

Wednesday 6 and Thursday 7 July
The important thing for us is uniforms. This year, once again, we have overalls and bibs. At the Dunhill Cup in 1985 John Paramor asked me and Peter Coleman into the caravan at St Andrews and said: 'The tour is getting very image conscious and to help your lads along wouldn't it be better if you formed an Association?' Neither of us really wanted to do it. But we did tell him there were only three things we needed. One was a ticket to get in with, a badge so we could identify ourselves to get our credentials; two, we didn't want hitting on the head on the practice ground (we don't have to fetch balls on the practice ground any more, so that's all right); and three, we didn't want plastic bibs or anything like that to wear. I've had terrible colds from wearing these bibs.

Also a bad thing for us to have to wear are overalls, which cover up our clothes. They may be fine for the organizers and sponsors, but they are crappy-looking overalls. And they give us bibs to wear on top.

At the end of 1985 I gave John Paramor a light jacket I had got at the 1983 Ryder Cup in the US. You can have what you like on the back, name of the player and/or sponsor. If it's hot you put the jacket on and you can't feel it. If it's raining you have your weatherproofs on and the jacket over the top so at all times the jacket can be seen; it doesn't interfere with us and it's not unhealthy as overalls are. We've had a report from the health people in Nottingham verifying this. But the tournament organizers keep trotting these overalls out.

This week I personally made my mind up just to wear the bib. A lot of the other lads had done so as well. In the PGA rules it says: 'Caddies are required to wear either uniform or bib with the sponsor's advertisements on it displayed at all times. Otherwise a fine of £50 will be imposed.' Either/or, not both.

I thought: 'Bugger it. I'll fight tooth and nail for this', and apparently a lot of other caddies had thought the same thing. John Davidson, the secretary of the European Tour Caddies' Association, had been in to see Paramor and explained all this and didn't get anywhere at all. So he said to Paramor: 'It's like this. Tomorrow there are going to be a lot of them not wearing their overalls.'

'Well, they'll be fined, then,' said Paramor.

So off we went. There must have been twenty-five or thirty of us who wore bibs, and nothing was said. But a lad called Nick Tarratt had been in to see Tom McEvoy, who supplied the overalls, and said: 'Don't give caddies that don't wear overalls any whisky.' There was half a bottle of whisky for us for wearing the advertising.

Tonight the first annual general meeting of ETCA was held in the Crown Hotel, Auchterarder. This instruction of Tarrant's came up. The consensus was: 'We don't care about the whisky. It's the point we're trying to make, to show everybody our feelings.' The overalls are very inefficient, don't look smart enough, are impractical and also a jacket is cheaper to make. We had to make our point and the PGA didn't want to know.

The next day I said to Nick Tarratt: 'You've noticed that I'm not wearing overalls. If you've got five minutes I'll tell you why.' I explained it all to him. Some of the story he didn't know, specially about the fine. The PGA had said to him: 'You're wasting your time talking to the caddies. You won't get any sense out of them.'

Then Alan Callan, boss of Keith Prowse and promoter of the Scottish Open, turned up. He was going to ask all the committee members of the ETCA what we wanted to wear next year. He wanted us to have something that was really smart and better than any other tournament. The upshot was that he promised that for next year Tom McEvoy would make smart practical uniforms, not overalls, for us. The same is going to happen with the Open – new uniforms made by McEvoy.

We can go to the sponsors every week from now on and say: 'We've got a 70-strong organization from eleven different nationalities including one Japanese. We're a responsible body.' We were finding out what everyone else knew – make representations, say you're an organized body and you get something. I hope it is going to continue. We're trying to establish credibility and to be recognized, which takes time. We've got to be patient like the lads were in America. We are affiliated to them.

Other matters came up at the AGM. There had been a deal with a fellow from Sweden for us to wear certain clothing, but it fell through. It was valuable experience nonetheless.

The subscription of £25 remained the same as last year. It was decided to impose a dress rule to start at the Benson & Hedges in August. From then members won't be allowed to wear jeans, track-suit trousers or collarless shirts on the course for the five days of a tournament, including the pro-am. This is to show people we mean business and we can be smart.

Our meetings are very orderly and well behaved. You wouldn't believe how orderly they are. Everybody gets a say and everybody listens. There is no shouting and slagging one another off.

Jimmy Bell, one of the old timers who used to caddie for Des Smyth at one stage, has been living near Marbella in Spain for a while now and the other day he got run over by a car. He was in intensive care. We have had a collection for him. In the room where the players sign their cards is a notice asking for money for him. We raised £118 at the meeting. We're going to convert the cash into a cheque, give it to Tony Jacklin and he'll take it to the hospital when he returns to Spain after the Open. That'll give Jimmy a boost.

Sandy played the first two rounds with Mark (Jesse) James and José Rivero. Fish Finger – real name unknown – is caddying for Jesse and Silly Billy for Rivero. Hilary couldn't believe her eyes when she saw on the first tee Fish Finger smoking a pipe and Silly Billy with the inevitable cigar in his mouth. And none of the three of us was wearing overalls.

Friday 8 July

I had spent two days slithering around because as caddies we're not supposed to wear spikes lest we damage the greens. Laughing Boy (Ken Brown's caddie) slid ninety-six yards from the 18th tee to the red spot on the fairway. 'Eddie the Eagle only managed ninety-one yards,' Laughing Boy said, when he told me the story. 'I beat him by five yards.' Even Big Brian had a fall, and we reckon he's one of the most stable human beings in golf. Apparently four spectators broke their legs on the first day.

I remember Big Pete, who used to caddie for Gary Koch, sliding all the way down from the 10th tee to the bottom of the slope at Augusta. Pete lost his bag halfway down and finished on one knee. Willie Aitchison broke his ankle in the 1969 Ryder Cup walking from the 17th to the 18th at Birkdale in the dark.

The worst fall I've ever had was at Cypress Point in California. It had poured with rain for several days and as I was walking down the slope from the 11th tee I thought to myself: 'I shouldn't be here' when I went *whooomph*. I was covered in mud from head to foot. The bag was plastered, so were the clubs. I had no chance of saving myself with a bag of clubs over my shoulder. One arm might as well have been tied behind my back. It was only our second hole so there were another sixteen to go. This meant I had to wait at least five hours before I had any chance to get clean.

After a while you get wise to it and plan your route. In the States it's easy. You walk down the cart path and never bother with the fairways. Or you walk in the trees where it's usually dry.

By now Sandy was fed up with me slithering around and so he went to the PGA and asked permission for me to wear spikes. Having got it, he went into the pro's shop and bought me a pair of Adidas shoes like he wears. They're very comfortable and easy to break in.

Saturday 9 July
Sandy began the day only a few shots behind Barry Lane, Roger Chapman and Peter Fowler. He'd had rounds of 69, 69 and 69 but was not striking the ball well. He actually shanked a full nine iron on the 12th hole in the third round. During the first nine holes today he fell back to six shots behind Barry, the eventual winner.

It was Henry Longhurst who talked about great players who had the ability to score well when playing badly. This is what Sandy was doing here. He was unhappy with his game but he didn't allow it to depress him and he made respectable scores despite it. He ended with a flourish, getting an eagle three at the last for a 68 that gave him joint second place with Rivero.

This was the only major stroke-play tournament in Scotland this year and the only chance the Scottish fans had to see the reigning US Masters champion. They made the most of it. About 80,000 of them turned up for the week and most of them seemed to be watching Sandy.

This morning I took an overnight bag with me to the course and Hilary took the rest of our luggage down to Blackpool in the car. I was off to St Mellion tonight to caddie for Sandy tomorrow in a challenge match with Nick Faldo against Jack Nicklaus and Tom Watson. Seventeen of us flew from Edinburgh to Exeter. It was a plane like the one we fly in from East Midlands down to London. Very comfortable. I had some whisky left from the Bell's and I passed that round. It didn't last very long. Somebody else circulated a bottle as well and so we called it a two-bottle-of-whisky journey.

On the way down we discussed the format of the match. The

BBC people said they wanted it to go eighteen holes and they were talking about having an aggregate. I said: 'Why don't you make it a four-ball better ball medal? Like the Dunhill Cup except you've got two on each side.'

So that was that.

Arrived at Exeter airport and spotted the Red Arrows lined up on the tarmac. Coach to St Mellion, arriving at midnight. We three caddies – Andy, me and Jimmy Dickinson, who was caddying for Nicklaus – were allocated accommodation just down the road from the club. Nicklaus had played a practice round with Faldo yesterday and Jimmy Dickinson had done the yardages for us.

The fourth caddie was Alan Bond, son of Hermon Bond, one of the two brothers who own St Mellion. Alan was caddying for Tom Watson. Set the alarm for 7 a.m. and awoke to the sound of rain pouring down and a cow chomping at some grass outside my window.

St Mellion Trophy, St Mellion, Cornwall

Sunday 10 July

The match was due to start at half-past nine. It had rained all night and it looked as though it was going to rain all day as well. It was heavy, continuous rain and a wind.

On the first tee they introduced the British pair first. 'Sandy Lyle, former Open champion and reigning US Masters champion. And Nick Faldo, the reigning Open champion.' After that, Watson turned to Nicklaus and said: 'The only thing that's "reigning" about us, Jack, is the weather.' Off we went, squelch, squelch, squelch.

After twelve holes, when we'd been going for three or four hours, the rain was getting in everywhere. I had my cap on and it was two or three pounds heavier than it should have been because of the rain. All the towels got used up and everything got greasy. Several of the BBC-TV cameras broke down and then Sandy's umbrella collapsed. One little lad asked me afterwards: 'Can I have Sandy's ball?' I replied: 'You can have his umbrella.' I thought the smile that followed the look of disbelief on his face would wear off when he tried to use it.

Sandy has cord grips on his clubs and that was the only reason he could keep hold of them. Nicklaus had leather grips and even though they felt dry they spun in his hands a lot.

Everybody made the best of it. A buggy followed us with flasks of coffee and bars of chocolate. It was a very important day for everyone at St Mellion and they had all gone to a lot of trouble. There were 800 invited spectators and most of them stuck it all the way round. Sir Neil MacFarlane, the former Minister of Sport, was one of them and he blamed the weather on the government. In the end the last hole made a good finish. Nicklaus sank a long putt for a birdie. Faldo then holed from fifteen feet for a bogey for him and Sandy to win by one shot.

We'd had seven hours in the downpour and it was a long job to get everything dry. It was four days before the inside of the bag was completely dry.

Flew from Plymouth to Blackpool that night in two small planes. Sandy and myself, Nick, and Andy and Tom and Linda Watson in one eight-seater plane and the rest in the other. Went to sleep, and when I woke up we were in bright sunshine flying over Hoylake, near Liverpool. A minute or two later Faldo spotted Birkdale so we all rushed across and looked. We could see the holes very clearly. Then we picked out Lytham and all the tents ready for the Open. We had flown over three championship courses in five minutes.

Open Championship, Royal Lytham & St Anne's, Lancashire

Monday 11 July
This morning Sandy wanted to play around 10.30. I arrived about 9.30 and found he was already there, practising his putting. When I caddied for Seve in 1979 I made two yardage books. The first one was rough and I then transferred the information in it to another book, writing all the details in ink. I gave this one to Dudley Doust of the *Sunday Times* when I was helping him with his book *Seve: The Young Champion*. I'm still waiting to get it back.

Because of the tv match I'd had no chance of measuring the course before Sandy played today. I'd remembered to bring my rough yardage book from 1979 so at least I had something to go on. When we got to the course I found that Sandy had been given a Strokesaver yardage book and that saved my bacon.

It's a very good book, the Strokesaver. Perfect size for a pocket and the maps of each hole are there. The measurements are good. For an amateur who comes here to play, this book would be perfect. It shows all the features and how far it is to the middle of the green from various points. But we need to know the distances to the front of each green. Also we need more reference marks. For instance, I know that on the second hole there is a sprinkler head that is not marked in this Strokesaver book. Yet it's a perfect distance for measuring from.

Andy North had still got his yardages from 1979. I bumped into him out on the course and saw him using it. That made me wonder whether they were still supplying the books. I said to him: 'Where did you get that plan from, Andy?'

'Last time I was here,' he replied.

I pulled mine out of my pocket, put it alongside and said: 'Snap.'

'Me and you can *really* caddie,' he said with a smile.

Andy had been flown over by this fellow with his own plane. He's worth pots and pots, this fellow. The only stipulation was that he caddied for Andy. Tom Watson spotted the plane at Blackpool airport when he landed there on Sunday evening.

When we were ready to play the Spaniards turned up, Olazabal, Rivero and Seve, and so we had a fourball. Sandy and Olazabal played Rivero and Seve – for lunch.

As we walked round Seve said to me: 'We had some fun here last time, didn't we? We do many crazy things.' He remembered the shots he had played and the shots he should have played and the strategies that he should have used. They say he drove it all over the place but he missed where he could miss. The great thing about his play which nobody ever noticed was the first nine holes. The first two days Seve played with Trevino and Ken Brown. The first nine holes were all downwind and

Trevino couldn't hold the ball on the greens because he was punching them in so low. But Seve could with his iron shots, even out of the rough because he hit the ball so high. That was a great strength of Seve's and enabled him to make a decent score on the front nine every day.

The fairways had sprinklers on them in 1979. But on the 3rd hole they watered the apron and left the green dry. That's the old trap that nearly all greens committees fall into. If a ball lands short of the green it stops; if it lands on the green it keeps going. Golf courses should be either running or holding, not both. Make your mind up.

When we got to the 13th Seve went and looked at the deep bunker on the right and explained to the Spaniards what had happened to him there in the last round in 1979. His drive hit the top of the hill on the right and rolled back down into the bunker away from the face a bit. He had a shot of only about fifty or sixty yards and there was a high bank in front. The flag was at the back of the green. His shot landed on the green but on a little slope and spun to the right just off the green. He holed it for a three.

On the 16th I recalled the details of Seve's drive in the last round, the car park shot. I said I hoped that one day someone would put in print how far it really was. It was fifty-four yards from the front of the green, thirty-six yards from the middle of the fairway. It's not wide by any standards, specially when you're twenty two years old, leading the Open by one shot on a bitterly cold afternoon. Anyway, Seve had played for that side of the fairway. Coming in from the right was the only chance he had of holding the ball on the green. He had figured that out earlier in the week. His ball was on the tractor path that runs across the course to the par three course, so he got a good lie. He inspected the green and then purposely played a sand iron to the most receptive part, which was about twenty feet past the pin. Holed the putt for a three and of course went on to win.

Sandy played here in the 1974 Open as well as in 1979 and he played in the Lytham Trophy a lot, too. As we went round the course he remembered what shots he had played and I remembered what shots I had seen and what different holes do. It's memory by association.

He doesn't do much practising around the greens. He is usually the first off a green ready to march to the next tee whereas someone like Langer is always the last. On the way round Sandy and Seve agreed about one thing: 'It doesn't matter how well you know this course. If you don't play good you're not going to win anyway. In this instance it's not knowing the course that's important. It's playing good.'

Sandy used his one iron a lot. He had no other choice – tight fairways and penal rough. The only two changes they've made since we were here last is they've made the 17th and 18th a bit longer, but the greens were slower than expected.

Another thing about Seve and Sandy is that Sandy will go to Seve and talk to him. A lot of people think to themselves: 'Is Seve in a good mood or a bad mood?' Sandy doesn't think as complicatedly as that. He just goes up to Seve and says: 'Hello Seve, are you married yet?' or: 'What sort of round have you had?' Sandy and Seve play a lot together. It's nice to see someone who can make Seve relax.

Sandy and Olazabal were dormie one up going down the 18th against Rivero and Seve. Olazabal was discussing what they were going to have for the first course – lobster thermidor was suggested. I said to him: 'Let's get the wine list straight first.' And Sandy said: 'It's going to be a corn beef sandwich.' They didn't get anything at all.

Sandy got all the interviews out of the way today. Seve always gets more requests. Makes you wonder what they find to say. Gary Player was the best at making up a story out of nothing.

Sandy doesn't like signing autographs. He has tried to avoid them, especially this week. He could stand there all day signing if he wanted to and it's far too tiring. People have even asked me for my autograph. 'You must be desperate,' I say to them.

Tuesday 12 July
The most time-consuming aspect of measuring a course is drawing all the features of each hole in your notebook. But with a Strokesaver this was already done. Rather than go around again with the wheel which is very difficult to do when everybody is practising, I got Brian Sibson to take the wheel

round for me while we were practising today and I wrote down all the measurements in a notebook. He's a builder and he did the alterations to our house. That's how I got to know him even though he's lived at Kirkby all his life, the same as me.

So there he is on the 1st tee, absolutely petrified because Sandy is playing with Seve and Langer. He was scared to open his mouth. 'There's nobody here yet,' I said to him, 'The stands are empty.' He grunted something like: 'There's thousands of folk all watching me.'

'Look, take the wheel and when you get to the green tell me what the reading is. When they've finished putting just wheel it across the green. Don't mind them.'

He was walking along shaking like a leaf and I said: 'Go on, wheel it across the green.'

'They're still putting,' he said.

'It doesn't matter. For one thing Langer doesn't know you're here yet. He hasn't seen you. If you went and hit him on the side of the head he'd only rub it and say where did that come from? Another thing: This is what we do every day. The players are used to people measuring and kicking their balls out of the way. Whatever you do nobody will bat an eyelid.'

'I don't want to get in anybody's road,' he said, nervously.

I introduced him to Pete Coleman and they chatted away to one another. Pete said to him: 'Why don't you come and do some work down in London? Builders down there make a fortune.'

After about five holes I said to Brian: 'Aren't you fed up yet?'

'No, no,' he replied. 'It's fantastic.'

'That's good. Because me and Peter are bored out of our minds and I was sure you would be.'

Willi Hofmann did about six holes with us one day when we were playing with Langer and then he vanished, so Pete had the wheel. Willi reappeared on the ninth green with a fistful of irons in his hand. 'You're lucky,' I said to Pete. 'You'll have to carry those.'

That's what Langer tried to make him do at one time but Pete had expressed his opinion often in the past about having to carry extra clubs. 'Enough clubs is enough clubs,' he had said, or words to that effect.

So this time they swopped clubs and Willi carried in the five Bernhardt didn't want. Sandy looked inside Langer's bag and said: 'You've only got three putters today. You must be putting better.'

On the 15th hole the BBC-TV people turned up. One had the hand-held camera and the other had the microphone, one of those dun coloured things about a yard long and covered in fur. They filmed everything including Brian walking up the fairway, head down, concentrating. He turned round and looked at me dead nervous, hands shaking, the lot. 'Can't handle all this,' he said. 'Too many people.'

'You wait until we get to the 18th,' I said.

'Have I got to measure that as well?' he asked.

'You wait until you see the stands there and imagine them full of people. One minute you can hear a pin drop when someone's playing. The next minute it's like Wembley stadium when a goal is scored in the Cup final.'

Sandy and Seve didn't play a match because you can't play a match with Langer. He won't do it. He was made to in the Ryder Cup but he wouldn't do it here. He was too busy concentrating and practising.

Went down to the Adidas stand in the exhibition centre with Sandy and got some sweaters, shirts and socks. Sandy swears by his Adidas shoes. He thinks they're terrific. Waterproof, lightweight. People at my golf club say they're the best there are. I don't know why they don't write it into Sandy's contract that I should wear Adidas gear as well. Pete Coleman's got it with Wilson. Makes sense doesn't it?

Wednesday 13 July
Read an article in the paper that said this is Jack Nicklaus's twenty-seventh consecutive Open. That's something we've got in common because it's my twenty-seventh too. The first one I went to was at Troon in 1962. I caddied for David Talbot, who was the pro at Hollinwell at that time.

I used to go caddying at Hollinwell a lot and when I started work I thought I'd like to go to a tournament to use my holidays up. The Open seemed as good a one to go to as any.

I took two consecutive weeks' holiday and the first week I went to see Hugh Monro, my old school friend, who had moved up to Scotland when he was fifteen. We toured around the Highlands. Walked up Ben Nevis one night. We were staying in a little house and the lady said: 'It's only a walk up there' and so we started at about six o'clock. Two hours up and two hours down. I've still got the pictures we took. We borrowed his dad's car, an old Hillman Minx. We drove past Loch Ness in the pouring rain and there was this chap sitting by the side of the road with a movie camera with plastic over it waiting for the monster to pitch up. We went over Rannoch Moor and right in the middle of the moor, miles from anywhere, was a parked van with a sign on it that said: 'Chris Jones, Church Street, Kirkby-in-Ashfield.' He was a builder. He must have been there on his holidays.

In those days everybody had to qualify on the Monday and Tuesday. We played one round on the championship course, which was Old Troon, and another at Lochgreen, a nearby course. The best 150 or so began playing on Wednesday and on Thursday the cut was a maximum of forty-four players. No ties. There were stories of someone on the course with a score that could knock out a whole bunch of players and everyone clubbing together and making it right with him before he reached the last hole.

The first time I saw Nicklaus was when he was playing a practice round at Lochgreen with Arnold Palmer, Gary Player and Phil Rodgers, who was on a hot streak. He finished third in the Open, behind Palmer. That was the first time I had seen any of them. Palmer got £1400 for winning.

The final two rounds were on a Friday to allow the pros to get back to their shops for the weekend because 90 per cent of them had club jobs. That was the only way they existed in those days.

1963 was my first Open at Lytham and this is now the fifth. I caddied for Brian Hutchinson in 1963 after Talbot had failed to pre-qualify. In 1969 I caddied for Lionel Platts, in 1974 for Roberto de Vicenzo, and Seve in 1979. 1963 was the year of the play-off between Bob Charles and Phil Rodgers – thirty-six holes on the Saturday. In 1966 the Open moved to four rounds on four days at Muirfield, ending on a Saturday. That was the first time that Nicklaus won it. They got so many people there they put the prize money up by 10 per cent during the week.

Sandy didn't play today. He decided to get his practice done early in the week when it's quieter. He needed a break from all the hullabaloo that accompanies the Open. He would have had a break on Sunday but for the tv match at St Mellion.

We're off tomorrow at 3.19. We don't know whether that's going to be good or bad as far as the weather is concerned. The only thing you can do when you're off late is sit and watch the golf on the telly. That's what he is going to do. Sometimes you can learn the line of the putts by watching on television. You can see the pin positions, how the others are playing. But if it's a bad day you can talk yourself into believing you're going to do a bad score. Like at Turnberry when everybody was way over par and Sandy felt obliged to go and join them. If you don't know how the course is playing you just go and play it.

I ain't going to sit watching the telly tomorrow. I'd like to do something more constructive but I don't know what there is. Andy is going to walk around the course. He likes to go and watch. He's due off with Faldo at half-past one.

Brian, his wife Sharon and son Glen are staying with us at an apartment we've rented in Blackpool. Andy is staying with us as well. We're going to the theatre tonight to see the comedian Frank Carson at the Winter Gardens. Hilary got the tickets weeks ago. We go to Blackpool every night on the trams. Brilliant. They go all the way to Fleetwood. There are slots on the seats and when the trams get to the other end they fold the seats over so they're facing the other way.

It used to be a good old-fashioned seaside resort. But now it's all video games on the Golden Mile. It makes you wonder what everybody did before they were invented. The whelk stall, Gypsy Rose Lee and coconut shies seem to have disappeared, which is a shame.

Thursday 14 and Friday 15 July

What is striking about Lytham is that the 1st hole is a par three with the tee in the trees and you have to be clear in your own mind of the wind direction before you get there. The way I do that is to look at the weather vane above the pro's shop. It's like an old blunderbuss with a golfer and a caddie on top.

The golfers finish their putting practice by aiming at a two-inch diameter hole on the putting green because this makes the regular-size 3½ in. hole seem bigger. This hole is the nearest to the first tee and the idea is that you have a few putts, look at the weather vane and go.

This year every match had a man accompanying them to rake the bunkers, men supplied by the Lancashire Green-keepers' Association. Also the rules officials wore white jackets so you could spot them easily. I think there is one on every hole. Rodney Foster and David Marsh were among them. They're both Sandy's mates from his amateur days and when they saw him they encouraged him.

By the time we started Seve had finished. He'd been round in 67. Do you think he was happy? He was on the putting green as we went out and I said to him: 'Do you want to come for another eighteen holes? You haven't got much to do.' He laughed.

Sandy didn't play particularly well on the first day but his bunker play was much improved. There was only one occasion when he didn't get up and down from a bunker and that was because his ball was buried.

The wind was no more than a moderate breeze on Thursday. It was no bother to us. For our last holes it was getting dusk and I can't focus in that sort of light. They're terrible conditions to play in. Sandy had a 73, just like Seve in his first round in 1979.

Friday was beautiful, a perfect golfing day. Sandy's second round, a 69, may have been only four shots lower than his first but he played quite a bit better. He hit two great one-iron shots on to the 15th and then finished bravely. After hitting his second into a bunker on the 17th he holed a long putt for a par. On the 18th he drove way right, luckily under a tv commentary box, hit a four iron to the side of the green, chipped to twelve feet and holed the putt. He had a par on every hole on the back nine. We're only five shots behind Nick Price, the leader. That's OK. Handily placed.

Saturday 16 July
We went to the course, myself, Andy and Brian, and as we were early we were able to get into the Dormy house car park,

which was spitting distance from the putting green. I knew the fellow on the gate. He knows my name. A lot of the security men go to all the tournaments. I've been trying to get in there every day. I pull up and ask: 'Is there any room?' He'll reply: 'You're lucky' or 'Sorry, you're unlucky.'

Into the caddie shed to watch tv. They had old films on of different Opens over the years. All the time it was raining. We were due out at 2.45 this afternoon, paired with Bob Tway, who's a very nice fellow. He's shy and hardly ever speaks. Sandy played with him in the TPC this year. Tway is a bit of an Andy North. He can either hit it four miles or nowhere because he's such a tall fellow.

But all the time it was raining hard. About midday somebody said: 'That's it, suspended.' The day's play was postponed two hours later.

The discussion then was whether it would be two rounds or not on Sunday. I couldn't see them doing it unless they cut the field to fifty. If they did, we'd have had a real good chance, two rounds in one day on a wet course. Sandy's strong, and bad weather is an advantage for him. Two rounds would frighten some people but they're meat and drink to him.

Since we finished in the early afternoon yesterday and are not scheduled to go out again until 2.45 tomorrow it'll be like starting all over again.

Tried to ring Sandy a few times to find out what was going off but he was never in the hotel. Had dinner with Wobbly and his girlfriend at a restaurant in the centre of Blackpool. Mike Chapman was there. He used to be the Mizuno rep but now he works for Maruman (another Japanese sports manufacturer). He sent us over a bottle of wine.

Sunday 17 July

According to the revised schedules we're due off at 2.45 again with Tway and Don Pooley. Two very tall men. Sandy said: 'I feel like a titch today because I've got two great big fellows playing with me. I feel like Woosnam.' Bob Tway called Pooley 'Ace' all the way round because he holed in one at Bay Hill in 1987 and won a million dollars. Nice blokes to play with. They're quiet and religious. On the first green the applause for Sandy was so loud they turned to him and asked: 'Are you a local here?'

There's been a lot of talk about caddies this week. They always say that Seve's better off with a professional caddie. I think he is, too. Vicente (Seve's brother) doesn't compare notes with any of us. We ask one another: 'How far have you got from here?', 'What club did you play on that hole?' It may be that you haven't got it yourself or what you've got is different. But Vicente or his brothers wouldn't know that because they never spend time with any other caddies.

Sandy played very well for a 67. In the first place it was relief at beating the cut. I know that sounds odd but when he started playing seriously in the States he had a string of very nervous Fridays. He always had one eye on the cut.

After watching Watson and Nicklaus playing bunker shots at St Mellion and Seve in practice at the beginning of this week, Sandy moved his hands forward at the address. When he did this he found he could take the club up steeper and get the ball out more easily. Sandy is a good watcher of other people. He spends as much time watching on a practice ground as he does practising. So he moved his hands forward for other shots as well. It brought back a lot of power he felt he had lost over the last couple of years. This helped him get rid of the heely cut shots he was complaining so much about at the Dunhill Masters last month. It also eliminated the hook shots off the tee with his one iron. As a result he was hitting shots more solid than he had been and he used his one iron on 3, 4, 10, 13, 14, 15, 16, 17 and 18, hitting the fairway each time. A screamer up the 18th.

Again he played three excellent bunker shots, on the 12th, 17th and 18th. The one on the 12th was nearly a case of playing backwards towards the tee because it was only a yard into the bunker and on a downslope. The one on the 17th he said was an easy shot. On the 18th his ball was buried. That means it's got to shoot forwards after he's played it and it ended six to eight feet from the hole.

He said he was pleased to be playing in three-balls because it's easier to lose his rhythm when playing in pairs. We don't play two-balls or singles very often and so he's not used to them.

We're three shots behind Nick Price now and there's one round to go. Seve was two shots behind Hale Irwin after fifty-four holes in 1979. I don't think I have any extra advantage I can give to Sandy because nine years ago I brought home the winner. The course is playing a lot different now. It was dry and running in 1979 and Seve won with only one under par. That ain't going to win this year because the course is wet for a seaside course and that makes it easier. The scores were a lot better today.

With Seve in 1979 it was a crusade, as it always is, life and death, specially playing with Irwin. Irwin's all right but the two of them never spoke a word for two days. Who was Irwin going to beat anyway with the scores he did at the weekend – 75 and 78?

If Sandy goes out and plays well he'll be satisfied, whatever the result. It'll be like last year's World Match-play. He was beaten in the final but he played well, whereas in the other three finals he felt he hadn't played so good.

When Sandy's playing well he doesn't say anything. He hits the ball like he did today, with no effort. He says a lot of golf is instinct, specially putting on greens like these. 'The first thing you see is the best thing to do. I can't understand why Faldo faffs about so much.' Faldo probably thinks that Sandy rushes his shots.

On the last afternoon in 1979 I can remember Seve saying: 'This all boils down to who's got the biggest heart on the back nine.' Different players kept coming on to the leader board – Isao Aoki, Rodger Davis, Ben Crenshaw.

I think there'll be a play-off tomorrow between two players and I don't think Nick Price will be one of them. He was swinging a bit fast when I glimpsed him on television today. Irish Dave (McNeilly, his caddie) said he chipped and putted a lot of times for par whereas I thought he was putting for birdies all day. McNeilly's got £20 each way on him at 100–1. I think the leaders are going to score pretty well as they did yesterday. There are four of them. They're not all going to shoot 75 or 76. And nobody from the back can shoot 63 on here.

I was optimistic at the start because we were playing ahead of our rivals. On the first tee Seve said the main threat was going to come from in front, meaning Sandy. And sure enough Sandy began by playing well, putting for birdies and eagles for eight holes. Trouble is the putts didn't drop. Then he missed a short one for par on number 9, drove into a bunker on the 11th and bogied that as well. That put him out of contention because Ballesteros, Faldo and Price were shooting unbelievably good scores, which got to him. He had gone out to win and it was hard for him to keep going after he realized that he couldn't win. Seve went on to shoot 65, an amazing score, to win by two shots from Price.

After the 11th I noticed that Sandy had become tired and jaded. Suddenly it had all caught up with him. A major title is exceptionally hard work for someone that's got a chance of winning. Everyone wants a piece of them – the media, autograph hunters, everyone. It's non-stop and very wearing. It makes you wonder how such as Nicklaus and Trevino have stayed at the top for so long.

It was an Open in two halves as far as we were concerned. The first half ended after our round on Friday morning, and the second half began after lunch on Sunday.

The best day was the Sunday when Sandy went round in 67 and there were loads of people there. Play-offs are always an anti-climax and that was the feeling we got over the last nine holes today when we were really surplus to requirements as far as the tournament was concerned. Everybody wanted to watch the match behind us where the interest was. Sandy probably felt that more than I did. Perhaps that's why he finished bogey double bogey for a 74, and a four-round total of 283, ten shots behind Seve?

At Home

Tuesday 19 to Saturday 23 July
My plans for the next few days are to sort out the garden, cut the grass, do the hedge. We've got rid of most of the weeds by

squirting fertilizer on them. I'll just potter about in the garden, go in the shed and appear to work. Don't do anything. You just move things about and keep out of the way. We've got some old furniture we're sanding off, two or three old chairs and a gateleg table. They've been in the family since the year dot. Sand them all down, re-varnish and re-assemble them.

Sunday 24 July
We decided to visit Scarborough for our day at the seaside this time.

We found Anne Brontë's grave. We walked from the South Bay where there's a nice beach and harbour, over the top where the castle is and down to the North Bay. When we got over to the other side a shower came down and so we dived into a bus shelter. In there a fellow turned to me and said: 'You're David Muscroft, aren't you?'

And I replied: 'No, not quite. I'm David Musgrove.'

'What are you doing here?' he asked.

'I'm trying to keep dry.'

Monday 25 July to Tuesday 2 August
I'll also do my accounts, all the paper work and play some golf. There's the heavy gang at Coxmoor on Monday, Wednesday and Friday. If there's three of them wanting a fourth and they know I'm at home they get in touch with me. So there's no trouble in getting a game. I play in competitions too.

Sandy's going to visit Jolande's father at Zandvoort, Holland, and then go on to the Adidas factory in Germany. He finds tons and tons of stuff to do at home, just to get away from the golf. He's good at that. He jumps on the lawnmower, drives up and down a bit and doesn't have to sign any autographs.

8

3 August–30 August

Why I like Fulford – On not going to the US PGA –
Ireland and the World Series

Benson & Hedges International, Fulford, York

Wednesday 3 August

This week isn't a hard one for me. I can stay at home and travel
up each day. I drove up today for the pro-am. Tomorrow and
Friday I'll have a ride with a mate of mine, Ted Bell, and his
sons. I get them tickets and a car park sticker and they drive. It's
a good deal.

There are days when it's very hard for me to go back to work,
specially when you have to pack and go to somewhere like
France or Italy. In France and Italy you get bread and jam for
your breakfast, the hotels we stay in are nearly always isolated
and the rooms are spartan. In the US by contrast you go for a
decent period of time generally, have a decent place to stay in.

I always find it harder to pack when I'm leaving home than I
do when I'm moving from one tournament on to another. You
have to make your mind up what to put in. When you're away
you just put everything you can see in your room into your
bag. It's rare for me to leave anything behind though I did
forget some shirts in a drawer in a hotel in New York during
the Westchester Classic in June and I finally got them back six
or seven weeks later. The customs had to open them, of course.

I'm looking forward to starting work again. I played in
several golf competitions during my two weeks off and did all
right. I finished with the ball I started with. That's my main
criterion for a round of golf.

Sandy came up to York yesterday but only to sign in, not to play. There's no point in him practising here because he knows what's involved. He must have played here ten times. Besides, who wants a four-to-five hour practice round. He's not going to learn anything more than he knows already. He has got a helluva good memory, memory by association. As soon as he gets to a course he can remember each hole, what shots he played there before, and a lot of times even which way the putts break.

I always keep my yardage charts from one year to the next. I crib a few measurements from someone else to check my own. Of course I could get round without doing it but it's important to be sure you have the right distances.

In the locker-room at York there's a fellow called Len Jackson, a former policeman. When this tournament started in 1971 he escorted Tony Jacklin and Peter Butler around. There was a lot of stuff pinched from the locker-room and they said they wanted somebody on duty in there. So he started to keep an eye on it.

One year Lanny Wadkins came in and said: 'Does anybody clean shoes in here?' Len cleaned Lanny's shoes himself and got a fiver for his troubles, which he couldn't believe. He thought to himself: this is all right. So every year he gets his shoe-cleaning stuff, cleans the players' shoes when they come in. He's there from six in the morning to eight at night. He's retired from the police force. He suffers from arthritis now and his two sons Andrew and Philip help him out. Andrew caddied for The Rat (Noel Ratcliffe) when he won last year.

There's a piece of paper in the locker-room asking for members who are prepared to give up their lockers for a week to a player. An old member at Fulford, Arthur Hopwood, who was also a member at Hawkestone Park, has been doing this for Sandy for years. He leaves his key with Len and in return Sandy leaves him some balls and a signed visor. Old Arthur, who plays every day, bores the members stupid all year by telling them what Sandy's given him.

Fulford is a marvellous venue. It's a good course, flat and easy to walk round. People make a point of coming here each year. The tented village is by the side of the 18th fairway and green and so it generates a good atmosphere. They used to call it the Benson & Hedges Festival of Golf. I thought that was a perfect title. I don't know why they changed it. You get around the course quick here. There's practically no walking in between holes and no really difficult holes. The greens are good. The standard of play is high. The speed of play is better than in many other tournaments. It seems to flow around Fulford.

I get the impression that nearly all the spectators are golfers. They've played golf and they've been here before. It's a good course to watch on. My mates say they feel as if they're nearer to the golfers in this tournament than in any other.

Am I making myself clear? I like this tournament. I've caddied for the winner twice − Vicente Fernandez in 1975 and Sandy in 1985. Every ten years I come good. Better than never, isn't it?

Thursday 4 August
These greens are usually the best in Europe to putt on. It's a heathland course and for six weeks before the tournament they cut the greens by hand. But with it being a wet summer this year it looks as though they've left it a little too late and then cut them down too rapidly. Today, when that cold wind was blowing they were difficult to putt on and not so good as they had been. Sandy seemed to cope all right, though. He had a 70.

Friday 5 August
I caught him out this morning. I had to get up at half-past five for an 8.40 tee-off time. I was in the locker-room getting everything ready when I heard Sandy come in and say: 'I've beaten that Musgrove here this morning.'

I popped my head up and said: 'No, you haven't.'

Sandy said: 'I can't ever flaming well beat you here.' He was probably angry at not having anything to complain about.

Sandy was playing with Mark James and Roger Chapman and on the first tee Ivor Robson, the starter, asked Mark whose card he had marked the day before. He replied: 'One-putt Lyle's.' They fell about laughing at that except Sandy who was dead indignant. Then Sandy goes and single-putts the first, second and third holes and Mark James was having hysterics.

After the round Mark said something very interesting about Sandy. 'Every time I play with him he scores well,' he said. 'He doen't play all that impressively, but he scores well. He's always two shots in front of the game when he's finished – two shots better than most people would be if they played the same golf. That's the difference between great champions and the rest of us.'

James and another tournament-professional Michael King (Queenie) have always been admirers of Sandy. The other morning Queenie said to me: 'Your man doesn't want to play like a wally, I see.' He was referring to this week's newspaper stories about Sandy saying he wasn't playing in the US PGA because he didn't want to go to the US just for one week for fear of playing badly and being made to look like a wally.

'Yes, that's right,' I said. 'He doesn't want to go all the way there and play like a wally. That's the point that most people refuse to get through their head.' All the press have given him a belting this week, apparently, because he hasn't gone.

He said before it became known: 'There's going to be a stink in the press but it will only last for a few days and then they'll all forget about it. It's me that's going to have all the aggravation of going, not them.'

Major championships, as described by Andrew Prodger, are a pain in the bum. Seve always takes the week off after one now. He said at the French Open last month: 'I've found out over the years that I just can't play the week after a major.' He's going to have a good go in Oklahoma and he's not playing in the Irish Open the week after. But Sandy wants to put up a good show here at York and not want to rush away afterwards. He feels obliged to the sponsors and spectators. Similarly, he wants to be fresh for the Irish, which he wouldn't be if he was returning from stiflingly hot weather in Oklahoma.

He's tried that over the years. He used to steam off to the US Open and the US PGA and never do anything and people used to ask: 'Why can't Lyle do any good in the States?' He's worked out his own way now, planning his schedule and playing only in what he wants to play in. At this time of the year he wants to support the European tour as best he can.

I see that Robert Green, the new editor of *Golf World*, gave

Sandy 'Divot of the Month' for not going to the US PGA. I'm going to tell him when I see him that there's another point of view. I don't think he could be bothered to try and understand Sandy's arguments. Either that or he just wanted to make some mileage out of it. He wrote an article listing eight reasons why the TPC wasn't a major. One of the reasons was poor press parking. He's scraping the barrel there. As if press parking makes a lot of difference to a tournament.

They asked Ken Schofield if Sandy's not going to the US PGA would stop other players getting invitations to play in tournaments over there. 'Sandy Lyle is his own man,' Ken replied. 'He plays in what he wants to play in.'

If you really weighed it up the Irish is a lot better event than the US PGA. Look at the place it's in. You couldn't wish for a more beautiful spot than Portmarnock on a sunny day with a wind blowing as it was last year. It's a good course, not a bloody tricked-up Pete Dye (the architect of Oak Tree, the site of this year's US PGA) job, and you know how the Irish are, living for the day. There's a friendly tented village. They've got their own post office, shops, catering and they usually run out of Guinness by mid-afternoon.

After Sandy won the Open in 1985 he had three special letters. One was from Bobby Locke, an outstanding colonial gentleman, welcoming him to the club. One was from Henry Cotton who said he had watched Sandy's career with great interest and welcomed another Englishman into the ranks of Open winners. And the third letter was from Seve. After the congratulations and saying he was one of Sandy's biggest fans, Seve said that from his own experience he knew that everybody would try and pull Sandy in different directions at once. 'Don't try and please everybody. Just suit yourself,' Seve wrote to Sandy. 'Don't try and do everything that is offered to you. The main thing is to please yourself and do all right by yourself.' Sandy has tried to do that.

What was it Polonius said in *Hamlet*? 'To thine own self be true and then it will follow as night follows the day thou canst not be false to any man.' That's what Sandy's doing, being true to himself.

'I've got that speech from Hamlet written down. Laertes is

about to sail to France and Polonius is giving him all this advice about clothes and lending money: 'neither a borrower nor a lender be.' It's like Kipling's 'If' poem, which I learned at the dentist's. When I was thirteen or fourteen, I had to have a lot of fillings and my dentist had it stuck up on the wall of his surgery. While he was doing the drilling or talking to his bookie on the telephone I used to read it. There was nothing else to look at. That's how I learned it. It keeps coming in useful.

For GCE English we had to read *Julius Caesar*, *Great Expectations* and a book of poems. I ignored the poems because I thought they were a load of rubbish and concentrated on the other two – and passed. I never answered one question to do with poetry.

I got five O-levels in English literature and language, mathematics, geometrical and engineering drawing and survey-ing. Mansfield Secondary Technical School, where I went, was about four or five miles from where we lived and it took twenty minutes to get there on the bus. It was a prisoner-of-war camp in the war and they just kept it on as a school afterwards. Our lessons were held in Nissen huts. I've still got my school cap at home. It fits me now better than ever. We had to wear it to and from school and the idea was to balance it on your head so that from the front it couldn't be seen. Then a prefect or a master would say to you: 'Boy, you haven't got your cap on.' You would tilt your head forward slightly and say: 'Oh yes, I have.'

The school has almost all gone. It's being engulfed by the hospital next door, which started off as the American military hospital – King's Mill, Sutton-in-Ashfield. The hospital is huge and it just keeps growing.

I don't ever worry that I might stop working for Sandy. He and I just keep plodding along. If I do then I do, if I don't then I don't. That's what makes the partnership so good. At any time either of us can say: 'I'm fed up with our arrangement'.

If I did stop working for him it would represent a considerable loss of income. But so what? It wouldn't be the end of the world. Something else will turn up. The house is paid for and everything in it. I pay into a pension scheme. Tournament golfers are in the same category as trapeze artists and deep-sea divers and can draw their pensions at forty. Mine matures when

I'm sixty. As I've said before, they can't take away from me the memories of all the places I've been to and seen, and all the things I've done. One door closes and another one opens. That's life. Nobody is indispensable.

I don't know whether I'd carry on caddying if I stopped working for Sandy. Pete Coleman has caddied for Langer and Seve and Norman, and when Langer isn't playing he doesn't try and get another bag. He's finding it hard. He probably looks at it as a come down to caddie for anybody else and he can't face that. I'd probably feel the same if I stopped working for Sandy. But needs must if the devil drives.

Saturday 6 and Sunday 7 August
Sandy finished sixth, rounds of 70, 67, 69 and 69, and was overshadowed by Peter Baker, who went on to win by getting eagles on the 18th, the 72nd, and then the 18th again in a play-off with Faldo.

At Home

Thursday 11 to Monday 15 August
I watched the edited highlights of the US PGA on television. As usual I looked to see who's caddying for who. I saw in the papers this week that Sandy got the anticipated pasting for not going to it, but nobody got it right about why he didn't go. But his feelings were such that when earlier in the year his sister asked him for a date when he would be free to attend her wedding he suggested 13 August.

After winning four tournaments at the beginning of the year and being in contention for so many more there's got to be a reaction, a time when you say: 'I've had enough. I want to be at home.' The only result that was any good to him was winning. And what's still within his grasp is the US money list. He wants to win it this year. If he'd gone to the PGA it would have helped him but only if he'd made the cut. He didn't want to go all that way and miss the cut, which was a real possibility.

Seve said recently: 'My real goal is to win at least once the US Masters, US Open, Open and US PGA. That's why I want to play in the US a lot next year to prepare properly. It is impossible just to fly over there and *expect* to win.'

Sandy is playing in the World Series. There are only forty-four in that and if you play anything like decent you can get a substantial amount of money and you don't have to worry about a cut. Also there's not the hullabaloo of major tournaments.

Sandy has been looking around for another car. He has ordered a 535 BMW like he had had before. Then, his family consisted of himself, Christine and their older boy, and for the three of them the BMW was big enough. Then they had another child and couldn't get everybody plus their golf luggage in the car. So he got a Mercedes to transport the family and a Porsche to run around in. When Christine left him and took the children he didn't need two cars. So he sold the Mercedes and then found that the Porsche was too small to get all the gear in. So that's why he has been looking for a BMW.

You can't say too much about Faldo's record through the summer. Second in the US Open. Came straight back and won the French, eagling the last hole to win. Then he went to Monte Carlo and finished sixth. He was third in the Open Championship, second in the Benson & Hedges having been beaten by two eagles. He then went to the US PGA and finished fourth and came straight back to the Irish and finished second. It's incredible. Yet somebody just turned round to me and said: 'But he's only won one.'

That reminds me of a mixed gruesomes (foursomes) story. A husband and wife were playing together. On the first hole the husband hit it 250 yards down the middle and left his wife with an eight-iron shot to the green, which she hit ten yards. The husband hit a wedge to three feet. The wife's putt was left short and her husband tapped it in. 'That's not very good, getting a five on a short par four', said the husband on the way to the next tee. So she said to him: 'Well, you had three of them.'

Carroll's Irish Open, Portmarnock, Dublin

Tuesday 16 August
Flew from East Midlands to Dublin and got a great view of

north Wales going over. Coming in to land you fly over the course at Portmarnock so you can see Ireland's eye, Howth Head, Portmarnock, Malahide and Dublin Bay.

D. J. Russell, Martin Poxon and Peter Baker were all flying in from Birmingham after me and so I waited for them and then courtesy cars took us to the house D. J. had rented 1½ miles from the course. They had all travelled in jeans and went upstairs to change into golf clothes. Martin Poxon opened his luggage and said: 'This is not my case.' It was full of ladies' underwear. The owner of the suitcase and Martin had arrived at Dublin airport with identical brand new suitcases with no labels on. I lent him a shirt and he borrowed a pair of D.J.'s trousers.

He played a practice round with Woosie and Baker and they had quite a crowd following them. Poxon was embarrassed because D.J.'s trousers were so much bigger they made him look like the Slimmer of the Month. He got the case back eventually with a nice note from this lady saying: 'Sorry about the mix-up. Shame the nightie didn't fit.' This will teach us to use labels in future.

The story of the mixed suitcases got into the Irish papers, which cheered Martin up. It was the best press he had had all year. Notoriety at last.

Wednesday 17 August
The pro-am for the Carrolls is different from other pro-ams. Initially 260 golf clubs go through three qualifying stages and end up with twenty-seven teams that play at Portmarnock. Sandy played with County Wicklow who donated a sweater, which I copped for. The format was the best two balls of the four to count but on the fourth tee Sandy was still trying to explain to one of the amateurs that it wasn't individual stableford. His famous patience was nearing its limit.

Thursday 18 to Sunday 21 August
Portmarnock is set on a peninsula with the sea on one side and a channel on the other. Years ago, when the tide was in, the only way in was by boat across from the mainland. When the tide's out you can still walk across and on the Sunday afternoon

people were walking across the mud flats with the Garda chasing them. We always have a good time in Dublin, drink a lot of Guinness. Have the last pint as we're getting on to the plane and pass it back down.

Met Dr Kevin O'Flanagan, the official doctor to the Irish team, who is a member at Portmarnock. He'd been at Muirfield Village for the Ryder Cup. Also met Renée and Michael Flannery, who I used to stay with. They live just up the road from Portmarnock. I saw the Halpins again – Dominic used to play professional football for Fulham years ago – and his daughters Anne and the gorgeous Jacqueline.

Then there's Jerry Kelly, who has been starting this tournament since 1975. I think he works for Dunlop. His style of starting is to say: 'This is match number 21, Jeff Hawkes of South Africa, Jerry Haas of the United States, Mike Clayton of Australia. Jeff Hawkes has the honour.' They all have their own ways, the announcers. The man at the Masters sits at the table and says 'Fore please, Jack Nicklaus now driving.' He nods off for a while, then says: 'Fore please, Sandy Lyle now driving.' That's the Masters. Ivor Robson is always spot on, very polished.

Sandy finished tied 17th. Had a bad last round of 77. The weather had started off OK but it got windier and windier as the week went on. By Sunday it was very strong.

There were the usual Irish stories. There's a little cabin for the caddies and a fellow called Wally giving out the sandwiches. He had the door and the window open and the wind was coming in through the window. He says: 'It's too windy in here,' and so he closes the door as if to stop it going out again.

I'm measuring the course with a wheel and a little old fellow with a cap looks at the wheel, looks at me, looks at the yardage book in which I'm writing everything down. 'That's fine,' he says when I've explained what I write in my book. 'But how do you know which way the wind is blowing?'

I said: 'You look at the flag on the top of the clubhouse and that tells you.'

He frowns and then says: 'But how do you know which way the wind's blowing tomorrow?'

NEC World Series of Golf, Firestone CC, Akron, Ohio

Monday 22 to Monday 29 August

Flew down to London airport and met Sandy in the executive lounge with David Feherty and Paul Way. All *en route* to the World Series in Akron, Ohio. Also met two gentlemen who were on their way to represent Jersey in the world seniors' championship in Colorado Springs. I later discovered the three Rey brothers from Crans were playing there as well.

I checked my luggage through to Pittsburgh at East Midlands airport. At Terminal One at Heathrow there's a BA desk and I always go there to get my seat allocation rather than have to queue up at Terminal Four. I asked for a centre aisle seat but was told all those seats had gone and that there was only a window seat left. I said fine.

In the executive lounge I had a coffee and a couple of Tia Marias to fortify the over-forties, and strolled down to the check-in desk. Every one was going through all right until I got there. Then the stewardess picked up my boarding card, typed on her computer and my heart sank. What's happening now, I thought to myself?

Then she said: 'We've upgraded you to club class.'

I said: 'Thank you very much, you're doing a fine job. By the way, how did you manage that?'

She replied: 'Because you're a member of BA's Executive Club.' At Terminal One I had given them my Club card just to see if it made any difference. Obviously it does – sometimes.

Paul Way was two or three places behind me in the queue and he asked if he could be upgraded, too. On the plane I looked around and thought to myself: 'This is great. I can work on the diary, read a book and there's plenty of space.' Then Way-Way comes over and says: 'They won't upgrade me. How much do you want for that seat?'

'I've never been upgraded before. I think I ought to see what it's like.'

He says: 'I'll give you a £100 if you'll change seats.'

I thought to myself: if it's worth £100 I'll stay here. So I declined his offer.

The plane was an old Lockheed 10-11 Tristar, which I used

to work on at Rolls-Royce in the late 1960s. It brought back old memories. The prototype flew over Derby and then Hucknall and we all turned out to watch it. They used to call it the whisper liner because it was so quiet. It had tin foil honeycomb sections around the engines to deaden the noise.

I stayed with Sandy in the Hilton Hotel in downtown Akron. It was converted from the old Quaker Oats factory and the round grain silos had been turned into rooms. So the rooms were circular. I've never stayed in a round room before. The bathroom was built into one quarter of the room.

The whole place was known as Quaker Square and had been converted into shops, restaurants, amusement centres and the like. I bought a mug for Hilary that said on it: 'I'm the one your mother always warned you about.' There was a place to have your photograph taken dressed up in Quaker gear or with a cardboard cut-out of President Reagan or Chicago gangsters with machine guns. Across the road, in what they called The Depot, was an engine, a real locomotive with a footplate, and inside was the most fantastic model railway. You walked to the middle of it and a sign said: 'Press me and I'll start.' Fascinating. All around the room were model engines and carriages behind glass cases.

Akron grew up around the Firestone factory. Firestone owned the course and the factory where they made tyres is still there but it's just their offices now. The tournament is sponsored by the Nippon Electric Corporation and has been renamed the NEC World Series of Golf. I can think of at least two other tournaments on the US circuit that are sponsored by Japanese companies. Is this another reason, we ask ourselves, why Tommy Nakajima and Isao Aoki don't always play fifteen tournaments in the US and never lose their cards?

I can remember when they started the World Series in 1962. Before that they had a tournament there called the Rubber City Open, believe it or not, and the first prize was $2800. They had press cuttings of old tournaments pasted in cases on the wall. I went to the World Series in 1978 with Seve who had qualified because he was leading the European order of merit at the designated time. It was the first tournament I had ever been to in the US. The south course is 7,100 yards, par 70. Enormous.

When we got there now, Sandy was a bit put out because he found that he was third on the money list. A week or so ago he'd been top and now he's $60,000 behind Joey Sindelar and $30,000 or so behind Chip Beck.

Off early in the pro-am. There was a Japanese gentleman with an unpronounceable name in the team so Sandy referred to him as Made in Japan.

Golf Digest had an experiment on the practice ground. They had two scales and asked golfers to put one foot in each scale and swing with a wood and an iron to show how much weight was actually transferred from one foot to the other. Sandy tried it. They recorded it all on computers and are going to publish the results. I took this opportunity to get the bag weighed. Fully loaded with two sets of waterproofs, two sweaters as well as all the clubs, it weighed 37 lb. It turned out to be the second heaviest of all the bags that were weighed.

Angus McNair is still working in the locker-room. He was born in Glasgow eighty-three years ago. Used to live in the same street as Willie Aitchison. Got married last month. I remembered him from my last visit and I had thought to myself: 'He must have retired by now, if he's still alive.' But there he was, fit as a fiddle.

Sandy put the Ballard harness on Paul Way and got him practising using it. He looked as though he'd taken to it and he's swinging a lot better. His game's not come together yet but at least it has given him something to work on. It's no good just standing on the practice ground and hitting ball after ball. All that is doing is practising your faults. You need a direction to go in. Before he started using the harness Sandy never had a proper direction, not something positive to practice. These days he spends 50 per cent of his time on the practice ground at a tournament giving other players lessons.

Sandy had a remarkable first round in the tournament. Bogied the first three holes. Then we reach the tough holes. He had a chip and a putt at the fourth for a par. A full-blooded shank with a six iron on the fifth tee, but saved himself with a pitch and a putt. Chip and a putt at the next. Good two putt at the seventh for a par. Par at the eighth. Hit a drive straight left at the 9th and it rebounded off a spectator's back on to the fairway and he made birdie from there. Holed from off the green for a birdie on the 10th. Four foot putt for a birdie on the 11th, a short par four. Then he chipped in on the 12th and parred in for a 69.

He was playing with Curtis Strange who started like a train and finished up so frustrated he threw his putter away at one hole.

Jeff Sluman's first shot in public since he won the US PGA was a stone-cold top from the first tee. It went all of sixty yards. It took him three shots to get past Mark McCumber's drive. Welcome back, he said to himself: 'I'm down to earth again.'

So that was the first day, Sandy shanking, Curtis throwing his putter away in disgust and Sluman topping his opening drive. Three champions of 1988.

Friday 26 to Monday 29 August
Sandy shot a good 67 and two frustrating 71s. He finished fifth and won $36,000. He was six under par after eight holes on the last day and five under played off. In the end Mike Reid, the shortest hitter on the US tour, won on the longest course the pros play all year by beating Tom Watson.

We were due to catch a plane at 6.40 that night from Akron to Cincinnati to connect with the London flight but there was a one-hour rain delay during the last round and that meant that we missed it and had to stay another night. Got to Heathrow at 9 o'clock Monday evening and stayed at Lyle Towers.

Ebel European Masters, Crans, Switzerland

Tuesday 30 August
Nearly missed the flight to Geneva because we got stuck in traffic on the M4. I couldn't live down here and face this traffic every day. I'd go mad. Left Sandy's house just after 8 a.m. and the flight went at 10.30. The journey shouldn't have taken more than half an hour. In fact, we only got to the airport at gone half-past nine.

My case came off the plane all right in Geneva but Hilary's didn't. I expect things like this to happen because I travel a lot, but for anybody going on their holidays it's very upsetting. Caught the Traveleads coach from Geneva to Crans to stay at L'Etrier hotel.

Here we are in the mountains again. We brought an end to the good weather, but then we always do. We did that in the US last week. 'You should have been here last week,' they all said. The thing about Crans is that the shops don't put prices on the goods in their window. If you want to know how much an item is, you can't afford it.

9

31 August–18 September

A week in the Alps – Caddies' gathering
at Sunningdale – Chasing Seve in Paris

Wednesday 31 August
In the pro-am we played with Pirmin Zurbriggen, the Swiss skier. They call him the Seve Ballesteros of the skiing world. He'd won three medals on these very slopes above the course at Crans in the 1987 world championships.

The third hole is a short hole, 180 yards, and it crosses a road. You have to be careful because there's cars and lorries whizzing up and down. In the pro-am last year Zurbriggen sliced his tee shot at this hole. There was a fellow coming up the road in an open-top car and the ball finished up in the back seat. All the fellow did was slow down when he reached Pirmin and hand him his ball back.

Zurbriggen looked quite a thin, wiry sort of bloke with fair hair and his eyes seemed sunk back in his head. Mac O'Grady eyes. He seemed very keen on golf. He can't have much time to play. So long as he enjoys it, that's the main thing. Same as everybody else. For an 18-handicapper he seemed reasonable, not too awkward. He could hit the ball, get it airborne. It's an experience to hit a ball up there. It just takes off on its own without any effort. It soars off and of course the mountains make it look as though it's going a lot further than it really is.

Hilary was in a state today because nothing seemed to be happening about her suitcase and nobody seemed bothered about it. It finally turned up in Crans at six o'clock tonight.

Thursday 1 September
Sandy had a terrible first round, a 76. It was windy but you

should still have been able to get round in a score. It was his third tournament in a row and by rights he should have been running into form, but he wasn't.

A meeting of the European Tour Caddies' Association. The main topic of discussion dated back to the Open when John Davidson (the Prof) wrote to the R & A in his capacity as secretary of ETCA and said now that we had a proper association it was high time we had tickets for the week instead of having to beg for them as we had at Muirfield. Why should we have to pay £10 or £15 as we're supposed to have been doing over the years?

We got two letters back, one from Michael Bonallack, secretary of the R & A, and one from the club. They said that we could have tickets for the week, car park stickers for those that need them, packed lunches every day and a small Portakabin for our use. We were to be allowed in the locker-room with our player to help him unpack his tackle and sort out his clubs and balls every day. We were warned that if anybody was found selling tickets that would be the end of it all. Here's a package, get on with it.

This is a major breakthrough for us. We like running our own affairs – that's one of the reasons why we've set up this association.

John Davidson was appointed caddie-master by the R & A. Another caddie, Rod Stewart we call him because he looks exactly like the singer, sat in the Portakabin all week because he didn't have a bag. We had a collection for him and raised £150. Also a television appeared, a cut-rate, hired tv that cost us £60. The ETCA paid by cheque for the tv. Then it leaked out that the R & A had paid £300 for the caddie-masters who had split the money between them without telling anyone.

When we heard this, a meeting was held at York and a sub-committee was set up to ask the relevant questions. It gave us its report in Switzerland. As a result it was suggested that the £60 to pay the television be taken out of the £300 from the R & A and the remainder be split as the committee saw fit. Then there was a motion of no confidence in the secretary, who didn't try and justify his action. So he was voted out, 18–14. We don't have a secretary now. That was one of the reasons why I voted to keep John Davidson – because I knew we'd have trouble finding a successor.

It was a difficult meeting. Pete Newby, a big lad from Liverpool who caddies for Peter Baker, was chairman and he did a helluva good job.

Friday 2 September

We're four over par, right up against the cut, which looks like being one under. The weather got colder and you could see the snow line coming down the mountains.

As it happened there was a rain delay and a fog delay and so we never started playing our second round until four o'clock. We stood in the tent on the first tee at half-past three and couldn't see a thing. I thought to myself: 'We'll never finish tonight.' Then suddenly the clouds lifted and off we went. Three under par for the first nine, which is at least giving it a chance. We were playing with José-Maria Olazabal and Mark McNulty who are both struggling. They need birdies to make the cut, too. It's getting darker but we look as though we're going to get somewhere near finished.

The holes you expect to birdie on the back nine at Crans are 14, 15, 16, 17 and 18, two par 5s and three short par 4s. On the 14th tee Sandy three-putts for a 6. Olazabal fails to make birdie and so does McNulty. Sandy is now three over par and Olazabal two over. We are standing on the 15th tee at the bottom of the hill in the gathering dark, Olazabal sitting on his bag with his head in his hands, Sandy staring out over the mountains looking as though he wished he could jump off them, and Mark McNulty says: 'What's the cut going to be?'

I said: 'There were seventy-two under par when we started out.'

'I thought the cut was going to be level par,' says McNulty.

'Well,' I said, 'if you can't beat par on this course you don't deserve to play at the weekend, none of you.'

At that Olazabal's head jerked up. Sandy turns round and says: 'I'd like to see you do it.'

'I'm not playing,' I said. 'You three are world-class golfers and you know in your own minds that if you can't break par here you don't deserve to make the cut.'

With that Olazabal jumps up and shouts: 'Yeah, we are the best in the world.'

Both he and Sandy birdie 15, the long one up the hill, 16, the short par four, and then Sandy holes a curler on 17 for another birdie and so does Olazabal. Sandy is now one under, Olazabal two under par.

We go up the last virtually in the dark, just able to see the clubhouse lights. Sandy and Olazabal need fours because we don't know for sure what the cut is going to be. Sandy hit a one iron and a wedge to the back of the green, putted up and tapped in for a par. But Olazabal had to hole about a four-footer for his par.

Michael Haarer, the tournament administrator, had come on to the 18th tee and given us the option of stopping or coming back in the morning. We said we didn't want to come back in the morning, thank you very much. You don't want to have to go back early the next morning to play one hole, specially if you miss the cut. That's the pits of the earth, that is. When you've been out in the gathering dark your eyes get adjusted to it. If you'd walked out on to the 18th tee from the clubhouse it would have seemed a lot darker than it did to us, having played all the way round.

Made the cut on the line. Sam Torrance did a similar thing. He had three birdies at the death on the other nine holes to make the cut, but McNulty missed.

Saturday 3 and Sunday 4 September
Sandy was first off with Steen Tinning and shot 35 on the front nine and 30 on the back nine, 65. We got down to the course at 7.15 a.m. and the temperature on Alex Sports shop said six degrees. Nobody kicking about, of course. We couldn't even get in the pro's shop to hit a few balls in the net. So Sandy did a few stretching exercises instead. The net in the pro's shop is Sandy's practice ground in Switzerland. He doesn't want to go down to the far end of the course and hit balls into that quarry. So he hits a few in the net, does a bit of chipping and some putting and that's it.

He was under four trees in his last round and all he could do was just chip out but he got par every time. Finished with a 69 to come twentieth equal. Afterwards I went back to the hotel and me and Hilary spent the afternoon around the swimming-pool. The weather had warmed up by then.

It represents just about the best value on tour, this week in Switzerland. We told our friend Tony Sher about it and he drove all the way up from Marbella and had a great time with us. He's used to living in places like Crans. He has homes in Boca Raton in the US and Sotogrande in Spain.

But for me a week is quite long enough. I always feel that a week in Crans is like eating too many chocolates or having too much sugar in your tea. It's too rich. It's a fantastic place to go to but you can have too much of a good thing.

At Home

Monday 5 September
Three planes landed at Heathrow in quick succession and the number of people coming through Terminal Two had to be seen to be believed! Had to fight our way out. Get me home, get me back to the East Midlands airport. Never any crowds there.

Drove home, arrived about 5.30 p.m. to find the gas was off. We were having our gas meter moved from the side of the fireplace in our front room to the outside of the house. For the workmen to be able to get in while we were in Switzerland we'd left the key with Mrs Unwin, the lady next door. They'd come last Wednesday to start work and a different crew came the next day. They didn't know where the key was and so couldn't get in and had left a card saying: 'Sorry you weren't in when we called, please make an appointment for a week's time.'

Hilary rang up. They arrived quite soon after that!

Panasonic European Open, Sunningdale, Berkshire

Tuesday 6 September
Drove down to London for the European Open and stayed with the Walkers at Twyford. Far too much traffic in this part

of the world (Sunningdale, near London airport) and the house prices are absolutely ridiculous. I first went to Sunningdale in 1963 for the old Bowmaker tournament before the Open. Caddied for David Talbot. The course hasn't changed much. There are one or two new tees and bunkers. It was a renowned course then and it's a renowned course now.

Sunningdale is the last remaining club where tour caddies can gather for the winter and know they'll get work. There was a nucleus of them at Southport at one time because there was plenty of work at Birkdale, Southport & Ainsdale, Formby, Hillside, and there was Wentworth and Sunningdale and the Berkshire. But Sunningdale is the only one left where you're guaranteed to see all the old familiar faces of the caddies.

There's the celebrated Ron Mullins, of course. He puts the top hat and tails on and goes in the enclosure at Ascot with Robert Sangster and company. He's been caddying at Sunningdale since God were a lad. Ginger Finch (who caddied for Dave Thomas), Seamus (for Christy O'Connor) and David Morgan (for Tommy Horton) are all there. Norman Stone (for Neil Coles) works in the clubhouse at Sunningdale now. Belfast Billy, one of the old tour regulars, is another. Snowball (for Michael King), who is the son of the famous Blondie (for Kel Nagle), is still around, and so is Blondie. I saw him not long ago.

Times have changed since Arthur Lees used to be the pro at the club. The pro's shop used to resemble a betting shop in those days and the famous old caddie-master was Jimmy Sheridan. The pro is Keith Maxwell, a real gentleman, a nice quiet Scot. He was assistant to Clive Clark and deservedly got the job when Clive left.

There's a canteen for the caddies just past the pro's shop, where you can get lunch, hot meals, tea, snacks. The kitchen had been renovated since I was last there for the European Open in 1986.

Behind the 18th green is the perfectly symmetrical oak tree, the club's symbol. The other thing we like at Sunningdale is the halfway hut, behind the 10th of the Old Course and the 9th of the New. It serves bangers, barley water and sandwiches, Mars bars, tea and coffee. A little gold mine, that is. It even serves champagne. Somebody asked the man behind the counter how many sausage sandwiches he sold during the week of the European Open and he said 8,236. It's good food. I prefer the sausages in brown bread.

This year there was a huge tented village. The tournaments are getting very corporate-minded with all those hospitality suites. It's getting so that the ordinary spectator can't see the last hole because of the corporate tents and the like. It was like that at York, too, and this is a shame because ordinary club golfers go and watch the tournament at York.

I had a drink of cider in the tented village. Hadn't had one for years. It was very refreshing. It was a hot week for a change. The Benson & Hedges and this one have been the only two nice weeks we've had in England all year.

Wednesday 7 September

Pro-am. One of the gentlemen in Sandy's team was Raghu Mody, captain of the Royal Calcutta Golf Club. Sandy called him M1 because he was a million-to-one when playing golf.

Terry Shingler and his wife were watching us. Terry is an old friend of Sandy's from his amateur days. He won the English Amateur in 1977 and still plays off scratch or one at Blackwell. It turned out that he and Raghu Mody were both in the same line of business: both work for Ferodo brakes.

Thursday 8 and Friday 9 September

Sandy shot 69 and 65, the latter including two eagles. He's not had a very good record at Sunningdale in the past. I think that when he plays Sunningdale or Wentworth, courses he knows well, he gets too aware of the trouble spots and he gets defensive. As he puts it, he can't let his hair down.

This week he got another one iron, about the fifth of the year. The one he's been using for the last few months wasn't working very well. He hit a load of bad shots with it at the World Series and they probably cost him the tournament. Then he found out that the decision on the square grooves won't be made until the end of next year, 1989, so square grooves are going to be legal for another year. It seems like bureaucracy is always determined to follow you around and bugger you about.

The first man Sandy saw at Sunningdale this week was Glen Batkin of Ping, and so he asked if he could have a one iron similar to the one he'd had before. It so happend that Glen had one in the boot of his car which Ronan Rafferty had just rejected, so he gave it to Sandy.

Sandy had a very hot ball in the first round. It flew at least twenty yards further through the air than it should have done. That's a big disadvantage because you can't judge it. On the 13th Sandy's shot went over the back of the green. Sandy said he thought that was just a flier. On the 14th he was in the rough and so he knew the ball was going to fly, anyway. On the 15th he hit a two iron very low. It landed in the middle of the green and just kept going over the back. He didn't hit his second shot very well on the 16th so though we suspected there was something funny about the ball we weren't sure.

The conclusive evidence came on the 17th. We had 140 yards to the flag and the ball lay on hard pan (hard, bare earth) so there was no danger of a flier. Sandy's shot carried over the green. It must have gone 155 yards through the air with a nine iron.

Sandy turned to me and asked: 'Are you sure of the distance?'

I said: 'Let's check it.' We went to the middle of the fairway, both paced it off and both came up with the same yardage – 120 to the front of the green. I've never come across a rogue ball like this one before.

On the Friday Sandy shot a 65 including two eagles in the morning. In the afternoon he had a barbecue at Lyle Towers with Woosie, Wobbly, Tony Sher and Lyle major and Lyle minor in attendance. Nice spontaneous afternoon.

Saturday 10 and Sunday 11 September
Hilary came down in the morning with her two friends from the golf club at home, Chris and Ken Gibson, policeman and policewoman from Mansfield. They instantly recognized the old car park attendant, a traffic warden in Mansfield who does a few golf tournaments each year. They were quite overawed by the big houses, the trees, the general area.

Jim Thorpe and Calvin Peete were there as well as Gary Koch. We played with Koch the first two rounds. He had won the Panasonic tournament in Las Vegas in the US so I suppose there was some justification in him playing here. But I think it was a complete waste of money for the others to be invited. What's the point in inviting American has-beens? We've got better players in Europe than they have in the US anyway.

Woosnam said at the barbecue: 'I wasn't paid a penny to play here this week so I'm going to take it out on their ribs.' It got Woosie all fired up. Left them for dead, he did, the old Woosie. Won the tournament, 20 under par. Sandy shot 67 and then a 65 and finished third.

It was a real good event. Nice weather, good competition, marvellous scoring. Because the weather was so good we had a great view of Concorde as she flew over every day.

Arrived home before 8 p.m. There were probably edited highlights on television but I didn't watch them. I liked to watch the Ryder Cup and the US Masters on video and Hilary also videoed the Dunhill Masters, but I watched it with very little interest even though Sandy won. My general reaction is: 'I saw enough of this the first time. What do I want to go through it again for?'

Lancôme Trophy, St Nom-la-Bretèche, Paris

Tuesday 13 September
Billy Foster, who caddies for Gordon Brand Jr, lives at Keighley and he picked me up on the way to the East Midlands airport. There were about eight of us from the tour on the plane, players and caddies.

Landed at Charles de Gaulle. Couldn't see any courtesy cars as last year so took public transport. The train service in France is excellent. Billy and myself bought tickets to Versailles, got on a train to Paris and changed at St Michel. Some of their trains are like double-decker buses, two-tier coaches. It was spot on time and very smooth-running and comfortable.

Arrived in Versailles at 5 p.m., and then it was only two minutes walk to the hotel, the Des Tournelles. Stayed in the same room – 31 – and the same bed as last year. Pete Coleman always asks for the same room. They've patched up the water leak from last year, put new wallpaper up.

This week I have the distinction in a room of three caddies of being the youngest. Big Brian is just fifty and Coleman is a year older than me – forty-six. Coleman is always good for a laugh. He can make even his troubles sound funny. Seve says: 'Every time I see Pete I have to smile.'

Down to the restaurant Athos every night. We have to get in there for 7.15 because there's only one lady serving, Monique – we've found out her name after about ten years of going there – and her mother is in the kitchen. We order Salad Athos, which is a speciality of the house with egg mayonnaise, tuna fish and tomatoes; boeuf bourgignon, pommes frites and petits pois; and the old vin rouge. Merci, madame. Every time she sees us she says: 'Ah, the Lancôme tournament.' Big snag is it never opens on a Saturday night. I went through the card one night. All you can eat and drink in a Parisian atmosphere for 81 francs.

Wednesday 14 September
Found out we're fairly early in the pro-am, 8.20. Can't get any breakfast in our hotel at half-past six so down to the bus station café at 6.25. Bonjour, monsieur. Café au lait grand, avec un croissant, s'il vous plait.

Thing that strikes us when we go abroad is that everything seems very expensive. Whichever country we go to we seem to be paying the earth, and the locals never seem to pay at all. We're convinced that we're financing them. They never get accused of putting any money on the counter.

Get to the St Nom-la-Bretèche course and there's Monsieur Richard Ferran, the caddie-master, who's been there for thirty-eight years, and the old locker-room attendant Gaspar. He gives me a locker and a combination lock the number of which has to be written in my yardage book every year. Same old faces everywhere. Rene Léfèbvre, the commissaire (head of the marshals), Patrice Galitzine, the starter. He goes into the usual long introductions about the players telling how many birdies and how many bogies they have had. He rattles on for ages about each player. He always calls Sandy le grand Alexander. Then when he stops talking the players turn round to him and say: 'Can we go now?'

The Japanese lady was there again, carrying her husband's ashes around in an urn while she played in the pro-am. The old apple trees between the 9th and the 18th are still there. Had to ask the locals which are the best apples to pick. Someone saw a spectator climb up the tree, open an umbrella and wave it round to knock down the apples.

Sandy got a new shaft for his sand iron, collected two dozen DDH HT balls from Mike Smith, the Dunlop rep, and off we went out on to the course. It has well-spaced out villas dotted on the wooded hillsides. Halfway up the 17th hole on the left is the Lacoste village. The weather vane is an alligator, like the symbol on their shirts.

Spectators turn out like it was a fashion parade every day. The clubhouse used to be a farm for the Palace at Versailles and the buildings form three sides of a rectangle. In the middle there's a lovely lawn which is now used as a putting green. There's a duck pond too. We caddies get a roll and a can of beer when we come off the course and halfway through the roll my jaws start aching so I go and feed the rest of it to the ducks. They can really move across the water when there's a bit of bread in it for them. It's the most picturesque clubhouse I've seen on the Continent.

Thursday 15 and Friday 16 September
Sandy had a 75. Missed only one fairway, and that wasn't bad. He just couldn't get on with his putter. Woosnam was putting well and I noticed that the triangle of his shoulders, arms and hands all moved. But Sandy was off line. So I said to him: 'Line yourself up. Keep your chest and shoulders parallel to the line of the putt.' I said it to him two or three times. He didn't want to take any notice. He wasn't very inspired.

The next day was a complete reversal. He played virtually the same off the tee yet shot a 63, a new course record. What a difference a change in attitude makes! Today he played as though he meant it. He's in line for a Rolex watch for the lowest round of the week.

Played with Chris Moody and McNulty. Sandy birdied the 11th, 12th and 13th but was still six shots behind Seve, so that was it really. Round in 68.

Packed the case on Sunday morning. Wobbly had arranged for Woosnam's courtesy car to come round and take us to the players' hotel where we got a lift to the course from Mark Mouland. So we only had to hump the case a short distance upstairs to the locker-room. I was reading a paper when Seve came in and so we sat there side by side reading the papers.

We were playing with Seve and Olazabal in the last round and Seve was struggling to concentrate, to keep his momentum. It's hard to motivate yourself when you've got a big lead. Olazabal was trying hard to make an impression but he couldn't. Sandy was playing erratically. Birdied the first, hit a flyer over the second with a sand iron and bogied that. Then birdie, bogey, birdie and bogey.

Seve was obviously beyond our reach. Olazabal was firmly in control of second place and Greg Norman shot a good score to get to six under par. Sandy was seven under par with three to play. Three easy holes. The 16th is an eight iron. He hits it to the right into a bunker. It's plugged and he has to come out away from the flag and does well to two putt. Didn't have a very good chance for a birdie on the 17th and on the 18th he drove into the left rough, where you shouldn't go because the water is on the left around the green. So he played to the right of the green, went into a bunker, came out of there maybe thirty feet from the pin and holed it for a four to share third place with Greg.

When you've worked all week and finished badly it's like a waste of effort, as it was in the Open. He played very reasonably all week and then dropped three shots on the last two holes and they cost him £20,000. It's not the money so much as pride of performance.

Then Ronan Rafferty birdied four out of the last six holes for a 63 to take the watch for the week's best round because he had a better last six holes, even though Sandy had birdied the last three. Anyway, he won £22,500.

In the last round we had three South Africans in front of us –

Jeff Hawkes, John Bland and McNulty, and we stood waiting on every shot. Finally Seve got really impatient and on the 9th he told a PGA man and we never had to wait again. Seve said: 'I'd like to be a tournament director just once. I'd pinch some bottoms.'

They got moving in Switzerland on that second day when it was getting dark. They moved a lot faster then than they would have done otherwise. Why can't they do it all the time? There are certain golfers that are known to be slow. I think being slow is discourteous to the other golfers, inconsiderate. Everybody knows who they are but a £50 fine in a half-million pound tournament is no deterrent. The only real deterrent is to give a two-shot penalty but you've got to be a hard man to do that.

Back in the clubhouse I had a shower, a beer, and on the bus to the airport I got the *Telegraph* crossword puzzle out. I was immediately surrounded by David Llewellyn, D.J. and Mark James and we did it in about ten minutes. The *Telegraph* crossword is very much in evidence with golfers and caddies.

10

20 September–14 October

*More trouble with bibs – Uncovering
a fireplace – Sandy wins at Wentworth*

German Masters, Stuttgart, West Germany

Tuesday 20 to Sunday 25 September

Wobbly and I stayed in the Hotel Ruf in Pforzheim. The hotel
was good. It was next door to a beer cellar and nearby was a
nice restaurant. The lady who was serving took a liking to us. I
like German food and beer, and the language is quite close to
English as well. You can pick it up very fast just by staying
there. There was a train station just across the road from our
hotel where we could get English papers. Bus from right
outside the door to the golf course every morning. It was
altogether a very handy week for travelling. The bus at the
airport went straight to the hotel. Come Sunday I took my case
to the course and then the bus left at 4.15 p.m. for the airport.

I brought my yardage book from last year but just to make
sure I bought a book off Ian Wright so I can double check my
measurements. Apart from a few new bunkers the course hasn't
changed at all.

'It's the one week of the year when we have sensible
bunkers,' Sandy says. Bernhard Langer took a lot of the sand
out last year. People don't realize that if you put new sand in
the bunkers the ball will plug and then be uncontrollable. There
are good rakes at Stuttgart, too. This is not always the case. In
Ireland the other week we had ordinary garden rakes with four
long prongs. They were hopeless. You couldn't make a proper
surface with them and we were slow using them because they

were so inadequate. Bunker rakes should be about $2\frac{1}{2}$ to 3 ft wide with small prongs so that you can get an even surface when you've finished.

Bunker raking is an art, and a very important one for a caddie. If you don't do it properly the bloke behind will say: 'Who's been in this bunker? Whoever it was didn't do much of a job in cleaning it up.'

I don't like the course very much. It's too hilly. There isn't a flat hole in it. There are probably some good holes but it's a bit clayey underneath and it's hard on the feet. Also they let the branches of the trees grow too close to the ground. A lot of courses do the same thing. Branches should be no lower than three feet off the ground so you can get in, find your ball and chip it out and not get your eyes poked out while you're doing it. At Coxmoor, my club, the branches grow along the ground, the grass grows up and you finish up with a barbed wire entanglement. You cannot get in, find your ball, play it or anything. What's the point? It's like this too at St Nom-la-Bretèche near Paris, for just one example. Sandy is always campaigning about it. And I've been going on about it for so long at our course that they've done something about it. Some of the branches of the pine trees used to grow horizontally.

For the first time for ages there were plenty of jobs going for caddies. Normally it's hard to get a bag. The reason is several of the regular caddies didn't go. It was too expensive. If you're going to live anything like decently, it's a £400 week.

Sandy didn't play particularly well but he finished joint fourteenth on level par so it was respectable if not spectacular. He said he felt partially brain dead after competing in six tournaments in six countries in six weeks.

Last year in this tournament we were given overalls to wear but I didn't like them for reasons already mentioned. This year I noticed jackets hanging up and I thought we would be given those. However, it turned out they were the tops of overalls which we pulled over our heads. On the back there was a big patch of plastic carrying advertisements for Boss, American Express or Mercedes, the tournament's sponsors. On the front were two more plastic advertisements, one on each side of the chest. And on more plastic strips across both the front and the back of the bibs was the player's name. Everything was attached by strips of Velcro.

I did what I always do, I modified my bib. I got a pair of scissors, cut straight up the front, thereby making it into a jacket. And I took the big plastic patch off the back. A lot of the boys did the same. Andy Prodger suffers from asthma and they're asking him to go round a hilly course with a big piece of plastic on his back. You can't breathe with a thing like that on. It's one thing sweating, but at least the air can circulate. You don't want it kept in as if you're in a suit of armour. Last year, after three weeks in overalls (the Dunhill Cup, World Match-play and German Masters) I was ill. That's why we call it the pleurisy patch.

Before we started on the first morning Andy McFee approached me. 'Have you got a problem with the bibs?', he asked.

'Not any more,' I said. 'I've modified mine up the front and I've taken the big plastic advertisement off the back. I've got Sandy's name and the sponsors' names on show and I'm comfortable. Last year I got very ill at this tournament. A lot of the boys were the same. We had to wear overalls with these big plastic patches on them and we got very hot while climbing the hills in all sorts of weather.'

'That's fair enough,' Andy said. 'But you shouldn't have cut it up the front. I'm in charge of this tournament. Why didn't you come to me?'

I said: 'We've been telling the PGA for years. Four years ago Tony Gray assured us we'd have no more plastic to wear.'

'That may be so,' he said. 'You should put it in writing.'

'John Davidson did put it in writing this year after the fiasco at Gleneagles. It has been discussed with the PGA.'

'I don't know anything about it,' McFee said.

'That's your organization's fault, not ours,' I said.

By the end of the second day it was coming to a head. Four or five of us asked to meet Peter German who stages a dozen or so tournaments each year on behalf of IMG. We said to him: 'If we can get our message over to you then you can set the standard and other people will follow.'

I told Peter that in 1984 the German and Swiss Opens were

back-to-back, and each week we had plastic bibs to wear and each week was very hot and a lot of lads got ill. At the end of that year we were assured there'd be no more plastic bibs.

I said how at the skins game before this year's Volvo PGA at Wentworth they had given us a pair of overalls, a bib, and a sweatshirt. It was ridiculous. I asked: 'Do we have to wear all this?' Richard Hills and Ken Schofield assured us then that if we wore them that day there would be full and proper negotiations as to what we need wear in future. John Davidson wrote to the European Tour on behalf of the caddies as well.

At the Belgian Open in June the boys were given plastic bibs and they refused to wear them. The organizers had to fly out cotton ones for the Sunday.

We also told Peter German we were being exploited by being expected to wear advertising for nothing. He agreed but said we were considered to be an extension of our players and one of our functions was to carry the sponsors' logo.

Peter listened sympathetically to our points of view. He's a very obliging bloke. Then he asked: 'Just this week, keep the plastic patches on the bibs on the first tee at least and the last three holes, which are televised, because the sponsors are very upset.' We agreed.

That evening the Caddies' Association received a letter from Andy McFee more or less accusing us of not cooperating, undermining the tournament, premeditatedly setting out to make everybody not wear the bibs. (In fact it was left to individuals to make their own decision.) McFee said that if we didn't stop immediately our Association would no longer be recognized by the PGA. That letter didn't go down very well as you can imagine, but we understood that McFee was under a lot of pressure.

When you talk to people like tournament organizers you realize they have tough jobs to do. We appreciate that Peter and Andy are responsible fellows doing tough jobs. They're not trying to make fools out of us or trying to make us wear stupid things. They have a lot to consider. But what they might not realize is we're on their side. We're all in this game together. We hope that we can understand each other's point of view a little better in future. And the only way to do that is better communication with one another.

Soon after that, John O'Leary (chairman of the European Tour tournament committee) sent a message saying he wanted to meet a representative of ours. At ten o'clock on the Friday night there was a meeting in the sauna of the Goldene Pforte hotel between O'Leary and Mick Maull representing the Association. O'Leary said he was very concerned about the whole situation and that there had been mistakes made on both sides. He wasn't happy with the PGA. He said that such as myself who had cut their bibs were out of order, but he understood it was born out of frustration as much as anything else.

Incidentally, nobody has ever apologized to me for messing my clothes up, either by dye going through on to sweaters, shirts or trousers, or having plastic bibs that cut into my neck. Nobody has ever said sorry except Peter German who said he didn't realize that plastic on top of linen was just as bad as plastic on its own.

O'Leary said that the sponsors were very concerned because caddies for the players in the leading matches hadn't been wearing the proper advertisements. The outcome was he asked us to comply as much as possible for this week and he gave his word that next year things would be better. So we are looking forward to a lot of dialogue during the winter and results next year.

As a result, a notice was put on the board from the Caddies' Association: 'It's imperative that the plastic patches be worn at least on holes 1, 16, 17 and 18 and if possible all the way round.' The boys tried to comply.

The caddies will discuss it formally again during the Volvo Masters next month. The point is that getting all our committee men together at a particular time is tough because they don't always go to each tournament. And if some of them are off in the morning and some in the afternoon and vice versa you might not see them all week. And there's very few tournaments when the caddies are all staying in the same town.

The members of ETCA are grumbling, too. It's difficult to say to them: 'All right, you've voted a committee. Leave them alone. Not just for a week or two. In this case it has got to be for years before any real results will be seen. But you must leave them alone instead of interfering.'

As far as communication goes I've had a lot of experience at Rolls-Royce and a lot more in this game. Even at Coxmoor, my golf club, it's tough. I remember when an extension to the clubhouse was being built. The architect was a member and during the building he got so much stick off the members that he resigned. He was sick and tired of them making criticisms. It's always the same. People who see something being built can always do it better. It's starting it from the off that's tough.

Hopefully, it will get to a stage where we can turn up each week and not have to wear crappy clothes. The ETCA have barred jeans for the pro-am and the four days of a tournament. Practising putting and hitting balls on the practice grounds are all illegal and fineable offences. We're doing our bit. The European Tour should be doing theirs.

So much for the German Masters. I don't feel particularly tired but I am beginning to feel stale. It's been a long year. I've been to sixteen events in the US, and eleven in Europe. It'll total thirty-two by the end of the season and that's enough for any man. I'm really looking forward to the Match-play. It's a classic tournament. Match play is always good atmosphere. The Open championship and any match-play event, specially the one at Wentworth, are always good. I've got to keep my legs strong for thirty-six holes each day. I do this mainly by playing golf but I have done a little bit of running in the past. Just keep active. Plenty to do at home.

As we've got a bye into the second round of the Suntory next week it's going to be a good pay day even if we lose our first match. It's the old saying: 'We'll either win money or be home early.' What a great feeling to start a tournament with!

At Home

Tuesday 27 September
Ever since I can remember there's been a gas meter in the front room of our house, and years ago, before we had electricity, we had to put money into it not only to keep the fire going but also for the light. When the light started fading you would rush downstairs, try and find the meter and shove the money in. If

you missed the slot with your coin it would slip between the floor-boards. When we were taking the meter out this time I found seven or eight pennies beneath the floorboards, one with Queen Victoria on, a couple of shilling pieces and a two-shilling piece.

The fireplace used to be boarded up with an electric fire stuck in front. We removed the board and Brian Sibson, who does all the work for us, took out the old fireplace right back to the chimney, built in a gas fire and tiled it up. At the same time I wondered if I could get the paint off the fireplace itself. Two tins of paint stripper and three days later we had got through several layers of paint and through the transfers down to the black lead and found a slate fireplace, dated 1904. A great discovery. Since then I've found out how to treat it.

There were two fellows working in the front room: a plumber altering the gas pipes and Brian rebuilding the fireplace. Somebody came to the back door saying that the house at the bottom of our garden is going to be pebble-dashed and they wanted my shed moving because it was near their wall. So I had to go down the garden, cut the grass as quickly as I could and empty all the stuff out of the shed so they could move it. What a day that was!

Monday 3 October
At last got a game of golf in at Coxmoor. I hadn't played for two months so I was due a game. Played with the heavy gang on a beautiful afternoon and got thirty-four points. Never threatened to win anything, but I think scoring over thirty points in a stableford with the same ball all the way round is quite a feather in my cap.

Tuesday 4 October
Got down to Lyle Towers at about 7 p.m. ready for the Suntory World Match-play.

Suntory World Match-play Championship, Wentworth, Surrey

Wednesday 5 October
Pro-am day. Our team of amateurs were valued customers of

NEC (Nippon Electric Corporation) who invited them. I haven't talked before about the caddies for the amateurs in the pro-am. They aren't caddies at all. They are people who work with or for the amateur player and they're having a day out.

The expression over-caddying comes from the sort of caddies you see working for amateurs in a pro-am. They blast their player with so much information he doesn't know where the hell he is. An amateur in our group today holed a good putt on one green, about ten or twelve yards, and his caddie ranted on about it for three holes. Of course, he was biting Sandy's earhole all the way round as well and when he did stop talking Sandy turned to him and said: 'Have you shut up or have I gone deaf?' Hal Sutton once fired a caddie in the States for over-caddying. It's nearly always amateur caddies who over-caddie. I restrict unnecessary comments like 'Good shot' to about three a week.

When we were going down the 17th Sandy saw the sponsor's big sign up on the right of the fairway. It's one of only four or five the sponsors are allowed by the BBC to put around the course. Sandy's mind went back to 1982 when he played Nick Faldo and came back from the dead (six down after eighteen holes) to win. Faldo drove into the trees on the right of the 17th and was in there for ages. His lie was unplayable but because there was an advertising board in front of him he claimed line of sight relief and got it. That sign is always there for the Match-play so anybody who hits into the right-hand trees from the 17th tee can usually get relief.

When Sandy saw the sign now, he shook his head and said: 'There it is again. They never learn do they?'

As we were starting in the pro-am, John Jacobs (the noted golf teacher and past Ryder Cup captain) arrived. He is designing a new course at Wentworth. I saw him again at the end of our round and we started talking, 'He's hitting in to out, of course,' Jacobs said. And I said: 'I'm glad you've said that because he wants a lesson from you.' So we got in the Range Rover, went up to the second tee on the East course, which they are using for practising this year, and John gave Sandy a lesson. He said Sandy had been swinging in to out which caused the variation in distances he'd been suffering from for the last three months. It also explained why Sandy hadn't been taking any divots and why he had shanked occasionally.

He tried to get Sandy to hit out to in and think he was going to fade the ball, which is beginning to straighten up Sandy's swing.

'I come here quite a lot because I'm working on the South course,' Jacobs said to Sandy. 'Any time you're at home and want some help don't hesitate to ring me.' Sandy is going to do that in the off-season. He and Bernard Gallacher are going to get together with Jacobs and do some work. Gallacher is a good fellow. I get on all right with him. Sandy says he tries to be a snob but you can't be a snob with Sandy.

Tonight went round with Judy Simpson, the cook at Lyle's house who was provided by the organizers of the World Match-play, to Ian Woosnam's house and Nino, the cook there, made dinner for Wobbly, Judy and me. Ian and Sandy had gone to an official dinner given by the sponsors. When Woosie came back he gave me a copy of his book *Ian Woosnam's Golf Masterpieces*. Sandy has just given me the US Masters book for this year so I'm getting quite a collection.

I'll treasure the Masters book along with another one about the same event called *The First 41 Years*. It came out in 1979. That was the first year I went, so I bought the book and got some signatures in it. It's all adding to my memorabilia of the Masters.

Thursday 6 October
Sandy likes to play practice rounds with Seve because, as he puts it, Seve gets on with it. He's there solely to play golf. Seve's motto is play as you practice and practice as you play.

They had a helluva good time, laughing and joking all the way round. There was quite a crowd following us even though four matches were in progress. Both Sandy and Seve got them involved in the proceedings, talking to them. At the halfway hut Seve said: 'Let's go and have a cup of tea and a sausage.' The spectators all trooped in too and one of them had great pleasure in buying us our sausages and tea.

Neither Seve nor Sandy spent too much time chipping and putting. The greens were so wet it was misleading. No point in practising on wet greens that tomorrow will be dry.

Then Seve and his fiancée Carmen came back to Sandy's

house for tea and scones and a look round. Everybody likes Carmen. You never think that people who aren't English are going to understand all you say, but a lot of them do. That always surprises me. Carmen speaks perfect English.

When I was at the World Series at Akron I asked Jeff Sluman, the US PGA champion, if he was coming to Wentworth and he said he was. Sluman's caddie was coming too, but by the end of the week he had changed his mind. By this time Sluman had left, not knowing he was going to be without a caddie here. So when I got back to England I said to Pete Coleman, who I knew had not got a bag for the Match-play: 'Sluman's caddie ain't coming and there's only me that knows. So get stuck in.' Pete got in touch with the IMG, the organizers of the Match-play, and that's how he got to carry Sluman's bag.

IMG have seen fit to give the French Open more status than the US PGA this week. In other words they have seeded Faldo, the winner in France, ahead of the PGA champion Sluman. Sounds daft to me after the fuss everyone made about Sandy not playing in the US PGA.

Tomorrow Sandy meets Nicholas Price, two old friends playing together. They first met in 1975 when the English Stroke-play championship for the Brabazon Trophy was at Hollinwell. I was at home and I thought: 'I'll go and have a look.' Before I got to the pro's shop Brian Waites said to me: 'Do you want a job?'

'I ain't bothered,' I replied. 'I've just come to watch.'

'The world junior champion is here and he needs a caddie,' said Waites.

'That suits me,' I replied. 'What's his name?'

'Nick Price from Rhodesia.'

So I went and met him. He was a nice pleasant lad and we wandered out to the practice ground for him to hit some balls. He must have shanked the first twenty balls, at least. I went up to him and asked: 'Can't you get out of it, then?'

'Don't worry about it,' he replied, boldly. 'I do it a lot.'

I tried to help him and as we set off I thought there was going to be a shank every other shot. Fortunately there wasn't. He might have had one in four rounds, but that was all.

The field for that year's Brabazon included Nick Faldo, Martin Poxon, Mark James and the winner was one Alexander

Walter Barr Lyle, a 16-year-old. That was the first time I had ever seen him play. He hit a drive and a seven iron to the last hole to beat Geoff Marks. The last hole is a long par four, or a par five as far as I'm concerned.

A couple of weeks later the Amateur championship was held at Hoylake and Vinny Giles defeated Mark James in the final. In between the Brabazon and the Amateur, Sandy and his parents invited Nick Price back to Hawkestone to stay. Sandy's dad gave him lessons. The two boys eventually played one another in the Amateur, and Price won.

Friday 7 October
It was all old friends today. As I've said, Sandy and Nick have known each other for a long time and I've known Dave McNeilly, Nick's caddie, for a good few years.

We caddies think this is one of our favourite tournaments because of the atmosphere and the difference between it and the long end-of-season run of stroke-play events. All of a sudden there's this one, and it sort of revives you. The Match-play week is usually slow to start and nothing much goes on for a couple of days, but then you're in there and it's all happening, specially with thirty-six holes with top-class golfers. There's a marvellous spirit.

George Hammond has been acting as starter at this event for years. He has a little table on the tee for his microphone, and a top hat he keeps all the tees in. He gives out the pin sheets and I always take two, one for the morning and one for the afternoon to help me compare the distances. Sometimes I can say to Sandy: 'This is exactly the same distance as you had this morning,' and he has an immediate feel for the shot.

The European Tour are very well organized in controlling this tournament. They have referees with each match and assistant referees go forward and tell the referee what has happened to each shot. It's all to avoid a repeat of the Faldo incident with Graham Marsh a few years ago when Faldo's ball was thrown back on to the 16th green. In overall charge is Tony Gray, the tournament director. He's watching it on television. So in effect you've got three points of view.

Incidentally, for televised tournaments the insides of the holes are painted white so they'll show up better on the screen. After the morning round you usually finish up with gooey white paint on the ball, hands and gloves.

The marshals have to be travelling marshals in that they move with each match, and the scorers take the number of each club from us. You have to flash the number to them and they relay it back to the scoring control in the press centre. Every so often a scorer will come up to me and say: 'Can you remember me from last year?' Over the years I've got to know some of them quite well.

I explain to them that Sandy carries a driver and a three wood, and that his one iron has got a brown beryllium head. The signs we make to the scorer are: first finger for a one iron, two fingers for a two iron, three for a three iron, four fingers for a four iron and four fingers and a thumb for a five iron. For a six iron I point my index finger at the ground, meaning I've got five in my hand and it's one more. Seven iron is two fingers pointed at the ground, an eight is three fingers pointed downwards, a nine is four fingers pointed at the ground. The sign for a pitching wedge is a clenched hand and for a sand wedge an open hand.

You wait until your opponent is at his ball or can't see you before you give these signs if you don't want him or his caddie to know. It's against the rules to help one another, but then there's a theory that no matter how much help you get you're the one who has to hit the shot anyway. In stroke-play tournaments we help one another a lot, probably more than we should. It's a known thing among anybody who goes out on the course. In the trade it's called: 'Giving a flash.'

Against Nick Price we were five down after twenty-one holes. Nick has got a fast swing but on the 3rd tee in the afternoon I noticed that he snatched at his drive. There was a blustery wind blowing as there had been the day before, so this was the 4th round in two days he'd been playing in a wind. And he was tired because he'd come from the States and he wasn't used to thirty-six holes. On the fourth he snatched at another drive and then Sandy won a hole.

On the 7th, Price snatched again. I said to Sandy: 'His swing's going. He's tired. He's snatching. I wish there were a lot more tee shots into the wind.' On the 9th Price's drive never carried the heather. No more than two thirds of a normal tee shot, say 180 yards. And on the 12th he hit the trees that stand 100 yards in front of the tee and had to take a drop. So I kept saying to Sandy: 'His swing's going. You've got him.' Even when we were behind I could sense that the pendulum was swinging our way. We finished up winning 3 & 2. Sandy played well. He never dropped a shot and had a load of birdies.

Saturday 8 October
Semi-final against Seve. This is the match that Sandy has wanted. Normally nobody wants to have to face Seve. You hope he'll be beaten before you have to play him. But this time Sandy hoped Seve would beat Tattoo (Mark McCumber), never more so than when Seve was four down. Sandy could sense that this was going to be his year and he knew he wouldn't get 100 per cent satisfaction unless he beat Seve himself.

Did he ever! Sandy gave the Open champion a dog's licence, beat him 7 & 6. He would have beaten anybody today. Round in 64 in the morning and he showed no mercy in the afternoon. On the 6th he wanted to hit a pitching wedge and I said to him: 'I think it's just right for a sand iron.' So he holed it. Sandy walked on to the green and took the flag out for Seve to have a putt. The crowd laughed at that.

You have to *bury* Seve. You must not give him a chance. He's looking for inspiration even when he's behind. The only chance that Sandy gave him was on the 7th in the afternoon and he didn't take advantage of it. Sandy's second shot ballooned up in the air and landed short of the bunker. It was caught by a rush of wind coming through the trees like an express train. Normally Seve's second shot would have been hit in to six feet but he pushed it out to the right. It was lucky it hit the trees or it would have ended on the toasted tea-cake stand on the 11th tee. So the hole was halved and Sandy wasn't threatened after that.

It was a very friendly match. They have a lot of admiration for each other and they talked all the way round. I don't suppose it'll be like that against Faldo in the final.

The lesson Jacobs gave Sandy has made a big difference the last two days. Sandy is getting quite pleased with the way he is playing and is looking forward to tomorrow. This is the thing the handicap golfer can't do – change his swing. Jimmy Ballard said it was a pleasure to try and help somebody like Sandy who can go out and do what he's told to do. Sandy can hit one shot, change his grip and then hit another – in a tournament.

Sunday 9 October

We were expected to play at 8.30 this morning. It had rained all night and so Sandy rang the tournament office and asked if there would be a delay. He was told there wouldn't be. We did our usual thing of playing the last four holes on the East course on the way in. People who drive along the road that runs between the 16th green and the 17th tee on the East course see Sandy playing in. Sometimes they do a double take. You can see they're thinking: 'We're on the wrong road.' I've known motorists reverse 100 yards just to watch Sandy tee off on the 17th.

When we got there we were told the final had been delayed until nine. Hung about for half-an-hour. Still raining.

Peter German, the tournament organizer, came in and asked Seve and Woosie whether they were really bothered about playing the third and fourth place play-off. If they wanted to play, he said, he would have to get two teams of greenkeepers squeegeeing the greens whereas if they didn't play then everyone could concentrate on the one match. Neither Seve nor Woosie seemed very keen and so they decided to shake hands and forget the play-off.

Another half-hour delay, then an hour. It was still raining hard. We had lunch, it continued to rain, the course looked saturated.

Weather delays are an occupational hazard in golf. The secret of coping with them is to learn how to pass the time and keep your patience. Sandy is very good at coping. He just switches off and it doesn't bother him at all. Generally what I do at times like this is read the papers, use the time to make travel arrangements for future tournaments. Today I whiled away some time by looking for Phil Sheldon the golf photographer in the press centre to try and sort out some pictures for this book.

I had a flight booked tonight from Heathrow to East Midlands. I was going to drive to Scotland tomorrow for the

Dunhill Cup and have Tuesday relaxing and doing some measuring ready for Wednesday. But it looks as though Tuesday's gone.

Returned to Sandy's. I went up to the red suite with the garden view and watched a tv programme about dreams and sleeping. I got into the spirit of it. I fell asleep. The next thing I remember was hearing Sandy come charging up the stairs: 'We're off at a quarter to three.' It was a quarter to two by this time. I thought we'd probably have time to get eighteen holes in.

At about a quarter to three we stood on the putting green having played ourselves in again – pitch shot to 16, then 17 and 18 with three balls. Chip shots, bunkers shots, stuff like that. We were standing on the green when they said: 'Come back in the morning at half-past eight.' Wonderful. We had to start all over again. But I'd rather play two rounds in one day, as we are going to have to tomorrow, than play eighteen holes today and eighteen tomorrow. Can't get any momentum if you do that.

Woosie was staying on in his house because he had to go to a pro-am in Kent tomorrow, and so he and Nino the cook from his house came and had dinner with us.

Monday 10 October
Off we went again. On the tee for 8.30. Beautiful day. As we played up the 18th on the East course the mist was rising from the fairway and Sandy remarked it would make a good photograph. Phil Sheldon has been threatening to go down and photograph Sandy playing himself in but he has never got round to it. As we passed the tournament office Peter German came out and asked if Sandy had enjoyed his practice session. He thought it was amusing that Sandy should want to play more holes than he had to.

When we reached the putting green Faldo was practising his putting. I said to him, dead serious: 'Excuse me. Are you on your own? Would you like a game?'

Faldo smiled and said, 'Yes, OK, I'll have a game.'

'Good,' I said. 'There's a chap here who wants a game. It's all right, he's a member here, too. Last year it was the Shropshire Plate. This year it's the Members' Vase.'

Faldo plays his own game. He's 100 per cent professional and he concentrates on every shot. He plays very economically and tidily, optimistically. He expects to birdie holes. You know he's hitting his second shot into a position for a putt for a birdie. He ain't playing for pars.

Sandy had that hot streak at the end of the morning round. He birdied the 14th and so did Faldo. Sandy holed a good putt for par on 15 and then a good putt for a birdie on 16. After Faldo had chipped close on the 17th and was obviously going to get a birdie, Sandy holed another big putt for an eagle.

On the last hole Sandy hit the worst possible tee shot, which looked as though it was going out of bounds. It went miles left and ended in some bramble bushes. I didn't think he could get over the ditch in two. It shows you how strong he is, because he hit a nine iron over the ditch, and came up short in three. Faldo made the front third of the green with two good shots and looked as though he was going to win the hole. But then Sandy chipped in from all of forty yards and Faldo did well to half the hole.

After lunch Sandy bogied a couple of holes so they were all square for a long time. Sandy was one down with six to play, had a good chance of a three at the 13th and missed, holed a good putt for a two at the 14th and this time Faldo missed from much closer.

Sandy had been hitting seven and eight iron second shots to the 15th all week and missing the green. This time he hit a poor one iron off the tee and had to play a four iron to reach the green. The ball finished three feet from the flag. Faldo three-putted.

They both got good threes on 16. Then you come to the crunch hole in the match-play, the 17th. It's like the 12th at Augusta – you don't want to be there. The worst place to be on the course is that 17th tee. The hole is obviously reachable in two most of the time but there's too many dangers. You can either hook it left and be out of bounds or push it to the right and not be able to get on in two. The tournament boiled down to who could hit a good tee shot on this hole? Sandy's went down the middle, Faldo pushed his to the right. Sandy chipped and holed from five yards. Faldo missed his birdie. So Sandy won 2 & 1.

This drive was one of two shots that Faldo missed all day. The other was on the 13th tee in the morning when it looked as though somebody had put him off by moving behind him.

There it was. Sandy had won all the classics, the Open, US Masters, winning side of a Ryder Cup and the Match-play. Fifth final and I've carried for him in four of them including today's win. Jimmy Dickinson caddied for him in his first final.

Afterwards there were just three of us left in the locker-room – Andy Prodger, Alf Sutton, the locker-room supremo who has been at Wentworth since God were a lad, and me. Alf's done every Match-play, twenty-five of them. He's a good old stick. He provides everything for the players, makes sure everybody gets a drink and the place is kept tidy. He can even do massage. We were away from the crowd. Nobody was bothering us. I find it difficult to slow down after the Match-play. After thirty-six holes a day for several days it's hard to stop yourself charging on to the next tee as it were. But sitting quietly in the locker-room having a drink was the perfect way to wind down.

Dunhill Cup, Old Course, St Andrews, Scotland

Tuesday 11 October
Had to drive 320 miles to St Andrews. During the drive Hilary did nothing but read this diary and check it. I came to the conclusion that it's a lot easier to do thirty-six holes in one day on the Burma Road than to write a book.

Hepburn Gardens, St Andrews, ready for the Dunhill Cup. We were with Andy and Pete in the same flat as last year. I'd brought a big photograph of myself and Sandy on the 11th hole at the Masters, taken by Lawrence Levy. I got Sandy to sign it and we will present it to Ivor Robson for him to put it up in his hotel in Moffat.

Wednesday 12 October
Alarm at 6.30 a.m. to check the measurements before the pro-am which started at 8.00. Andy went with me. You start on the second hole because the first hole at St Andrews never changes. The greens change a little from year to year because they

bring them out (make them bigger) in the summer and take them back in the winter, but the features on the hole remain the same.

Me and Andy had a wheel each and we got out to the 8th tee, the furthest point possible, about two miles from the town, when it started to rain, cold, wet, big white drops. There was a PGA man there for some reason, checking the pins, I suppose. He said to Andy: 'Nick Faldo's starting time has been changed. He's now off at 9.00, not 10.50. His amateur partner is something to do with Volvo and has to leave at dinner-time.' Andy was taken back in a buggy and he got wet just sitting in it. Meanwhile I was stuck out there in the slashing rain doing my measuring.

As it happens Walter Woods, the course superintendent, was out with another fellow, cutting the holes. I thought, 'Bugger this for a game of soldiers, I'll ask Walter for a lift in.' I used to play with Walter at Coxmoor when he was the greenkeeper at Hollinwell. 'Is there any room in the back of that jeep?' I shouted. 'Yes, jump in,' Walter replied and he took me to the Old Course hotel where Sandy was staying.

Sandy did half-an-hour's practice with me holding an umbrella over his head to try and keep him dry. I had my back to where he was hitting and every four or five shots I would say: 'Good shot.'

'You've not seen one shot yet,' Sandy said.

'No,' I replied, 'But they sound all right.'

Players were walking in off the course the conditions were so bad. Then I heard that the pro-am was to be cut down to the first five holes and the last five, the boozers' loop. This was just after eleven. In the States the whole thing would have been called off at nine o'clock.

We got out to the first tee and there was Ivor Robson with his waterproofs on, holding an umbrella. Nobody has ever seen him with his waterproofs on before so it just shows you how bad the weather was. While we were waiting to tee off Sandy went to the tournament office to get some car park tickets for Saturday, and during this time they called it off. Lyle's luck prevailed once again.

Andy and I were very tired so soon after Wentworth,

specially coming up here to the sea air. Had a hot bath when I got back to the flat and that night I couldn't get into bed fast enough.

Thursday 13 October
Played Thailand. Sandy had a hard match. His opponent was Somsakdi Srisangar, a happy-go-lucky sort of fellow. He was out in 37 and most of the way round he was only one shot behind Sandy. In the end Sandy shot a 70 and beat him by three or four shots. Srisangar got a great reception at the 18th. I think he was happy just to have been there.

Friday 14 October
We weren't off until two o'clock and so we went down the bottom end of the town to the harbour and the cathedral and made our annual homage to Tom Morris's grave.

The Old course is the most interesting golf course of all – not just in Scotland or Britain. Anywhere. At this time of the year it's not quite so demanding. The fairways and the greens are soft but when it's firm and running it plays more difficult. I like it best in midsummer when the fairways are hard and it's a test of patience and skill. I loved it the way it was for the 1984 Open.

Played England, the auld enemy, and just for a change we faced Nick Faldo. Captain against captain. That meant I was up against the Prodge for the second time in five days. On the course Andy is very intense and difficult to fault. Not only does he have to measure the shots and read the putts, he has to make sure the rest of the world comes to order while Faldo plays.

Sandy and Faldo got off to a terrific start. Sandy birdied the first three holes and Faldo birdied two of them. Then Sandy birdied the fifth and Faldo put his second close on the sixth. And so it went on.

As we were going round Sandy kept remarking on how well Colin Montgomerie, the third member of the Scottish team, was playing even though he was two or three strokes behind Mark James at one stage. It's his first year as a pro and his first year on tour. Colin lost by two shots (71 to 69) but he was still under par. Sandy thought he did very well. And Gordon

Brand Jr, who beat Barry Lane, 71 to 73, has always been the cornerstone of the Scottish team in this event. He's won thirteen of his fifteen matches. With Montgomerie losing and Gordon winning, this meant it all depended on Sandy.

He and Faldo had only one bogey between them and that was Sandy's on the 17th. In fact it was the only bogey Sandy's had in two rounds and he got quite mad with himself about it. Last week it was the 17th at Wentworth and here it was the 17th again. Faldo drove to the left and then Sandy hit it even further left. You mustn't go where Sandy finished. He opened the door for Faldo, who played a brilliant pitch to one foot and holed for a four.

Faldo beat Sandy by holing a good putt for a three on the 18th. It was fifteen feet and downhill. That gave England victory by 2–1. I was surprised at the emotion Faldo showed when it went in. He leaped into the air. Compare that with what Sandy did in the Match-play. He just holed his putt and shook hands. Sandy is always approachable whether he's won or lost. He gets upset, but he doesn't show it.

So the week ended sooner than I had expected, but I looked at it like this: even though we lost I was not sorry to be going home – especially after having won last week. We had a good week at Wentworth, a phenomenal week. It was someone else's turn here. Now we can go home and have Sunday off. I'm getting back the day I lost at the beginning of the week, if you like. Winning is not the be all and end all, after all.

11

16 October–17 November

Birdie-less in Spain – Tracing my schoolmates –
Earthquake in California – Coffee with Phoebe

At Home

Sunday 16 to Sunday 23 October
For some years we've had surplus furniture stored in different rooms around the house. We got rid of three easy chairs and a chest of drawers by giving them to a young lad who is in the Army and lives two doors away. He's going away for six months and he needed furniture to put in his house so he could let it.

The next day we went to MFI in Mansfield and bought a couple of units. I had a day constructing them. You do so much and leave it for the glue to set. They never give you enough glue by the way. I went down to the last shop in Kirkby that goes back to the old days. You go in and it's all wooden floors and higgledy-piggledy but they know exactly where everything is. You always have to have a conversation with them. It's great fun.

Mrs Unwin, our 82-year-old next-door neighbour, has a garden that has been a little overgrown. It's not surprising, because obviously she can't do it herself. It's unsightly and the weeds are going to come across into our garden if we don't do something, and so we made a start on it. I got rid of a lilac tree. Terrible job that was. I cut it down and then sawed it up, roots and all. It weighed about two tons I think, dear me!

Over the years in the local paper the *Notts Free Press*, I've seen these pictures from thirty, forty or fifty years ago of old school classes. And all the pupils are named. I've got a tin full of old photos and one of them is of my class taken when we were all about nine years old in the garden of the headmaster's house across the road from where we live. I think the photo was taken in 1952. I thought to myself: 'I'll have a go at trying to write everybody's name down.' There were forty-one in the class plus Miss Pike our class teacher who is still alive, and the headmaster Mr Mollard. I got most of them but there were still half a dozen missing. I had all the lads' names; it was the girls I couldn't remember. I only keep in touch with Hugh Monro who lives in Scotland.

Walking past the library one day, I thought to myself: I've not been in for a while but when I used to go to the library there was a girl in there I am sure I was at school with. But I've never plucked up courage to say, 'Are you Sheila Culley as was?' This time, though, I went in. Mrs Jean Low, the lady behind the desk, is the wife of a fellow I play golf with.

'Is there a lady called Sheila working here?' I asked her.

'Yes there is.'

'Was her maiden name Culley?' I asked.

'I don't know. I'll have to telephone her and ask. Why do you want to know?'

I explained and Mrs Low rang this lady called Sheila. 'Were you at school with Dave Musgrove?' she asked.

'Yes, I was.'

'He's here and he's got something to show you,' she said.

'Is it a photograph of me when I was about nine?'

She came down and we went through all the class. I remembered a few more names and she got the rest. 'That girl there,' she said pointing at the photograph, 'Janet Bowler as was, works in Brays china shop in Station Street.'

I go in there and I recognize her not from school but from seeing her walking up and down the street.

'I've seen you many a time,' I said.

'Yes,' she replied, 'but you've not shown any recognition.'

We got the photograph out and all the customers came crowding round in the shop. They've all known me since I was eight or nine years old. Eventually we get all the names and I wrote them down on a bit of paper. Dubious spelling of course.

I'm going to wait until I'm fifty in 1993 and then I'll stick it in the newspaper and say Happy Birthday to all the class.

Volvo Masters, Valderrama, Sotogrande, Spain

Monday 24 October to Tuesday 1 November
Sandy didn't decide to play in the Volvo Masters, the last event of the European season, in Spain until the match-play and we had trouble getting tickets because the flights to and from Gibraltar were full. Traveleads couldn't help so we rang Randy Fox (another travel agent specializing in golf) and finished up with club class tickets for myself, Hilary and Andy from Gatwick. This week we are eccentric millionaires travelling club class.

Every other tournament appears to want to be called the Masters of some description. The Dunhill Masters, Ebel Swiss Masters, German Masters and now Volvo Masters. It's like *Jaws I*, *Jaws II* and *Jaws III*. Can't they think of any other name than Masters?

Our friend Tony Sher invited us to stay with him in his house at Sotogrande. He also fixed up an apartment for Woosnam, Poxon, D.J. and Baker as well as three of the rats, Wobbly, Prodge and Paul Stephens. He met us at Gibraltar. The last time I was here I caddied for John Fitzpatrick, Jimmy Cousins, Manuel Pinero's caddie, caddied for his partner and we had a nice day out. That was a long time ago. John Fitzpatrick lives here now.

I've met some old reprobates this week – Alan Hazlehurst who used to keep a pub near Reading, Patrick Ryan from the 19th Hole bar in Puerto Banus, Michael Balfour, the old actor, and Bruce Forsyth were here, too. On Thursday night we had a barbecue at Tony Sher's. The old Prodger did the barbecue. What an artist! During the evening I met a fellow called Des Marriott and after we'd been talking for a while it turned out we had both worked in the same offices at the National Coal Board at Huthwaite, near Mansfield, twenty-five years ago.

While I was doing the garden at home last week, Sandy went to Japan to play in the Bridgestone tournament. He's welcome to that. It's like having to live standing on your head for a week and then turning the right way up again and coming off nights, all at the same time. He had a few shanks out in Japan. One went out of bounds. On another hole he shanked again. It hit a tree and came back about twenty feet further on. From there he wedged to the green and made four. He finished well down the field. Even Langer with the yips beat him.

Sandy's shanking is becoming a thing with him. He is getting anxious about it and it's affecting me as well. I had a dream one night. We were playing around Valderrama in the tournament and came to one hole and decided it was a seven iron and he refused to hit it. So I had to hit the shot and with a seven iron I shanked it.

In the pro-am I thought I'd have a bit of fun with Tony Sher, who's in charge of Sandy's gallery marshals. We were coming up the 18th and I said to him: 'Tony, go and hold the pin.'

'Who, me?' he replied.

'Yes,' said Sandy. 'Go and make yourself useful for a change.'

Tony went and held the pin and was probably thinking: 'This is easy' when Sandy said to him: 'What's the line?' That threw Tony, and Sandy's ball finished twelve foot wide of the hole.

Seve won the pro-am and said: 'I only win pro-ams now. At my time of life it's all I can do.' We all felt sorry for him.

I thought Sandy played remarkably well in the pro-am considering he had only just arrived after a horrendous flight from Japan. He made a film on Monday, left that night and got here late on Tuesday night.

First round 68, four under par. Sandy putted well. He said that after the Koria grass greens in Japan he found it a great relief to putt on these greens even though they were spiked up. He said when he played here in January with Gallacher and Jacklin the greens were fantastic. Now there are whole bare patches, brown, and they're losing some of them. They have been cut down too fast.

If you take a course like Harbour Town on Hilton Head island in the US, the greens are small but flattish. You know where you stand. The other extreme is Augusta National where the greens are big and have big slopes on them. Here they've tried to combine the two, which is not surprising since Robert Trent Jones, who designed Valderrama, also did some work at Augusta National. The result here is there aren't many pin positions. Also, the rough around the greens which is made of bent and Bermuda grass apparently, gives terrible lies. That's why the scoring is so high, because chipping from just off the greens on to these fast surfaces is murder. There were only four men under par on the first day – Sandy, Seve, Ove Sellberg the Swede, and Roger Chapman. The bunkers are chipped marble as well. It's not sand at all.

Sandy had a 71 in the second round and led by one shot, five under par, from Seve. The only other player to beat par on both days was Anders Sorensen. The cut was ten over par, the highest of the year, which gives you an idea how hard the course was playing.

This is a limited field, only eighty players. Yet it didn't move any faster than a field of 150. We were still waiting on almost every shot. It must be the severity of the course.

Sandy's got this new driver. It's the most desperate-looking club anybody could imagine, but he's convinced that it keeps the ball down low and he's happy with it. What can I say? I can't see it lasting very long. I kept talking him out of using it in Scotland but he apparently took it to Japan where it performed OK. He's hitting his three wood well. He hit a shot with it on the seventh in the second round that carried 260 yards. It's his iron shots that are bothering him.

In the third round Sandy had a 75 and went for eighteen holes without a birdie. Can't remember when he last did that. Played with Seve, who had a 74. Neither of them had any inspiration at all. As Ian Wright, Seve's caddie, said: 'It was about as interesting as watching paint dry.' They're joint leaders, two strokes ahead of Faldo, who has caught up well. A two-horse race has become a three-horse race. Sandy was still in good spirits afterwards. 'I'm going to the practice ground and try and sort myself out,' he said after his round. He was helping Peter Baker for twenty minutes, then he went to watch Phil Sheldon who was hitting balls. By this time we were getting eaten alive by gnats, which had been a bad feature of the week. Finally we dragged him off the course in the gathering dusk. He'd hit a few shots, all rubbish.

It has been a helluva long year and a lot of the golfers were beaten before they started. They couldn't get out of here fast enough. A lot of them threw the towel in. They were 670 over par after two rounds, I understand, an average of eight over par. Sandy couldn't understand that. 'Here we are on a good golf course in good condition and in nice weather, and most of them have given up,' he said. 'It's good for them that don't, but it's a bit of a ridiculous attitude.'

A tournament like this is a lot easier to win for a good golfer. It's not like the Swiss, say, because everybody is going to shoot a good score there. Valderrama is a good course and you've got to be a good player to play well round it. The cream has come to the top, Sandy, Seve and Faldo plus Woosnam, Canizares.

Before the tournament started Sandy said: 'This will be decided among the players who have done well in America and there's only three of us here – myself, Seve and Nick.' And after three rounds that was exactly it. Sandy and Seve were joint leaders and Faldo was close behind them. Sandy didn't feel he was playing very well. He was frightened to death of shanking, he was hitting too many bad shots. Sandy thought that Faldo was the great threat. At this point in the season he thought that Faldo was a more consistent player than Seve.

The last two days at Valderrama, Sandy played with Seve and neither could make any impression on Faldo who just kept steadily climbing up the field. He'd been six shots behind after thirty-six holes, two behind after fifty-four and he took over the lead from Seve on the 11th of the last round and went on to win by two shots.

Sandy had nine straight pars on the front nine on the last day and that wasn't good enough. He went for thirty-nine holes without a birdie and he hasn't done that since the Pope was an altar boy. I can't remember the last time he didn't have a birdie in eighteen holes, never mind thirty-nine. Even in Ireland in 1985 in the famous 89 that might have been, he had a birdie.

Tony Sher was getting his wife to tape the television coverage and he'd ring her every so often and ask her how many times she'd seen him because he'd wangled it so that he marshalled for Sandy. On the Saturday night he rang and asked: 'Have you seen me much on tv?'

'We've seen you a bit, but if you get closer to Sandy tomorrow we'll see you a lot more,' she replied.

So on the last nine holes, which are the tv holes, he never got more than six feet away from Sandy. What a poseur!

The good thing that came out of the tournament was Sandy's fighting finish. Woosnam was on one over par in the clubhouse when Sandy was level par with four holes to play. Sandy managed to par the last four holes to stay third, one shot ahead of Woosie.

Sandy was aware that he could pass Des Smyth and possibly McNulty in the money list with a good finish. By coming third on his own he did so. He won nearly £21,000 which was enough for him to jump from seventh to fifth, ending with official earnings of £186,017.98. Not bad for a part-time player. He played twelve official events and also the Dunhill Cup and the World Match-play in Europe. Fourteen in all.

By the end of the year he will have played thirty-three tournaments – fourteen in Europe, seventeen in the US, one in Japan and one in Australia. He's hoping to get it down to thirty next year.

There was an end-of-term feeling about this event. The last week in September used to be the Dunlop Masters and the first week in October was the match-play and that was it, full stop. I said 'So long' to loads of caddies – Jimmy Cousins (Pinero's caddie), Silly Billy, Manchester Stewart, the Professor, General, Pedro, Zebedee, Sandwich Sam, Captain Kirk and McDivot – because I shan't see them until the PGA next May when Sandy plays in Europe again.

The first flight we could get back was on Tuesday, and we actually caught an earlier plane than we were booked on. We got back to Winifred Villas in Kirkby just before 10 p.m. having dropped Andy Prodger at Rickmansworth station on the way.

I don't feel too tired, actually. We had a long stint in America earlier in the year ending with the Heritage. That was a tough seven weeks. Then we had that spell when we had six tournaments in six countries in as many weeks – starting with the Irish Open at Portmarnock in August and followed by the World Series in Ohio, USA, the European Masters in Switzerland, the European Open at Sunningdale, the Lancôme in Paris; and then the German Masters in Stuttgart.

I were ready for going home after that. I'd had enough. I didn't want to see another aeroplane, another airport terminal, another motel room. But since then we've had the Match-play, with a week off before it, the Dunhill and a week off afterwards, then we went to Spain where the sun shone. It has been a gentle run-down to the end of the season.

At Home

Saturday 5 November
At home in England for bonfire night for the first time since 1979. I used to stay down in Portugal and Spain after the European tour and do some caddying at the qualifying school and in occasional pro-ams. I would stay there until mid-December, get home for Christmas, ready to leave for the US again in the new year.

It's going to be a long day tomorrow flying to San Francisco for the Nabisco Championships of Golf at Pebble Beach. But I've got plenty to read on the plane and there's always the chance of being upgraded to club class. I'll ask as soon as I get to Heathrow and flash my BA Executive Club card. I didn't have that technique before I went to the World Series. You never know what you might get if you ask for it. Got to make yourself available, that's the trick.

Nabisco Championships of Golf, Pebble Beach, California

Sunday 6 November
On the flight I was thinking about the money involved in this tournament. It's incredible. The total prize fund is £1.2m and the first prize could be nearly £300,000 with bonuses. I can't keep track of it all.

In a tournament like this I don't look at the top money, I look at the money for last place because that's what we're guaranteed. Last prize is $32,000 plus the bonus. I ain't worried about what the first prize is at all.

All I know is it's a tidy sum and Sandy as the only European eligible to play here could become the first European to top the US money list if he wins. He is currently lying third, $130,000 behind Chip Beck. He is leading the points for the Golfer of the Year award and is a leading the putting averages but only by .04 from Don Pooley. Sandy is going to have to putt well this week to stay ahead of Pooley; and Pooley has the advantage of not playing, so his average can't get worse, whereas Sandy's can unless, as I say, he's near his best on the greens this week.

Sandy led the money list for more than four months during the year, a fantastic achievement considering he only played sixteen tournaments and missed the cut in three of them.

All to play for, as they say.

Monday 7 November
Up early. Always am after transatlantic flights east to west. I had a good flight yesterday and wasn't particularly tired. I was in my motel room by 4.30 p.m. whereas Sandy didn't arrive until 11 o'clock last night. Woke at 5.30 a.m., watched a film on tv and walked to Denny's (a restaurant chain) for breakfast. The door hadn't closed behind me and a bloke said: 'You here for the golf?'

'Yes, I am,' I replied.

'Thought you were,' he said. 'Is your man playing?'

'Yes. Where do you come from?'

'Cheltenham.'

Weather was beautiful. They said they hadn't had any rain for eight months and parts of the course were brown. 'We'll soon sort that out for you,' I said. 'Put your buckets out. It'll be coming.'

Went to caddie registration, and guess what? Had to wear overalls. Wow! So I said: 'What do we do when it rains?'

'We'll think of something else when that happens,' was the reply. Typical!

Sandy was the first man on the course – at 10.00 a.m. We

worked out between us that the ball was too far forward in his stance. When he moved it back that got rid of this feeling that he was going to shank every shot. He was quite happy with the way he was playing. He knew Pebble Beach quite well from playing in the AT & T pro-am.

Tuesday 8 November
Election day. They were prattling on about it all day. Filling an election form here takes about ten minutes because you vote for the Senate, the local mayor, and all sorts. People were standing in line for two hours at some polling booths.

Yesterday and today we raced round the course in less than three hours despite sometimes playing three balls. It used to take nearly six hours in the Crosby. We got a whole new perspective on the course. Plus it wasn't as wet as it usually is at the beginning of the year. They'd hollow-tined the greens twice and put sand down and so they looked very suspect.

In the evening I was in Bud's Pub waiting to meet some friends who originally came from the Isle of Man but live in Carmel now – Ray Hughes and his wife. Every time Sandy plays nearby Ray turns up and a load of Scotsmen come down from San Francisco and Sandy's Uncle Jimmy comes down from Canada. So it's home from home. While I waited I watched a tv programme about the election. The winner would be the first man to get 270 electoral college votes. By half-past six George Bush had got 222, Dukakis had got 22 and only a few constituencies had not reported. The television interviewer turned to an expert in the studio and asked: 'Can we have a prediction?'

The expert said: 'What do you want me to tell you? It's going to be over in half an hour.'

The election had taken two and a half years and cost a mind-bending sum. I was telling an American that our elections lasted three weeks. He said: 'How can you get it all done in three weeks?' 'Three weeks is more than enough time,' I replied.

Wednesday 9 November
Sandy was off first in the pro-am with Mark Calcaveccia and two amateurs, one of whom was Dick Estey, who had been

runner-up to Charlie Green in the British Seniors' this year. They played stableford and added everybody's points together after each hole. Mike Reid and his team won with 150 points.

The two amateurs shared a caddie, Bob Robare, who had been caddying at Pebble Beach for fifteen years. 'Call me the dawg (dog),' he told me. He gave Sandy the lines of the greens and it confirmed our suspicions that grain was a factor in the reading of putts. As I say, 'Dawg' carried two bags, which is known in the trade as a double bagger and is worse than hard work, I can tell you.

As the room rate in my motel was going up from $40 to $60 at the week-end I decided to move out. It was a real rip-off. The people in the Monterey peninsula are the same as the people in Scotland when the Open is on. They automatically think that everybody going to a golf tournament is fair game and so they double and triple the prices. It'll be the same at Troon next year for the 1989 Open.

I had one bit of luck, though. I made a lot of phone calls, to Hawaii, Palm Springs, San Diego making reservations for this winter's trip with Hilary. When I went to check out I said I had some phone calls to pay for. 'I've got no record of you making any phone calls,' said the receptionist. That was a result. I didn't hang around after that.

I moved into a hotel in Marina, half an hour's drive to the north, and teamed up with Keith Duckworth, a golf photographer from the Lake District. I've known him for a long time. At nine o'clock he said: 'There's an earthquake.' It sounded like a lorry going past, to me. The windows shook a bit and pots rattled. It turned out there had been a tremor of 4.7 on the Richter Scale at San José.

This tournament was the old story. We got up early in the morning because of the early starting times. By the time we'd finished playing and had had a bit of lunch and Sandy had done with practising, it was getting dark and that was the day gone. No time to do anything else. A lot of people ask me: 'Do you ever play golf with Sandy?' I always say that even if I had time that would be the last thing I'd want to do.

There just isn't time for anything. You have to make a conscious effort to fit in everything as it is – doing the laundry, making travel arrangements weeks in advance, that sort of thing.

Thursday 10 to Saturday 12 November
The scoring in the tournament was absolutely phenomenal. The first three days all produced 64s – by Curtis Strange, Mark Wiebe and Payne Stewart. On the first day Sandy had a 72, level par. He played good but he couldn't hole any putts. On the first day he got a nose bleed on the 13th. Isn't that caused by a build up of pressure? He had one on the second day, when he shot 71, and one on the third day as well. After his second round, a 71, he was on 143 and beating about five men.

In the third round he had a 68 and got to halfway up the field. He was five behind. Sandy and Gary Koch started at 8.28 and were finished for 11.30. Koch comes from Tampa, Florida, and before he left for California a journalist asked him: 'How do you feel about playing for all that money in the Nabisco?'

'It's like this,' Koch replied. 'Even if I finish last I shall still have won more in one week than I did in the whole of 1987.'

Everyone had bunched up. Joey Sindelar, who was lying second in the money list, was doing all right. Tom Kite was going well. So were Calcavecchia and Ken Green who were right behind Sandy in the money list.

Word came through that Chuck Van Linge, Sandy's friend and partner in the AT & T, had been put on the reserve list for next year's tournament. They were getting rid of all the old stagers and putting AT & T men in their places. Sandy made his feelings known – that he wanted to play with Chuck next year.

Sandy was due to go on to Australia to captain that England team in the Ashes series against Australia but after the long trip over here he said to me: 'I don't feel like fifteen hours on the plane to Australia. I wish I could pull out.' Then he got the nose bleed and rang London and said he didn't want to go. That must have been Friday night. When I got there on Saturday morning he was quite chuffed.

Sunday 13 November
But by this morning he'd a lot of faxes from London overnight. They said that if he didn't play the tournament the organizer

would call it off and IMG might get sued. Sandy didn't want to let the rest of the team down. He thought they were bluffing, but then Greg [Norman] said that if Sandy didn't play he would lose all credibility in Australia.

So Sandy went out and waved to Greg that he had changed his mind and would play. Greg seemed relieved and he then went and ran round the course with Mark O'Meara in an hour and twenty-five minutes. They were last, and whatever they did the breakdown of money was such that they couldn't win much more than the minimum.

You pay to learn. Sandy won't make the same mistake again. He'll play his fifteen tournaments in the US next year, make his statutory appearances in Europe and choose what else he plays in more carefully.

Our tee-time was 10.46 and as we'd been going round in just over three hours all week I worked out I would catch my plane at 3.10 p.m. from Monterey to San Francisco with the greatest of ease and the 5.20 p.m. from San Francisco to London. While we were on the putting green several newspaper men came up to us and told us that Seve had won in Japan, Gordon Brand Jr in South Africa and Bill Glasson in Florida. Because we were so far west, we were able to receive Sunday's results, which we would normally only get on Monday, before we started, on Sunday morning.

The wind was howling and people were saying to Sandy: 'If you shoot 65 you'll be ten under par.' But 72 is a good score here in a wind. We were soon to find out that the 9th and 10th were unreachable in two even though they're par fours.

Off we went and who should be in front of us but Scott Verplank? They talk about Brown and Langer being slow, but you ought to go and see him perform. He takes root. Very selfish attitude. We were playing slower and slower. A storm had been forecast for days and it would arrive at one o'clock, the weather men said. That was spot on. We could see the rain coming for about an hour, and it started when we were on the 13th.

Sandy and Koch played on steadily even though it was tough to hold the club in the rain. On the 16th green the electronic scoreboard said play had been temporarily suspended but we hadn't heard a siren or seen any PGA men. On the 17th tee word came through: 'Play has been suspended.' All the others went back to the clubhouse but Sandy and I went to the beach club and somebody brought us a club sandwich and a plateful of hot chips and two cups of coffee. There was a log fire and I could dry the clubs.

We started again at half-past three, played the last two holes and that was four o'clock. I'd had it for my plane. The leaders just got in in daylight. Kite birdied the 18th and Strange bogied the 17th so they tied. Kite had the best score of the day, a 72.

But it was too dark for a play-off that night so it was held at nine o'clock the next morning, which has got to be the greatest anti-climax. Strange won with a birdie on the second extra hole, thus becoming the first man to earn more than $1 million in one season on the US tour.

Sandy had a 76. He was pulling a lot of tee shots and he only had one birdie and that was after a two-inch putt on the eleventh. He finished on 287, one under par, eight strokes behind Strange. Green, Calcavecchia, Kite and Strange all overtook him on the money list. He ended up coming seventh, disappointing but still a fine effort from comparatively few tournaments – seventeen.

Sandy was flying to Australia at about 6 p.m. I went with Keith Duckworth to San José and the next morning he took me to the San Francisco airport for lunchtime. While I waited, I sat reading about Richard Burton's life with Elizabeth Taylor in *Life* magazine. Real entertaining.

Then I had more bad news. Not only was I a day late but the plane had to go to Vancouver on the way to London and so it was going to be a thirteen-hour flight. And by the way, I didn't get upgraded to club class, not on the way out nor the way back. Got to London and had to circle for half an hour because of the fog. So we were on the plane for fourteen hours, which is enough for anybody.

At Home. Kirkby-in-Ashfield

Thursday 17 November
Called at Coxmoor to scrounge a cup of tea from the heavy gang. Unlike Wentworth, who have doubled their subscription to £1000 this year, our subs aren't going up at all for 1989 – the first year since 1966 there hasn't been an increase.

At eleven o'clock there was the usual tapping on the wall from Phoebe Schofield, our 80-year-old neighbour. When my mother died, she decided to adopt me. The knock on the wall is her signal that coffee and cakes are ready. In her copy of the *Sun* I read a report of how Sandy was trying to placate the Australians for what he'd said about them when he announced he was pulling out of the Ashes series. I'd told him last week I would think about him – and so I did. He's welcome to it.

Had a final meeting with secretary and ace author because this diary has to be delivered to the publisher tomorrow.

This weekend Hilary and I will be going to see Aunty Fanny Musgrove. She's 84 and fit as a flea. She will prove once again that wherever you travel in the world there's nothing to beat her home cooking.